ONE MALLORCAN SUMMER

PETER KERR

summersdale

CONTENTS

Follow me to the island of calm, where men are never in a hurry, women never grow old; where words are never wasted, the sun shines all day long, and even the moon, as though caught up in its idle activity, moves more slowly.

From *L'Illa de la Calma* by Santiago Rusiñol
(Antoni López, Barcelona, 1913)

- One -

COCKERELS AND MUSSELS

General Franco had developed insomnia. Or maybe he just sensed the approach of spring. Whatever the reason, the diminutive cockerel with the autocratic name and a bossy attitude to match was suddenly bent upon making his early morning presence well and truly felt... *and* heard.

Thus the feathered *generalísimo* put paid to the soporific luxury of the long, silent nights which had become an accustomed treasure of winter at 'Ca's Mayoral', our little farm nestling among scented groves of orange, lemon and other exotic trees, in a lush valley hidden away at the foot of the towering Tramuntana Mountains of south-west Mallorca. The cocky little bantam who ruled the roost over at the *finca* of our neighbour, old Maria Bauzá, was clearly determined to ensure that, when he was awake, every living creature in the entire valley would be awake also. And just when everything about our new lifestyle seemed to be settling nicely into place at last…

For it hadn't been easy developing the *tranquilo* attitude so necessary for living at the relaxed pace of the Mallorcan country folk, into whose midst we had so recently moved – an island way of life so laid-back, a Spanish temperament so enviably dilatory that we had very soon come to realise that we had put down roots in a place that deserved to be dubbed Mañana Valley. And we loved it!

Admittedly, it had been something of a shock adapting to the mainly-manual working methods of a small Mediterranean fruit farm after the highly-mechanised arable practices which we'd been used to 'back home' in Scotland, but we were getting there gradually, or *poco a poco*, as the locals put it. *Hombre*, it was the only way to go! And while our resolute struggles to communicate with our rustic new neighbours in Spanish must have raised many a hearty laugh when they talked amongst themselves about the *familia extranjera* that had come to live *and* work in their secluded, close-knit community, they showed nothing but courtesy and patience when conversing with us one-to-one.

Even my wife Ellie's penchant for ignoring small but vitally-important idiosyncrasies of their language was always politely, if sometimes mischievously, overlooked. Yet her habit of neglecting to pronounce the Spanish letter 'ñ' as though it was an ordinary 'n' with a 'y' tagged on (as in 'canyon'), almost landed her in trouble on one occasion.

It was in early January, when Ellie was making her first visit after the New Year holiday to the shops in the nearby market town of Andratx, cheerily wishing the various shopkeepers her well-rehearsed compliments of the season as she stocked up on depleted comestibles. Only when she returned to the car after a sojourn to the fishmonger's did I suspect that something was amiss.

'You look a bit peeved,' I remarked. 'What's up?'

'It's that fishman,' she stormed, slamming the car door. 'He's got an attitude problem, that's all!'

'How d'you mean? I've spoken to him a few times in the bar next door on market days, and he seems a genial sort of guy.'

'Well, everything was sweetness and light until I called "Happy New Year" to him on my way out of the shop.'

'Uh-huh?'

'Yes. Then his face turned puce, and all the women in the queue started to giggle.' Ellie gave an umbrage-induced snort. 'OK, I didn't understand what he shouted at me, but it certainly wasn't "Have a nice day", that's for sure!'

'Ehm, I take it you wished him Happy New Year in Spanish, then?'

'Of course. *Feliz Ano Nuevo* – what else?'

I stroked my nose, trying to hide the smirk tugging at the corner of my mouth. 'Right, so you said *ano*, pronounced 'anno' – not *año*, pronounced 'anyo'?'

'Of course. Why?'

'Because the poor fellow's just been in hospital for a haemorrhoids operation, so it's no wonder he got the hump.'

Ellie's brows knotted into a puzzled frown. 'But why should having his haemorrhoids seen to make him fly off the handle at being wished a Happy New Year?'

'Simply because you said anno instead of anyo.'

'So what?'

'So you didn't actually wish him a Happy New Year, that's what.'

'I didn't?'

'Well, no. What you actually wished him,' I spluttered, tears of hilarity welling in my eyes, 'was a Happy New Arsehole!'

Now Ellie's face turned puce.

No doubt we dropped piles of other such linguistic bloomers without even being aware of them. But that was to be expected. And if we did accidentally say something offensive at times, none of the local folk – with the understandable exception of that poor fishmonger – reacted in a discourteous way. The fact that at least we were trying seemed to be appreciated, and that was fine by us. After all, our priority was to restore our run-down little farm to *somewhere* approaching the state of esteem in which it had once basked, so we were content just to scale the learning curve steadily, encouraged by our apparent acceptance by our *vecinos*, our new neighbours in the valley.

But now General Franco was spoiling everything by putting the mockers on my much-needed beauty sleep for the third night in a row. All right, it wasn't as if I hadn't been brought up with the morning crowing of a family rooster in my ears, but the encircling proximity of the craggy Mallorcan mountains seemed to amplify such commonplace country sounds to a nerve-jarring level. And to make matters worse, Franco wasn't even good at the job. His early morning efforts sounded more like the wobbly vocal acrobatics of an adolescent Swiss folk singer than the macho call of a strutting chicken-coop supremo.

The little general yodelled up another of his broken-voiced reveilles.

'What in God's name has got into that deranged bird?' I groaned, squinting at the bedside clock through the shuttered darkness. 'Hell's bells, it's not even five o'clock yet! He's getting earlier every bloody morning!'

Ellie curved herself into a foetal ball and pulled the duvet over her ears. 'Shut up and go back to sleep,' she mumbled. 'It's the middle of the night.'

'Tell me about it!'

My wife's annoying talent of being able to sleep through just about anything short of a Richter Eight earthquake had been inherited by our two sons, eighteen-year-old Sandy and his twelve-year-old brother Charlie, whose muffled snores I could hear penetrating the thick bedroom walls of the old farmhouse.

Then came another warbled clarion call from the bantam *generalísimo* in the little farmyard up the lane. And now his grating outbursts were being echoed by a bestirring legion of other territorial cockerels, all crowing in tip-toed, wing-flapping anticipation of the new day about to dawn on their individual poultry provinces – the rickety hen runs on a score of little *fincas* scattered around the pine-clad slopes of the previously silent mountains.

Ellie started to snore too.

I lay there, staring blindly into the dark void of the ceiling, wishing for sleep, while a growing choir of waking birds began to twitter in the nearby orange groves as enthusiastically as if auditioning for the chorus line of Brer Rabbit's 'Zip-A-Dee-Doo-Dah'. And still the cosy sounds of family slumber surrounded me. It seemed that

I was the lone wakeful human soul in the valley, doomed to lie there listening to Mrs Van Winkle & Sons snoring away blissfully in a blacked-out nightmare aviary.

Then old Pep's dim-witted dog Perro barked in the little higgledy-piggledy farmstead across the lane. He barked again, yelped as if in pain – a pain induced, no doubt, by a timely kick in the *cojones* from his under-slept master – then fell silent once more. But the damage was done. Perro had succeeded in launching the entire canine population of the valley into confused, contagious yapping and baying, each chained-up mutt dutifully warning off the packs of wolves, bandits and bogeymen that they imagined were skulking in the wooded darkness around their isolated farms.

Well done, Perro! At a stroke, he had developed plumate bedlam into total pandemonium. Nature's quietly passing night-train had gone right off the rails.

Ellie and the boys snored on regardless.

I sighed in despair. 'Ah well, if you can't beat 'em,' I muttered, hauling my reluctant body out of bed and pulling on my clothes. 'I'm going for a walk!'

Outside, the musky scents of the Mediterranean night were still lingering intoxicatingly in the damp early morning air. There was a dream-like quality about the view from beneath the beamed, open *porche* at the front of the house. The ancient almond trees that stood in the nearest field were only just visible in the dim half-light, their twisted black branches rising through a gossamer lake of mist like the distorted arms and spidery fingers of sad, silent ghosts.

I shivered, pulling the collar of my jacket round my ears, and wandered almost hypnotically towards the sleeping orchards beyond. Here in the open, the sounds of waking animal life seemed somehow less irksome, totally at one with the surroundings, in fact, and gradually becoming less frenzied, too. At length, I found myself standing by the old rubble-stone well in the corner of our farthest field, and I turned to look back over the gently-rising terraces of orchards towards the house, its ochre-tiled roof just perceptible through the lifting gloom, its shutters still securely closed against the fading night. Everything was silent now, a total stillness having descended on the valley, enveloping it in the grey-shadowed hush that precedes the magic moment of dawn.

A southerly breeze whispered through the fruit trees, carrying on its balmy breath the fragrance of wild myrtle and thyme from the green hills rolling gently away towards the coast, and I half imagined, half scented the faint, hot aromas of Africa, lying dark and mysterious far over the horizon on the other side of the Mediterranean Sea. I no longer envied Ellie and the boys their undisturbed sleep. General Franco had done me a favour.

My gaze was drawn upward to the high mass of the Sierra Garrafa, where a lone star still glowed in the inky emptiness above the peaks, their serrated outline silhouetted now against a spreading ribbon of light. This was Mallorca as I had never seen it before, awakening in all its serene magnificence. And I was witness not just to the birth of another day, but also the beginnings of a new season.

Suddenly it was spring, and the signs of its arrival were everywhere. Green and petalled things were popping joyously all around me. And there, on the exposed limb of a nearby pine tree, a young cock sparrow was practising his juvenile copulative technique on a consenting fir cone; while over there by the adobe wall of the old water *cisterna*, a pubescent male hedgehog was trembling with myopic ardour while passionately sniffing the blunt end of an upturned scrubbing brush. Oh yes, it was spring all right!

I don't know how long I stood there, leaning against the parapet of the well, my senses delighting in the subtle charms of the nascent day, but by the time I started to wander back towards the house, warm sunlight was already flooding the valley floor, filtering through the lush foliage of the citrus trees, fragrant with *azahar* blossoms, and humming with honeybee melodies.

'Bees are the cupids of the orchard,' old Maria Bauzá had told me, shortly after our arrival in the valley. 'Without them, the act of love between trees, the *matrimonio* which leads to the birth of the fruit, would not take place.'

I remember marvelling at such a poetic description of what, to most people, is just an accepted, if not totally taken-for-granted, detail of nature's ways.

'You need a beehive,' Maria added while I was still silently pondering this unexpectedly romantic turn of phrase from our feisty neighbour.

She had already told me that I needed a pig, some hens and a donkey. The pig and hens had certainly been added to our shopping list, albeit a tad half-heartedly, but a donkey – to old Maria's utter dismay – would never replace a tractor in my league table of essential farming aids. And I was quietly of a mind that the beehive would be joining the donkey in the rejected ideas bin. God knows, I had enough to learn about the complexities of Mediterranean fruit growing, without further complicating my life by plunging my over-taxed brain into the mysteries of the ancient apian arts. No, our lover-boy trees would have to rely on the little arrows of someone else's winged cupids.

It was nice to hear them buzzing away in the blossoms, though, and comforting to know that their dedicated labours were sowing the seeds, so to speak, of our next harvest. The bees were obviously happy with the arrangement, and their owner (if indeed they had one) could look forward to a supply of citrus-blossom honey gleaned for free from somebody else's trees. It was an 'everybody wins' situation, and I savoured the notion of it as I continued my stroll back towards the house.

Although it was still barely seven o'clock, workaday mechanical sounds were already beginning to echo round the valley – another sign of spring and the advent of warmer weather. And, with the lengthening days, we would drift soon enough into the stifling heat of summer, when the work of the countryside, by necessity, would be undertaken in the relative coolness of early morning, late afternoon and evening.

Down the lane towards the village I could hear the two-stroke rattle of the baker's little Citroën 2CV (Juan the *pan* man's van, we called it) starting out on the day's deliveries, while the nasal rasp of a Mobylette moped announced the first of the village-domiciled *campesinos* making his daily journey from house to *finca* somewhere higher up the valley. No doubt he would already have 'breakfasted' on a couple of *coñac*-laced coffees with a few *amigos* in one of the village bars, and he exchanged a cheery

'*Weh-ep!*' greeting with old Pep as he scooted past our neighbour's farm across the way. Although hidden behind the ancient wall running along the lane-side boundary of Ca's Mayoral, the sound of Pep roaring obscenities at his dog, and the tinkling of a score of tinny bells told me that he was already setting off, with his little herd of sheep, for one of the many 'meadows' of weeds on the high *bancales* where he enjoyed grazing rights.

Then the hollow 'chug' of a diesel tractor started up, unseen among the trees of a distant field.

Morning had broken.

Ellie and the boys had their backs to me as I entered the kitchen – Ellie at the hob making coffee, the boys at the table wolfing down bacon and eggs worthy of the name, courtesy of old Maria's fig-fed pigs and orchard-pecking hens.

'Morning, Dad. Been having a lie-in, have you?' Sandy enquired, glancing up momentarily from his matinal feast. 'Didn't think you'd be needing it, judging by the snores coming out of your room all night.'

'Yeah,' Charlie agreed without interrupting his food-shovelling. 'I'm bushed. Hardly got a wink's sleep because of all that racket you were making.'

Saying nothing, I stood there, slowly nodding my head while I awaited Ellie's inevitable clincher.

'The boys are right, dear,' she eventually confirmed, not a trace of remorse in her look as she turned to bring me my coffee. 'You really will have to get yourself seen to, you know.'

Being a Wednesday, it was market day in Andratx.

Sandy had volunteered to do this morning's 'brat run' – his term for driving his younger brother the seventeen miles or so to school, along with three even younger kids whom he'd pick up en route. Not that he particularly enjoyed acting as chauffeur to four bum-scratching little slugs, as he described them with the lofty disdain of the 'mature' eighteen-year-old, rather that he'd do almost anything to postpone embarking on the day's field work with our tiny Barbieri tractor. In comparison to the mighty four-wheel drive beasts he'd been used to driving, he somewhat cruelly regarded our dinky diesel as a motorised donkey... without a saddle. And, in truth, that's almost all it was: a little two-wheeled workhorse which you walked behind, as you would a donkey, and controlled with handlebars instead of reins. But it was a machine ideally suited to working in the tight confines of those tree-crowded little fields, nonetheless. And, on the plus side, as Jaume, another of our venerable neighbours, had so eloquently put it when first recommending that I purchase such a tractor, 'Unlike a donkey, Don Pedro, it will not shit on your boots.'

That was good enough for me, but all purely academic as far as Sandy was concerned. The demeaning image of trudging over the land behind this putt-putting Mickey Mouse contraption was clearly not one that he fancied nurturing. Or so he liked to imply...

In any case, our sons set off in the relative comfort of our 'family' Ford Fiesta, while Ellie and I dropped the back seat of the 'farm' Seat Panda and loaded it to the roof with crates of oranges, today's order for Señor Jeronimo – not the Apache chief reincarnated, as Charlie had originally hoped, but merely our friendly fruit wholesaler along the coast in Peguera.

'Handy having the two cars,' Ellie stoically puffed, doing her best to make herself comfortable in the Panda's pushed-fully-forward passenger seat, with a plastic crate thumping into the back of her head and several plump Valencias landing on her lap every time I braked on the twisty *camino* that led through Sa Coma village to Andratx town.

'Mmm, I'd still be happier if we had the reg. papers, though,' I muttered, retrieving a flying mandarin from the dashboard. I recalled our friend Jock Burns' assurances when he'd nodded us in the direction of his second-hand car dealing *contacto* up the island.

'Dead leery, Enrique is,' Jock had confided as he winked me one of his keep-it-shtum winks. 'Gets the best deals ye could imagine outa the big car-hire companies, see. Year-old motors, mint, low mileage, been serviced every week, fifty per cent off the new price. Magic. Cannae whack it, son.' Another wink, verging on the Masonic this time. 'Contacts, know what I mean? Contacts – that's how ye survive on this island, by the way.'

However, fully three months had now elapsed since we'd taken Jock's advice and become the proud, though somewhat anxious owners of our mint, low mileage Fiesta and Panda cars. And still the registration documents hadn't turned up.

'*No problema,*' Enrique had assured me at the time, giving my back a series of confidence-inducing pats with one hand, while stuffing my eagerly-accepted roll of *dinero* into his breast pocket with the other. I was not to concern myself with such a trifling detail as the absent papers for these *coches estupendos*. *Coño*, this was Spain and these things took time. He lowered an ear towards a raised shoulder and dropped the corners of his mouth into a what's-the-big-deal? facial shrug. 'You know what these big car-hire companies are like, *amigo*. A law unto themselves, no?' I should just relax, be *tranquilo*. The *documentos* would be in the post soon enough. Probably even *mañana*. '*Ay-y-y, no problema, eh!*'

Jock, a fellow Scot who had worked as a schoolteacher on the island for many years (as well as being a popular hotel entertainer and well-known Mr Fixit in his spare time), had reiterated Enrique's philosophy on the several occasions I'd mentioned my concerns to him during the ensuing weeks.

'Dinnae get yer breeks in a fankle, son,' he'd said. 'Look at it this way – as long as ye've no got the papers, ye cannae register the cars in your name, right?'

'Right, but that's what's bothering me. I mean, I can't tax them either and –'

Jock raised a silencing hand, an enquiring look on his face. 'And as long as the cars are no registered in your name...?'

I looked at Jock blankly as he awaited my answer in true schoolmasterly fashion.

'Ye don't get ma drift, do ye, son?'

I shook my head.

Jock shook his head too, tutting in exasperation. 'Have ye ever tried parkin' in Palma city centre when Ellie's dragged ye off tae the shops on a Saturday mornin'?'

I nodded my head.

Jock nodded his head too, smirking smugly this time. 'It's a bugger, intit? Cars everywhere. The polis dishin' out parkin' tickets hoalis-boalis, right?'

'Yeah, but I don't see what...' Then it dawned on me. 'Aw, wait a minute – what you're saying is that I can park wherever I want, because the previous owners of the cars will be –'

'Sent *your* parking tickets,' Jock grinned, delighting in the sweetness of the scam.

'Hmm, but –'

'Hmm, but nothin'! Listen, what d'ye think these car-hire companies do wi' the dozens o' parkin' tickets they're sent every day on a holiday island like this? Forward them tae their long-gone, never-tae-be-seen-again clients in Britain, Germany, Scandinavia or wherever? Fat chance! Nah, they bin them, pal – straight intae the old shredder. And that's what'll happen tae yours an' all, so park on in immunity while the goin's good.' Jock pulled an Enrique-type shrug. 'Par for the course here.'

I wasn't entirely convinced. 'Well... maybe. But, anyway, there's the traffic police. I mean, what if they suss the cars' road tax is overdue?'

Jock patted my cheek and gave me a condescending smile. 'Just try tae look daft for the polisman. Shouldnae be too difficult in your case, eh? Ye say in a very loud voice, "*No comprendo!* Speako only English! Car no mine-o! Hire company's!" Then ye get the wife tae flash him a come-tae-bed look and a tantalisin' wee glimpse o' the *melones* – never fails wi' the Spanish polis, that – and bingo! – ye're off the hook.'

'Or off to the nick for soliciting,' I ventured meekly. 'As well as sundry vehicle-related offences. I could go down for months – years, even.'

'Nah, nah,' Jock laughed. 'Hey, get leery, son. Bein' leery – that's how ye survive on this island, by the way.'

I'd had enough bother trying to learn to be *tranquilo* (and, to be absolutely honest, I still had some distance to go before I would be even halfway to mastering that most Spanish of attributes), and now Jock expected me to 'get leery', a trait which he reckoned should be second nature to me anyway... 'bein' a Scotsman and that, know what I mean?'

Just as I instinctively knew he would be, a municipal policemen was directing traffic, standing four-square in the middle of the crossroads just outside Andratx, as Ellie and I trundled towards him in our orange-laden Panda. He signalled me to stop, then ambled over, his demeanour a study in uniform-wearing intimidation. Any trace of natural leeriness that may have been lurking in my tartan genes quickly took the high road.

The inscrutable lawman walked slowly round the car, scrutinising everything inside and out through his mirror shades.

'For Christ's sake, don't flash him your *melones*,' I muttered to Ellie out of the corner of my mouth.

'I *beg* your pardon?' she gasped, dudgeon ascending rapidly.

'Just, you know, try to appear calm. Keep... keep natural and everything.'

'I *am* natural and everything! Calm too!'

'Yeah, but, I mean... no papers for the car and all that...' I was whispering now.

'Don't be such a numpty,' Ellie scoffed. 'Even if he does ask to see them, what's the problem? Just tell him the truth. You haven't done anything wrong. Just drop that Enrique guy in it if there's any hassle.'

As ever, Ellie was right. The flawless logic of the clear conscience. Something else I had to learn, apparently.

A sudden fracas between a young tractor driver and an old *campesino* with a donkey and cart, over who had the right of way at the road junction, diverted the policeman's attention. Mallorcan road rage had bridged the generation and technology gaps in the nick of time. The frowning *policía municipal* waved us on – a mite grudgingly, I reckoned – blew his whistle at the tractor-versus-donkey combatants and swaggered off to sort them out. All oncoming traffic was held up in the meantime, of course, and being market day, this quickly led to a rapidly growing tailback of coaches ferrying tourists into town for the popular weekly event. Offering a silent prayer to the god of tax evaders, I drove off as fast as the little Panda would go, while an orchestra of coach horns blared a futile fanfare of protest against the three-man shouting match now raging back at the crossroads. The donkey, as I noticed in the rearview mirror, had already fallen asleep.

Leaving Andratx behind, the road to Peguera rises steadily towards the Coll d'Andritxol, a gentle ridge linking the wooded lower slopes of the Biniorella and Garaffa Mountains, and the location of one of the most prolific wells in the area. Normally, you had to keep a weather eye open for one of a regular procession of huge, water-laden tankers exiting the narrow track from the well-head, but the only traffic joining the main road this morning was a battered old Mobylette, ridden by a slightly-built Mallorcan farmer with a smile on his face, a cigarette in the corner of his mouth, and a shopping bag dangling from his moped's handlebars.

It was Jordi Beltran, a real Andratx character, who lived in the town, but cultivated one of a clutch of *huertos*, or small market gardens, occupying a narrow sliver of flat, fertile land that clung to the mountainside adjacent to the Coll's rich source of water. Jordi, who boasted a commendable line in foul-mouthed English, had become a good chum and a valuable source of advice and local information since my chance meeting with him a few months earlier, in the newspaper shop down at the Port of Andratx.

I hooted the Panda's horn and waved. A grin of recognition spread over Jordi's lean features. He pointed towards Andratx and made the thumb-to-the-lips, pinkie-in-air, Mallorcan sign for imbibing. Then, taking my thumbs-up as confirmation of message-understood, he twisted open the Mobylette's throttle and tootled merrily off downhill in a swirl of blue exhaust fumes and cigarette smoke.

'That's *your* market day taken care of, then,' said Ellie dryly.

I elected to remain circumspectly silent.

A bustling holiday resort, a burgeoning *urbanización* which had been little more than a scattering of fishermen's huts prior to the advent of mass tourism, Peguera is the very antithesis of sleepy old Andratx, and therefore nothing like the 'real' Mallorca which we had come to know and love. But for all that, we had made Peguera a regular port of call, basically because at that time it contained the nearest decent-sized supermarket, a branch of the Palma bank that we used and, of course, Señor Jeronimo's wholesale fruit business.

I dropped the cramp-crippled and orange-bashed Ellie off at the *supermercado* on the outskirts of town and proceeded on my way, stopping outside the Bar El Piano for a few moments to exchange pleasantries with its proprietrix, the ever-jovial Señora Esperanza, who was mopping the terrace in preparation for the day's trade. Essentially a large and unpretentious off-the-main-drag eating place, El Piano's 'bar' is used mainly as a post-prandial brandy-downing post by the groups of building workers and vanmen who crowd in every lunchtime to enjoy Esperanza's renowned *menús del día* – three generous courses, including bread and a manly *garrafa* of wine, and all for the price of a 'starter' in the average British eatery. Not surprisingly, the resort's legions of mainly German, retired expats hadn't been slow to recognise the obvious merits of patronising a restaurant where you would be served the better part of your day's required nourishment for no more outlay – and considerably less bother – than you could prepare the equivalent in your own kitchen.

The cosmopolitan and socially-eclectic Bar El Piano had long since been added to our ever-growing list of Mallorca's bargain lunch venues, too, and Esperanza's recitation of today's bill of fare had me feeling hungry already. But there was much to do before any such thoughts could be entertained, so I bade the Señora *adiós* and continued on round the corner to Jeronimo's little warehouse.

As ever, the cramped premises were milling with people: farmers depositing their wares, shopkeepers, restaurateurs and hotel cooks weighing up and selecting their respective requirements, delivery men lugging full crates to their vans, and in the midst of it all the unflappable Jeronimo, taking money with one hand and doling it out with the other. In keeping with the best Spanish country traditions, all transactions were being conducted in cash, and whatever records were being kept appeared to exist only in Jeronimo's head. Pity the taxman who tried to fathom the financial intricacies of such an apparently imprecise system, which, also in keeping with the best Spanish country traditions, could have been precisely the reason for the apparent imprecision. Though only if a less honest businessman than Señor Jeronimo had been involved, of course.

'*Lo siento, señor,*' he said with an apologetic raising of his shoulders after running an eye over my array of oranges, 'I can take everything you have today except the two crates of Valencias.' He gestured towards a stack of crates at the back of the warehouse. 'All Valencias, Señor Peter. It's late in the orange season and, as Valencias are a late variety, there is a glut.' He shrugged again. 'I have bought too many already this morning.'

'Ah, well,' I smiled, trying not to appear too disappointed, 'I suppose that's the fruit farming business for you.' I thanked him for the little wad of notes that he counted carefully into my hand, then turned to leave, lugging the two crates of unwanted oranges back to the car.

'*Momentito!*' Jeronimo called after me, running out of the warehouse with a handful of short green stems that looked not much thicker than grass. 'A little gift for your wife.' He surveyed my puzzled expression for a moment, frowned, then asked: 'She does not like, no?'

'I don't know,' I said, staring blankly at the flimsy shoots. 'No offence, but I mean… what is it?'

'You do not know?'

I shook my head sheepishly.

Jeronimo was patently aghast. '*Hombre*,' he gasped, 'this is beyond value – the caviar of the Mallorcan countryside!'

'Well… well, thanks. Thanks very much,' I said, none the wiser. 'What, uhm… what do I do with it?'

'You do not know how to prepare the *espárragos*? *Dios mío!*'

'Oh, asparagus! Right, of course,' I bluffed, taking a closer look at the spindly stalks. And, sure enough, it *was* asparagus, but looking like an extremely anorexic version of the plump spears I was accustomed to. 'They, uh, look very nice.'

'Nice? *Nice?*'

I had clearly offended Jeronimo, so I apologised profusely, admitting my hitherto total ignorance of this priceless example of the island's vegetation.

This Mallorcan asparagus, he then went on to explain, regarding me with the slightly pitying expression of a man who believes he's talking to a complete idiot, was without doubt a gastronomic luxury of gargantuan proportion.

'Despite its modest size,' my mouth flippantly blurted out before I could slip my brain into gear.

Treating my clumsy quip with the disregard it deserved, Jeronimo proceeded to tell me that the *espárragos* grew wild on the island, and the young, tender shoots – like the ones which he had given me – were eagerly sought by people of educated palate every spring. That was why, at this time of year, every roadside and patch of scrubland was painstakingly scoured by aficionados of this rare gourmet delight.

'The French may boast of their truffles,' he added with a derisory grunt, 'but, *hombre*, those over-priced lumps of smelly fungus cannot compare with the culinary treasure of Mallorca which you hold in your hand right now. Sautéed in a little butter, lightly seasoned and perhaps touched by the slightest caress of garlic, and... I tell you, *señor*, some people would kill for it.'

Suddenly I felt a bit guilty about accepting such a prized and scarce delicacy, and I tried to tell Jeronimo so. 'Look,' I began, 'please don't take this the wrong way, but your own family... I mean, wouldn't you rather –'

Jeronimo raised his hand and shook his head in a placating sort of way. 'Please, I know what you are going to say, but I promise you, you are more than welcome to have the *espárragos*, my friend.'

'Really?'

'Sure.' He gestured dismissively towards the little green bundle in my hand, then started back towards his warehouse. 'Personally,' he called over his shoulder, 'I can't stand the taste of the damned stuff.'

Being a subscriber to the belief that one good turn deserves another, I stopped again at the Bar El Piano in passing and gifted one of the crates of Valencias to Señora Esperanza, who accepted amid a squealed deluge of *muchas gracias*, while insisting that she must pay me for such lovely oranges. Why, growing *naranjas* was my business, she pointed out, and it was only right that I should receive payment. Respectfully declining her offer of money (I knew full well that, in an over-supplied market, I probably wouldn't be able to sell them to anyone else, anyway), I suggested that she might be able to make use of the other crateful as well. But no, Esperanza stated with a courteous smile, she could not possibly accept an even more generous gift of oranges than the one already given, and no doubt the *señor* would find a more worthy recipient for his *benevolencia* elsewhere.

I wasn't so sure about that, but I did know that Esperanza wouldn't forget my little gesture, even though her storeroom was probably already overflowing with cut-price Valencias. When a suitably polite period of time had passed, she would repay us in kind. And, although not looking for any such reciprocation, we would, when the time came, accept with grace, but without fuss. It was, as we'd already learned, the Spanish way.

'A pity you hadn't left them on the trees,' Ellie commented, glancing at the still-full crate as she helped unload her supermarket trolley into the car. She rubbed the back of her head. 'Hmm, would have saved me a few bruises on the journey here today, too.'

She was right on both counts. Oranges do keep best if left to hang where they grow, even when perfectly ripe. I'd been told that by our near neighbour Jaume, right at the outset of our Mallorcan fruit-growing adventure, and by just about every other *campesino* in the valley many times since. Yet it had taken my first experience of a saturated market to make the advice finally sink in.

'So, what are you going to do with them?' Ellie asked, an overtly supercilious hint to her tone.

I resisted the temptation of giving the obvious answer and pointed the little Panda in the direction of Andratx.

The market place of Andratx is situated on the outskirts of town, in a wide, tree-lined avenue overlooked by the imposing bulk of Son Mas Castle, for centuries the baronial pile of wealthy landowners, but now the unashamedly grand seat of the *Ayuntamiento*, or Andratx Town Council. Times, politics, and, therefore, fortunes change.

I dropped Ellie off for her weekly rummage round the rows of stalls, selling everything from farm-fresh produce to sheepskin carpet slippers, from live boiling fowls and roasting rabbits to pots and pans and pruning saws, from caged canaries to fake snakeskin belts touted by swarthy Romanies shouting, 'Lookee, lookee, lady!', and from plastic sacks of steaming mule dung to music cassettes featuring the perennial hits of the Spanish holiday hotspots. Costa classics like 'The Birdie Song', 'Agadoo' and, of course, the essential, 'We're Having A Gang Bang Against The Wall' were blaring out across the bustling scene.

Despite being so early in the tourist season, the market place *was* surprisingly busy – chicken-prodding country women rubbing shoulders with sombrero-topped holidaymakers; leather-faced old farmers being elbowed aside by pot-bellied bruisers in football shirts; shifty gypsy youths dipping open handbags or palming bulging wallets protruding invitingly from passing hip pockets. Roll on the autumn, when Wednesday mornings in sleepy old Andratx would return to being 'normal' again. I gladly left Ellie to it and drove off towards the main square.

The Plaza de España is tucked away in the centre of town, a pleasant open space in the midst of a right-angle network of narrow streets, the pervading maze effect exacerbated for the stranger by a confusing, though necessary, one-way system. Even after almost four months as an adopted native, I would still often lose my bearings in Andratx. But this morning was all right. I parked the car near the corner of the square and headed for the Bar Nuevo.

'Ay-y-y, bloody 'ell! How you being doing today, man?' Jordi called from his seat in the sun outside his regular haunt.

Exchanging greetings and handshakes, I joined him at his table and ordered two beers from Guillermo, the attentive proprietor, who had appeared in the doorway of his bar on hearing Jordi's salutation.

'No, no, bloody 'ell, don't putting me a beer!' Jordi protested.

'OK,' I said to Guillermo, 'a beer for me, *por favor*, and a *coñac* for Jordi. Or gin, Bacardi – whatever he wants.'

Guillermo cast me a you-won't-believe-this look as Jordi redoubled his protestations. Although by no means a drunkard, I'd never known Jordi to refuse alcoholic refreshment when he was relaxing, so what he said next took my breath away.

'*Zumo de naranja, Guillermo. Sí, solamente zumo de naranja, eh!*'

Orange juice? Straight orange juice! What had happened to Jordi? Was he unwell, I enquired?

'Been being in hospital, oh yes,' Jordi confided in hushed tones, his accent when speaking English falling engagingly somewhere between Karachi and Coventry, having worked for sixteen years in the English city, while living in a mainly Asian community there. 'Two weeks in bloody bugger *sanatorio* up the mountains, man.'

Somehow this revelation didn't come as a complete surprise. Jordi had been a lifetime heavy smoker of strong Spanish cigarettes, after all, and now that he was past his sixtieth summer…

'A *sanatorio?*' I said, genuinely concerned. 'Lung problem, is it, Jordi?'

The little fellow shook his head, pulled out another cigarette from his shirt pocket and lit up, not the slightest suggestion of a telltale cough emanating from his scrawny chest. I could tell from his delay in replying to my question, however, that he was searching for the right word. Jordi loved speaking English, and although his vocabulary wasn't particularly extensive, he hated to be found wanting. He was never stuck, though. If in doubt, throw in anything, and in this particular instance the throw-in word was 'tripe'.

'Tripe?' I asked, totally bamboozled. 'They put you in hospital for… *tripe?*'

'Bloody 'ell! What bloody bugger lingo you being speak in Scotchland, Crice sake?' The best form of bilingual defence was obviously attack as far as Jordi was concerned. He pointed agitatedly at his midriff. 'You know – thing in here what going well with onions. Like I been being say… tripe!'

Then it dawned on me. The onions connection was the breakthrough. 'Oh,' I said, trying desperately hard not to even smile, let alone laugh, 'you, ehm – you mean liver, right?'

'Yeah! Like I been being say… liver! Jordi's bloody damn baster liver been becoming crap!' He wrinkled his face into an aggrieved scowl, crossed his spindly legs, took a deep drag on his cigarette, then muttered through a cloud of exhaled reek, 'Is bloody ridickliss!'

It didn't take much to persuade Jordi to reveal the full details of his recent infirmity, and, not surprisingly, my initial suspicion that his liver problem had been drink-induced proved to be absolutely correct. A little over a fortnight earlier, he recounted, he had popped into the Bar Nuevo on his way home from his *finca* – 'just for the drinking a coupla bloody swift ones' – as was his wont of an evening. It was then that cruel fate stepped in (not an unusual occurrence in bars). This time fate had taken the form of Wayne Murphy, a hard-drinking Aussie who, between spells working as a roughneck on Middle East oil rigs, holed up with a seen-better-days Swedish sheila in an ex-shepherd's shack outside Andratx. Wayne had just arrived back in Mallorca after a three-month 'dry' stint in the Gulf, with, as he had put it, 'a swagful a' petrodollars, mate, and a thirst that'd start a bleedin' bushfire in Sydney Harbour'. Trouble was, a bloke needs a cobber to have a yarn with while puttin' away a few cool ones, so Wayne had a problem, since he didn't speak the local lingo and none of the locals in the Bar Nuevo that evening spoke his… until Jordi arrived.

Well, Jordi and Wayne had had a couple of memorable beer-ups in the Andratx bars on previous such occasions, so it had seemed only natural to Jordi that he should join his sometime chum again. A few bottles of San Miguel, a good old chat in English and, of course, the chance to pick up a few rare expletives from a real expert like Wayne. No harm in that, Jordi had decided.

But, as the night wore on and the intended few bottles of beer graduated into several litres apiece, it had appeared a splendid idea, when Guillermo finally put up the shutters, for the two intrepid carousers to proceed to Jordi's house for a quick nightcap. A random handful of Wayne's pocket-burning petrodollars had then been converted into a modest take-away of six one-litre bottles of Fundador *coñac*.

Jordi woke up three days later. He was at home. He knew that because he recognised the kitchen floor he was lying on. But how long he had been in that position, or even what had happened after they'd left the Bar Nuevo, was a complete blank. All he knew was that his head was thumping fit to burst, his mouth tasted like a Bedouin's Y-fronts (an expression he *thought* he must have picked up from Wayne), and there was a terrible burning pain just below and to the right of his ribcage. Wayne was gone, and so was the brandy, although the six empty bottles lying strewn around the floor told their own story.

'Damn baster doctor been coming my house,' Jordi grunted, then took a tiny sip of his orange juice, which I thought for a moment he was about to spit out again. 'Been sending me up the *sanatorio*, oh yes. Right away – *ambulancia* – lights been flash – hoot horning – big emergingcy.' He stared silently into his orange juice for a few reflective seconds before adding, almost as if to himself, 'Bloody 'ell! Poor Jordi been being nearly bloody stiff city.'

'A wee touch of alcohol poisoning, eh, Jordi,' I ventured sympathetically, immediately realising that I'd probably just uttered a contender for the understatement of the century prize.

Jordi said nothing – just sat there thinking his own thoughts.

'And what about your pal Wayne?' I asked after a while.

Jordi looked up, a sudden twinkle in his eyes, a look of quiet esteem lighting the smile that now played at the corners of his lips. 'Oh, he been being OK all right. I been seeing him yesterday – over there in Bar Balear, other side the bloody square. And still being drink the Mahatma Ghandi, him. Yay, guts like a tin shearing shed, that bugger being have,' Jordi chuckled, a faint Aussie whiff to his accent now. 'Oh yay, stone the bleedin' lizards, mate. Bloody 'ell!' His bony shoulders shook in a wheezy little snigger.

'So, uhm, you – you're off the hard stuff, then, Jordi?'

The glum expression returned to his face. 'Hard stuffs, wine, beer, everything stuffs. Baster doctor been tell me straight, no more drinking the alcoholics for you, Jordi – else you being dying, for sure.' Jordi paused and looked at me, tears in his eyes, his bottom lip quivering. 'Like I been being tell you already... Jordi's tripe... fucked.' He shook his head in undisguised self-pity, then concluded in an emotional croak, 'Is bloody ridickliss.'

I was spared the difficulty of having to think of something appropriate to say by the sight of Ellie struggling into the square, weighed down with even more bulging plastic bags. I did wonder, though, how long a dedicated social imbiber like Jordi would be able to stick to fruit juice. But, looking at Ellie, I wondered even more how it is that a woman can spend half the morning stocking up with a trolley-load of stuff in a supermarket, then immediately spend another hour doing exactly the same in a street market.

'Ah, hello, lady – please be sitting,' Jordi said as Ellie approached the table. He stood up, bowed his usual stiff little bow, gestured Ellie towards a particular chair, then graciously beseeched her to 'plank her arse down there'.

Ellie did as beseeched, while flashing Jordi a demure little 'thank you' smile. She'd been in Jordi's company on a few brief occasions before, and she knew that the milder swear words which he reserved for a lady's presence were intended to be taken purely as a mark of respect and chivalry. And, fair enough, not once had I heard Jordi using anything stronger in front of Ellie than his trademark 'bloody 'ell' or, as today, 'arse'. Quite the gallant *caballero* was Jordi.

'So, lady, what you been being buying?' he asked, once satisfied that Ellie was comfortably planked.

'Well, you know, just the usual bits and pieces. But, ehm, I did buy some mussels from the fishmonger. First time I've been in there since I wished him Happy New –'

'Muskles?' Jordi exclaimed, a delighted grin wrinkling his lean features. 'Bloody 'ell! Jordi too!' He bent down and pulled a small net full of the shiny black molluscs from his shopping bag and held it up proudly. 'Mayorky muskles. The most best ones, oh yes.'

'Yes, I thought they looked nice and fresh and everything. But, I mean, I've never bought them here before. And mussels... well, I just sort of wondered...'

'You knowing how to cooking them, lady?'

'Uhm, yes. I usually just sort of –'

Jordi wagged a forefinger at Ellie. 'Parding me the interrupts, lady, but Jordi being have the best recype for the muskles from many time. From old grandmother of Jordi – he been being one sailor in the fishing boats, OK?'

While we tried to fathom that one out, Jordi proceeded to spell out his special mussels recipe, insisting that Ellie write it down 'in case she being forgets'.

'MEJILLONES Á LA JORDI'
('Jordi's Muskles')

1 kilo of fresh mussels, washed, de-bearded and put into a large saucepan over a medium heat.

Add:
1 large glass dry red wine
1 lemon, halved
1 large onion, finely chopped
3 garlic cloves, sliced
1 large tomato, chopped
Few drops wine vinegar
Handful parsley, chopped
Black pepper, freshly ground
Tomato purée – sufficient to thicken sauce

Cover pan and bring to the boil, then reduce heat.

Simmer, shaking frequently, for five or six minutes
(until the shells are open) and serve with crusty bread.

As Ellie scribbled the final few vital instructions onto the back of an envelope, Jordi leaned towards me and whispered, 'Is bloody marvliss recype, man.' He winked. 'The baster bollicks of the dog, oh yes!'

After such a colourful critique, I could hardly wait to cover that pan and start shaking frequently. In fact, I could feel the tremors coming on already. Or was that rather because I'd just noticed the traffic policeman who'd pulled me up earlier ambling into the square and stopping beside our car? Again he carefully scrutinised the outside, checking the number plates, back and front, then peered inside, a wicked little smirk spreading beneath those unfathomable mirror shades. Nicked, I thought. God, and I'd forgotten back then at the crossroads – I hadn't yet completed the lengthy procedure of obtaining my Spanish *residencia* certificate, which would at least have made my selling of oranges legal. So, what was I going to say if he asked me where all the crates that had been in the car before had gone? Gave them away to an orphanage? Nah, didn't know of any handy waifs' homes. A nunnery? Nope, hadn't any connections there, either. Don't panic! Just sink low into the chair and try to look invisible, that was the answer...

Jordi wasn't slow to notice my reaction to the arrival of the lawman. He made a dismissive swatting movement with his hand. 'Ay-y-y-y, don't worrying about him,' he scoffed. '*Policía municipal?* Pah! You need only worrying about *Guardia Civil*, bloody 'ell!' He gave a chesty chortle.

'*Sí*, and even them not be shooting so many peoples now'days.'

But despite this bravado pronouncement, Jordi hurriedly excused himself and beat a prudent retreat into the sanctuary of the bar when the policeman wandered towards us, pausing en route to survey Jordi's old Mobylette, illegally parked, as it usually was, on the pavement. My heart skipped a beat as the officer then sauntered directly up to our table.

'*Ah-h-h, buenos días, señor*. That is your car, no?' he enquired with a scarily cordial air, nodding in the direction of our little Panda.

I tried to make eye contact, to look for a flicker of compassion through the mirror lenses of his sunglasses, but all I saw was my own reflection – the face of a guilty-looking foreigner – in stereo.

'Ehm, *sí, sí... Mi coche... sí*,' I falteringly confessed, dark images of the notorious dungeons of Bellver Castle on the outskirts of Palma rising in my mind. Damn – and I had a glass of beer in my hand, too. No car documents, no car tax, no work permit, and now I was a Breathalyser candidate to boot!

Ellie cleared her throat and flashed the policeman a disarming smile. 'A *problema*, sir?' she asked in fluent Spanglish.

The policeman removed his shades to reveal a pair of big brown eyes, which were about as threatening as a koala's. '*No problema, señora*,' he smiled. No, no, he continued, making reassuring movements with his hands, as if smoothing out a tablecloth – no, it was just that he had seen the magnificent Valencia oranges in our car earlier and had intended asking if he could buy some. Then that silly old *campesino* with the donkey had started the fracas with the *chico* with the tractor and... Well, he had just noticed that we still had some Valencias in the car and, being a *valenciano* himself, he always looked for his native oranges at Andratx market, but hadn't seen any as good as ours today, so –

'They're all yours,' I blurted out, taking the startled copper by the arm and guiding him towards the car. 'All of them. Please... be my guest.' I opened the boot and thrust the full crate at him.

'No, *gracias*, but all I need is –'

'No, I insist.'

'But – but, I must pay. How much for–?'

'No, no – I don't sell them! Oh no, we just, you know – we have so many, we just give them away to – to, uhm, friends. Yes! And you're more than welcome... eh, *amigo*.'

'But the crate...'

'Don't worry about the crate. Just, well, just hand it in to Guillermo at the bar sometime. But, no hurry – no hurry at all. Just, you know, whenever you happen to be passing.'

A delighted grin spread over the policeman's face. '*Muy generoso, señor*,' he beamed, then leaned towards me to quietly confide: 'And if you ever pick up a parking ticket, you know where to come to have it, er... dealt with, *sí*?'

Valencias had suddenly become my favourite variety of orange.

'See what I mean?' Jock would surely have said. 'Connections and leeriness. That's what ye need tae survive on this island, by the way. Aye, ye cannae whack it, son!'

His twin criteria had certainly helped make my day, albeit a mite fortuitously, and by the time we settled down in the *porche* that evening for our first alfresco family dinner of the year, even General Franco's yodelled crowing sounded relatively tuneful. Maybe it was the wine, maybe it was the balmy fragrance of the citrus trees drifting up from the orchards on the warm evening breeze, or maybe, as with old Maria's cockerel, it was just the arrival of spring. Whatever the reason, I felt contented with my lot, and although nothing was said, I knew that we all finally realised that we were more than a little fortunate to be living in such an enchanting place.

And what of Señor Jeronimo's *espárragos*? Simply done in exactly the way he had suggested, they were indeed an absolute delight – more tender, succulent and delicate of flavour than any asparagus I'd had before, or have tasted since… except on the rare occasions when we've been lucky enough to find a few of the magic Mallorcan shoots growing in the untilled corner of a field, perhaps.

Jordi's mussels recipe, too, was given a unanimous vote of approval. Another gem of simple Mallorcan cookery which I implore everyone to try. Jordi's seafaring grandmother will be universally applauded, I promise you.

'Well, Dad,' a well-sated Sandy said, mopping up the last delicious dregs of his mussels liquor with a chunk of bread, 'going to entertain us with more of your snoring tonight, are you?'

I poured myself another glass of wine and settled back to watch the sun dipping behind the crest of the mountains on the far side of the valley. 'Yes,' I replied through a contented grin, 'I think I very likely will at that.'

Ellie and Charlie groaned in unison, while a choir of crickets began their nocturnal chorus from the depths of a fig tree at the side of the house. Another sign that spring had truly sprung.

- Two -

WOOD FOR THOUGHT

'There's a five-foot blue tit hanging upside down in one of the orange trees.'

'There's a *what?*'

Ellie didn't really drink, so I knew she had to be sober, but I'd heard about opium poppies growing wild in Mallorca, so I wondered if she'd inadvertently sniffed one.

'I'm telling you,' she persisted, '– a thing like a giant blue tit, dangling from one of the trees in the far orchard. Come out here and see for yourself.'

I joined her on the balcony and followed her gaze down over the lines of trees that filled the gently sloping fields. And she was right. She wasn't hallucinating. There *was* something down there – a brightly-coloured creature which, from that distance, did look remarkably like an overgrown titmouse, moving about in the innards of an orange tree and flinging great bunches of twigs and even the occasional branch onto the ground.

'See what I mean?'

'Yeah, I do,' I gasped. 'But if that's a blue tit, it must have been crossed with a woodpecker on gorilla hormone-replacement therapy. Look! It's tearing the tree to bits! Right then, I'd better get down there and see what the hell it is.'

The one snag about an orchard on such occasions is that, from ground level, you truly can't see the wood for the trees. Indeed, traversing each little field at a trot, all I could see ahead of me was row upon row of tree trunks and citrus foliage drooping to almost knee-height. But, try as I might, I could catch not a glimpse of the giant blue tit, the noise of whose tree vandalising grew ever louder as I approached. The sickening crunch and groan of wanton timber destruction seemed to fill the valley now, the usual serenity of our nook of Mediterranean paradise transformed, aurally at least, into something more akin to the clamour of a lumber camp in the Canadian Rockies.

And the sight that greeted me when I finally reached the far field took my breath away. There, right before me, was what I had considered until then to be the healthiest orange tree on the farm – a large and prolific mandarin, reduced now to an almost leafless skeleton, some of its inner limbs and several outer branches lying scattered around what little remained of its once handsome form.

Carnage.

'What the blazes is going on here?' I shouted.

'Ah, *buenos días, señor*,' crooned the blue tit… or, rather, what still looked a bit like a blue tit, even at this close range.

But the creature dangling in the remains of the tree was no bird. It was a man – a wiry little man in his fifties, with a blue-and-white baseball cap on his head, wearing a yellow T-shirt and blue jeans, his 'tail' a selection of saws, knives and snippers hanging down from a stout belt around his waist.

'I am Pepe Suau,' he smiled, dropping lightly out of the mandarin corpse and offering me his hand. 'I have come to prune your orchards for you.'

Pepe went on to explain that he usually attended to old Maria's trees first in this valley, but as those of the *Señor de Escocia* were in such a neglected state, he thought it best to start with them instead this year. His voice was soft and reassuring as he informed me that there was much work for him to do here. '*Hombre, mucho, mucho trabajo.*'

Didn't I know it! Soon after buying the farm of Ca's Mayoral from Francisca and Tomàs Ferrer, an upwardly-mobile Mallorcan couple who had inherited the property from Francisca's parents, we had been told by well-meaning neighbours that the health of the orchards was not all that it might appear to *inexperto* fruit farmers like ourselves. Although Francisca's father, old Paco, had prided himself in maintaining the farm in prime condition all of his days, old age and the heartbreaking loss of his wife had gradually sapped his energy and the will to carry on. The result was that, in recent years, the orchards had become more and more neglected. Although the trees may have looked all right to the untrained eye, the fact was that many were now suffering from disease, and all from a serious lack of essential pruning. We had to face the truth: in our innocent ignorance, we'd bought a lemon of an orange farm – a run-down, though idyllic, pig in a poke, which would test our resolve, stamina and, we guessed, our financial resources if we were ever to restore it to its previous position of high regard in this valley of similar little farms.

I remembered how crestfallen I'd felt when old Jaume gently broke the bad news to me during a casual inspection stroll through rank upon regular rank of our trees one sunny December day, when the calm of the benign Mallorcan winter weather was suddenly at odds with my feeling of rising panic. Had I brought my family all this way to a foreign land, invested so much of our capital in a form of farming I knew nothing about just to fall at the first hurdle, the victim of my own impetuosity – and, maybe, the dupe of the wily Ferrers? I'd feared then that I had, despite Ellie's ever-optimistic words of encouragement.

But there was no turning back. We had burned our boats, and there was nothing else for it than to grit our teeth, roll up our sleeves and get on with the job. After all, we'd been faced with a similar challenge back in Scotland many years before and had achieved what we'd set out to do by sheer determination and hard work. So why not here? Surely, when all was said and done, the only differences were the language and the climate. Well, if we discounted the fact that we knew nothing about what we were doing, that is.

Yet it took the kindness and understanding of our old Mallorcan neighbours in the valley finally to convince me that I hadn't made an irreparable mistake.

'Everything will turn out all right in the spring, Don Pedro,' old Jaume had said on that unforgettable December day. 'This is Mallorca. Just be *tranquilo*, and everything will come right, you'll see.'

Sound advice for a fellow *tranquilo mallorquín*, perhaps, but easier said than done for a fish-out-of-water northern neurotic like me.

'All you need is a true maestro of the trees to help you,' Jaume had then said, laying a sympathetic hand on my shoulder and ushering me off through his immaculate lemon groves for a *tranquilo*-inducing tasting session of his home-made *vino tinto*. 'And my *amigo* Pepe Suau is the tree maestro of tree maestros around Andratx here. Just leave it to me, Don Pedro. I will arrange everything.'

A midday gutful of Jaume's 'robust' vintage had certainly introduced me to the necessity of the daily *siesta*, but the nagging doubts about the prudence of having hitched our wagon to a potential white elephant still haunted me throughout the remaining winter months, despite gradually feeling totally at home at Ca's Mayoral and at one with the valley and its people.

And now, when I looked at the drastic surgery that Pepe Suau had found it necessary to perform on what I'd rated our healthiest tree, those doubts escalated into near panic once more. How would we get a citrus crop the following winter if all the orange and lemon trees ended up looking like this? Even the most ardent of bees couldn't arrange a *matrimonio* if there was nothing left for the blossoms to grow on. And worse still, there were all the other summer and autumn-fruiting trees to consider in the interim – the apricots, the quinces, the persimmon, the figs, pomegranates, loquats, plums, cherries and pears – not to mention the almonds and carobs. How would we survive with no fruit to sell till God knows when? Hell's teeth, it would take years for the trees to recover from near-terminal amputations like this!

I felt a bead of cold sweat begin to trickle down my forehead, just as one of General Franco's harem of hens laid a timely egg in old Maria's farmstead a couple of fields away, her post-natal cackle sounding at that moment suspiciously like a derisive chuckle. And maybe she was right. No matter how integrated I thought I'd become, I was still the *loco extranjero*, the daft foreigner, like all the others who, some Mallorcans reckoned, left their brains at the airport on arrival. Yes, let's face it, I had laid an egg far bigger than Maria's laughing hen could ever have popped in her wildest dreams. And it hurt.

Pepe Suau gave a little knowing chortle, his kindly eyes observing me closely. 'You think I am murdering your trees, Señor Peter, no?' he murmured.

A spoken reply would have been superfluous, so I simply shrugged a resigned shrug, my body language suggesting, no doubt, a somewhat pathetic '*que será, será*' – 'whatever will be, will be'. I was rapidly sinking into a quicksand of doom.

Pepe's smile spread into a broad grin. 'You thought this old *mandarino* was one of your best trees, *sí*?'

I nodded gravely.

'And it gave you *mucha fruta*, no?'

'*Sí, mucha.*'

Pepe gestured towards the sad amputee. 'And now you wonder how it will grow any more *mandarinas*... ever, *sí*?'

I heaved an affirmative sigh, dropping the corners of my lips into a negative smile.

Ah, but that was the trick of trees, Pepe disclosed, directing my attention to the tangle of branches and mounds of leafy twigs surrounding the base of the subject's trunk. 'Left to their own devices, they just grow and grow, the network of branches becoming more complicated and entangled. For a tree is like a child, *señor* – left unchecked and untrained, it simply grows wild. No less beautiful in some ways, perhaps, but unruly, less productive and, usually, its own worst enemy.' He bent down and picked up a straight, thin shoot, almost as long as he was tall. 'And, just as you would a child, you must protect the tree from bad company, from hangers-on like this sucker here, which will eventually steal all that is good from the tree.' And when health problems struck, as they inevitably would, no matter how attentive the farmer, the tree had to be nursed until it was better. '*Sí*, just like a child, Señor Peter – but even more difficult.' He put a finger to his lips. 'For a tree cannot talk.' Then he pointed to his eye. 'So the farmer must be *muy observador*, no?'

Jeez, and I'd thought mothering week-old orphan calves back in Scotland had been a headache! Still, at least a tree couldn't skitter diarrhoea down the front of your jeans, or bellow to be bucket-fed warm milk in the middle of the night, so that was a bonus.

'Yes, well, I get the theory, Pepe,' I admitted, 'just common sense, in a way. But to be honest, I don't see how mutilating a tree as severely as this can be good for it. Or the farmer, for that matter. *Or* his bank manager.'

Pepe took my point, and blunted it with a little giggle. 'Aha, but just like the wayward child, this tree will reward you soon enough for having saved it from the folly of its own ways. All you have to do is water it and feed it throughout the summer, and let nature do the rest. By November, this tree will give you a good crop of *mandarinas* – maybe not so many as this year, but bigger, juicier and,' he paused to rub his forefinger and thumb together, '– the most important thing... heavier.'

To my inexperienced eye, it seemed that it would take some sort of minor miracle to validate Pepe's prediction, but our very survival was now entirely in his hands, and all I could do was trust him and hope for the best.

He went on painstakingly to explain why he had cut several fairly stout limbs from the centre of the tree. You had to keep the heart of the tree open, he said, to allow the light in and encourage new fruit-bearing growth to develop. 'Such intrusive branches should have been removed years ago,' he disclosed, talking in a whisper and glancing over his shoulder as if old Paco, the former owner of the farm and a once-renowned tree maestro himself, was somehow listening. 'But the tree has already given you a reward for rescuing it, Señor Peter,' he grinned, trying, I suspected, to lighten the mood which my glum expression was doubtless imparting.

'It has?'

'*Sí, claro!* Look at this, my friend.' He bent down and picked up one of the thicker branches that he'd cut from the tree. 'Trim off all the thin shoots and twigs, cut what's left into half-metre lengths, and what have you got?'

'Logs?' I tentatively ventured, half wondering if it had been a trick question.

'*Sí!* Logs! *Estupendo!*' The little chap laughed aloud, giving my back a slap so congratulatory that you'd have thought I'd just won the final of *Mastermind*. Ah, *sí, sí,* he enthused, next winter I would have the joy of sitting by a blazing fire which was sweet with the scent of oranges – lemons too, and cherries, quinces, everything! *Coño,* by the time he was finished in these orchards of mine I wouldn't need to buy firewood again for years!

Well, at least we would starve to death in comfort, I told myself by way of consolation, my mind's eye conjuring up images of our fields looking like some post-nuclear battle ground in the wake of Pepe's 'curative' *trabajo.*

'*Ahora!*' he said, girding his tool belt and adopting a business-like air. 'Now, Señor Peter, I must continue my work. But look.' He swept his hand in a wide ark. 'All of those orange trees which still have fruit – I will leave them till last so that you can pick them clean before I prune them. *Sí*, there is much work to be done here. *Mucho, mucho trabajo.*'

He didn't have to tell me again. For the next ten days Ellie, Sandy and I – Charlie, too, at weekends and after school – worked like fury to keep ahead of the sawing and snipping Pepe, accompanied sometimes by his son Miguel, who had clearly inherited his father's gift for tree doctoring. It seemed that they hardly needed to give a tree even the briefest of inspections before setting to with their tools to perform a barbering job at least, and at most a complete makeover. The speed of their technique was formidable, but, fortunately for us, pressure of other work meant that they only came to Ca's Mayoral in the mornings, so we had every afternoon and evening to try to catch up – picking the last of the oranges, hauling out the 'log-able' wood from the rest, trimming it, then piling the waste material into heaps for burning later.

And as the spring daytime temperatures crept inexorably into the mid-twenties, we were given an ominous foretaste of the working conditions that awaited us in a month or two. As it was, we were struggling at times to keep toiling away in heat which, although still temperate by Mallorcan summer standards, was about as much as we'd normally had to cope with even in the sunniest of Scottish haymaking seasons. Also, in Scotland we'd had machinery to do much of the heavy work, whereas here, in the confines of the orchards, manual labour was almost totally the order of the day. Even the essential *siesta* had to be forfeited in the quest to keep just one step ahead of the flashing blades of Pepe Suau and son.

'Think of the pounds you're shedding,' I said to Ellie by way of encouragement one particularly sticky Saturday afternoon, when a humid southerly breeze fanned the flames of the bonfire that we were feeding with the now tinder-dry heaps of tree debris. 'Better than a sauna, this.'

Ellie said nothing, but the look which she gave me while wiping the ash-smudged sweat from her forehead with the back of her arm spoke volumes.

'I'll settle for a sauna,' Sandy grunted, heaving a hefty apricot branch onto the little trailer attached to the rear end of our tiny Barbieri tractor. 'And a proper tractor... with four wheels... a hydraulic front-end loader... a cab with a seat in it... *and* air-conditioning!'

'I'll settle for a seat and air-conditioning,' quipped Charlie from his look-busy-and-nobody'll-notice position, faffing about with a few lightweight branches at the windward side of the fire.

I decided to keep any further man-management words of inspiration to myself.

But we were making progress, even if *poco a poco* as ever, and our dogged hard graft was not going un-noticed by our neighbours.

'In the old days we would have saved the twigs too,' declared old Maria Bauzá, Jaume's ancient mother-in-law and the owner of the next-door *finca*, which Jaume worked for her since retiring from his *profesión* as a waiter in one of Palma's top hotels. Maria, clad in her habitual black – except for a battered, wide-brimmed straw hat of the type favoured by Mallorcan country women of her generation – had hobbled, unseen and unheard, to the drystone wall which separated our two farms. She stood looking over at us, trusty mattock hoe in hand as usual, while resting her diminutive, stooped frame against the smooth trunk of a shady lemon tree.

We had long since learned that Maria's favourite topic of conversation – or, more accurately, lecture subject – was her precious 'old days' and everything associated with them.

'*Buenos días*, Maria,' we chanted in panted unison, anticipating her latest dissertation with no great relish on this particular occasion.

'And you should save all that wood ash once the fire is out,' she further advised. 'Put it in sacks or boxes and keep it in a dry place.'

'*Sí?* Come in handy for something, does it, Maria?' I puffed, dodging back from a long tongue of flame that licked out greedily from the bonfire on the hot breath of the breeze.

'In the old days we would have saved the twigs, even the smallest of them, for kindling the house fires in winter,' Maria said reprovingly, while slipping effortlessly into her confusing conversational custom of reverting to the penultimate topic without first completing the last. Talking to Maria was to play a game of verbal leapfrog – in reverse.

I blinked at her through the stinging wood smoke. 'Good idea!' I replied, feigning enthusiasm. 'Maybe we'll do that another year, Maria. But, well, for the present, as you can see, we're a bit too busy to –'

'And what does that noisy tractor give you to burn in the house when the weather turns cold?' she cut in, a frown gathering beneath the rim of her straw hat as she pointed the handle of her hoe at the little machine.

I took a deep breath, preparing myself for one of her favourite tractor-versus-donkey diatribes. 'Well,' I sighed, 'I suppose we could burn the spent engine oil. But in the house, that wouldn't really be a good –'

Maria thumped the blade of her hoe on the wall, abruptly shutting me up in mid-flow.

'*Mierda de burro!*' she declared at the top of her squeaky voice.

Ellie and Sandy sniggered quietly at their work. Charlie guffawed. I searched for a reply which would neither cause offence nor convey to the mischievous old woman that I was about to take her bait.

'Ehm, sorry, Maria – *no entiendo*. I don't quite understand what you –'

'She said shit of a donkey, Dad,' Charlie piped up wide-eyed, an approval-seeking grin bisecting his face like an upturned slice of melon.

'Good to know your Spanish studies are progressing so well at school, Charlie,' I muttered, 'but I managed to fathom that translation out for myself, thank you very much. Now, just you get on with what you're doing and let me handle this, OK?'

'*Mierda de burro!*' Maria reiterated, even louder this time.

I decided to risk mixing it, leapfrog-wise. 'So, what you're suggesting, Maria, is that the wood ash and the *mier–*'

'Who mentioned wood ash!' she yelled. 'I'm talking about things to burn in your fire during the winter! *Madre mía!* Never listen, you young people – that's your problem!'

I suppose I should have been flattered at being called 'young', but then everyone under the age of eighty was young in Maria's eyes. I forked another pile of leafy twigs onto the fire, prompting Maria to mumble a string of words in her native *mallorquín* – derogatory-sounding words which, although I didn't understand them, required no elucidation. I was already convinced that she'd made her mind up long ago that I was a *loco extranjero* of the first order.

'Did you not have hand-made logs in *Escocia?*' she eventually called out, reverting to standard Castilian

Spanish, which was, in effect, a secondary language to her and her fellow rural *mallorquines* – a 'foreign' tongue which they sometimes had to think about before speaking, and then did so relatively slowly. This suited struggling Spanish-speakers like us just fine.

'Hand-made logs?' I scratched my head. 'No, I don't think so. Well, yes... now you mention it, somebody did once invent a little machine for making burnable bricks out of old newspapers, I think. Never caught on, though. More trouble than it was worth, I suppose.'

'More money than sense,' was Maria's muttered response. *Vale*, she knew nothing of newspaper logs, but the principle was the same. Make use of everything. Waste nothing. That was the motto on these little Mallorcan farms. 'Mark my word,' she added sagely, 'you will find out soon enough, *muchacho*.'

While I didn't doubt the wisdom of Maria's advice for one moment, under the present circumstances it would have cost us more than a few packets of firelighters to have kept Pepe Suau hanging about while we laboriously separated out, bunched and carted off countless trailer-loads of twigs. Clearly, our impish old neighbour knew this perfectly well, too, but she saw the matter as a good vehicle for today's 'conversation' – distinctly one-sided though it was bound to be.

'*Gracias* for the, ehm, eggs, Maria,' Ellie said, attempting a change of subject in her characteristic Hispano–English. 'The, uh, boys – *hijos* – yes, the *hijos* here had them for breakfast the other *mañana* there. *Sí, muy* lovely, the, you know – eggs... *gracias*.'

Whether Maria had made much sense of any of that, it was impossible to determine, but as she saw Ellie as some kind of fairy princess from the romantic frozen north, she appeared to take the stumbled mumbo jumbo as a compliment, anyway.

'No, no, *Señora de Escocia*,' she sweetly smiled, a gently reproachful forefinger tick-tocking in front of her nose, '*gracias a* ti! Thank *you*!'

But this interlude of welcome digression was short-lived. As I suspected, Maria was not about to be so easily diverted from the main avenue of her thoughts for today. The frown returned to her face as she shifted her attention from Ellie back to me.

'*Mierda de burro!*'

More muted titters of anticipation from my hard-at-work wife and sons.

Inhaling a heavy sigh of surrender, I stuck the three wooden prongs of my Mallorcan pitchfork into the ground, clasped my fingers over the end of the long handle, adopted the legs-crossed resting position, and gave the old woman my undivided attention. Better to get this over with once and for all.

'*Bueno*, Maria,' I exhaled, combining the words with a slow, you-win nodding of the head, 'you'll have to spell it out for me. What's the connection between twigs, dry leaves, donkey dung and winter fuel?' I awaited the predictable answer, while Maria wheezed a triumphalist titter to herself.

It was obvious to anyone of reasonable intelligence, she declared, leaving me in no doubt that I didn't qualify as a member of that particular club – during the waning moon of May you crunched up the dry leaves and smaller twigs, mixed them with some straw, the donkey droppings and a little water (she paused to do pat-a-cake movements with her hands), you left the resultant moulds to dry in the sun for a while, and '*Oye!*', you had your hand-made logs. '*Mágico, no?*'

'Yes, well, I can see now why you must have been so disappointed when Jaume swapped your donkey for a tractor,' I diplomatically conceded, trying to appear impressed.

'*Sí*, and another thing,' she added as an inspired afterthought, 'you *modernos* could do well to revive that practice from the old days.'

'Well, maybe, Maria – but these days it could be a bit too time-consuming to go about looking for enough donkey sh–'

'*Barbacoas!*'

'Barbecues? Sorry, you've lost me again.'

'They are the modern craze, the *barbacoas, sí?*'

'*Sí*, but I don't see what –'

'*Mosquitos!*'

'Barbecues and mosquitoes... yes, that can be a bad combination, certainly.' Despite myself, I was becoming a bit exasperated. 'But what's that got to do with logs made out of donkey turds? I mean –'

'A very crafty creature, *el mosquito*.' With a gnarled forefinger, Maria tapped her temple to emphasise the point. Then she tapped the side of her nose. 'For it will fly nowhere near the smell of *mierda de burro* smoke.'

The old woman's face creased into a huge grin, her lips parting to reveal her distinctive oral graveyard of five teeth – two up, three down. The first time I'd seen this full-blown smile of Maria's, I remember thinking of it as a visual tickle, and that was how it struck me again now. Irresistible and totally contagious.

I started to smile. I couldn't help it. Then, as Maria's grin developed into one of her tinkling giggles, I began laughing as well. Inevitably, the catching jollity spread to Ellie and the boys, yet the only one who really knew what all the hilarity was about was the perpetrator herself.

Had she merely been pulling my leg about donkey-dung, mosquito-repellent logs? I suspected so. But then again, I *had* heard of Australian cattlemen in the bush burning dry cowpats on their campfires to keep the flies off, so maybe she hadn't been kidding. Anyway, I wasn't about to go roaming the country lanes with a bucket, shovelling up lumps of donkey droppings in order to put Maria's quirky recommendations to the test. For, knowing her as I was beginning to, that was more than likely exactly what she wanted me to do, just so that she could have another good chuckle at the expense of her favourite *loco extranjero*. I guessed that the pro-donkey propaganda element of her lecture would have been genuine enough, though – a supposition confirmed by the telling glower that she directed at our tractor as she turned to leave.

'Spent oil?' she grunted. 'Pah!'

'At least we were spared the wood ash bit,' I muttered to Ellie.

'Yeah,' Sandy concurred, 'maybe that backflip grasshopper memory of hers has hopped the twig at last.'

Some hope.

'*Oiga!*' Maria called over her shoulder. 'Do not forget what I told you about the wood ash. Sprinkle that around your cabbages, *amigos*, and they will never be attacked by slugs.' She paused and spun round to deliver her customary parting shot, her hoe raised like an executioner's axe. 'But for the best ashes, you should have burnt your twigs in the waning moon of November!'

I mentioned this moon-phase fixation of Maria's to Pepe Suau one morning when he was snipping the finishing touches to the last of our orange trees.

'I can just remember my grandfather going on about all that waxing and waning stuff,' I said, 'but I doubt if there are many farmers in Britain holding onto those old beliefs any more. To be honest, a chemical spray company's tips are about all the younger ones abide by these days.'

Pepe smiled a knowing smile. He used such sprays now too, he confessed – but only when absolutely necessary. Many of the older orchardmen totally rejected the application of such 'poisonous' modern concoctions, of course, but used responsibly and in moderation, he saw no great harm in them. '*En realidad*, some of those sprays can work miracles,' he insisted. 'They can save a sick tree which would have died in bygone times.' He pointed to a black, mouldy substance clinging to the leaves of the tree he was working on. 'A fungus caused by insects which also carry virus diseases,' he explained. 'These *parásitos* will have to be controlled with chemicals. And look there.' He gestured towards an apricot tree that he had cut back so severely that it looked as if it had been struck by lightning. 'That one has an *enfermedad* of the limbs which had entered the wood through old pruning cuts.' Pepe lowered his voice, glancing furtively about him again. 'Old Paco should have seen to that years ago,' he whispered.

'And will it survive?' I anxiously enquired, having noticed several other apricot and plum trees in the same 'close-cropped' condition.

Pepe raised his shoulders. '*Vamos a ver*. We shall see. But only with the prudent use of sprays and *por la gracia de Dios* will it be possible.'

So, I silently pondered, even in a devoutly religious country like Spain, God had to rely on back-up from the likes of Bayer and ICI for agricultural miracles nowadays.

'Well, I can certainly manage a prayer or two, Pepe,' I said, 'but when it comes to administering chemicals to the trees, I wouldn't even know where to start. I mean, I can't even identify the diseases yet, far less prescribe the cures.' I was getting that old sinking feeling again.

Laughing quietly, Pepe gave my shoulder a reassuring pat as he moved on, saw in hand, to his next patient. 'You will soon pick up the knowledge, Señor Peter.'

'I could kill off all my trees in the process, though,' I meekly suggested.

Pepe gave his mellow little chuckle again. '*Usted tranquilo, señor*. I will keep you right for this first year, never fear.' He stopped sawing for a moment and looked me in the eye. 'But there is one golden rule which you must learn from the start.'

'*Sí?*'

'*Sí*.' He cupped a hand to his ear. 'Do you hear their music?'

'You mean the bees?' I ventured, surprised that the industrious little insects were still able to find enough blossoms to attract them to our decimated trees.

'*Sí*, the bees. *Las abejas*.' A sentimental smile lit Pepe's face. 'The little musicians of the orchard, we call them in Mallorca.'

First old Maria had called them cupids, now Pepe described the bees as musicians. The affectionate, almost soft-hearted feelings which these ostensibly no-nonsense, hard-working country folk had for such a lowly creature both surprised and touched me.

'And the golden rule?' I prompted.

'The golden rule is that, if you are going to spray your trees, always wait until the evening – until the bees have gone home after their day's work. Otherwise, *señor*, you will only risk killing the best little friends a fruit farmer has.'

Simple but profound advice indeed, and something I hadn't even considered before.

'And what about the moon phases?' I asked, half jokingly. Pepe's reply was notably serious, however. 'Your grandfather was right. You don't live on an island without treating the influence of the moon with respect.'

Now that *was* interesting, because my grandfather had been an islander too – a farmer from Sanday, one of the outlying Orkney Islands to the north of Scotland, situated close to what has been described as perhaps the most treacherous area of sea round the British Coast. And now that I thought of it, he had told me how he'd combined the raising of cattle and crops with fishing – the latter not on a commercial scale, just setting out alone on a little sailing dinghy whenever a catch was required for the family table. Being familiar with the effect that the lunar stages had on tide and wind would have been absolutely crucial to him.

I listened closely to Pepe as he went on to tell me how he had been brought up to heed the phases of the moon for just about every task that had to be undertaken on the farm throughout the year. The grafting of the almond trees in the waxing moon of January, hoeing the *huertos*, the market gardens, in the waning moon of the same month – all of these rules had to be adhered to. And so it went on – sowing, planting and grafting in the growing moon, weeding, cutting and pruning in the diminishing. And it was the same with animals. Why, even tasks like the castrating of lambs and calves had to be undertaken in the waning moon, while it was universally accepted that the mating of goats and sheep would be most successful when 'arranged' to take place during the waxing phase.

'It is simply following the rhythm of nature, Señor Peter. And, for me, I believe in such things. *Bueno*, it is difficult these days to find time to follow all of the old beliefs, but I have forgotten none of them and I have already passed them on to my son.'

'And the spraying of chemicals? Is there a time that's best for that?'

Pepe gave a resigned shrug. 'Many of the ancient rules of Mallorcan farming date back to Roman times, to the writings of Pliny.' He chuckled again. 'But I doubt if even he in his great wisdom would have risked an answer to your question, my friend. No, just wait until your little musicians have packed away their instruments for the day – I think that is the best advice you are going to receive on the use of chemicals, no?'

The little man pushed back his baseball cap to mop his brow, and the sun illuminated his placid features. He had a kindly, contented face, and without the swarthy skin and dark hair colouring so typical of a mainland Spaniard from, say, Andalusia. No, his was an islander's face, possessing, like so many of the native Mallorcan country people, features more akin to folk from the Northern Isles of Britain, for instance, than the dusky descendants of Moors who populate much of Southern Spain. No doubt the bold seafaring Norsemen of old had scattered their seed widely... and successfully.

I watched Pepe make the final few deft cuts to the last orange tree, then looked back with him over the results of his *trabajo*. Perhaps our orchards weren't quite the post-nuclear wasteland I'd feared they might be, but neither were they any longer a verdant delight to behold. I silently hoped again that Pepe's skills would turn out to match his reputation.

'They will soon recover,' he said, reading my facial expression, then drew my attention to the nearest ranks of trees. 'And as you can see, I have left some trees only lightly pruned. They will recover even quicker than the others, ensuring you a good crop this year, no matter what. But next year it will be their turn for the surgery *mas extenso, sí?*'

'Whatever you say, Pepe. I'm entirely in your hands.'

Despite having attentively watched Pepe's work as often as I'd had time to, I still hadn't much of a clue about the intricacies of his skills, although I did notice that several particularly overgrown trees had been left completely untouched. I pointed them out to him.

'Ah, *sí, los higos.*' He shook his head. '*Hombre*, by the look of them, those old fig trees have not seen a pruning saw for many, many years.' Of all the fruit species, he proceeded to explain, the fig tree was the one which had to have its growth controlled rigidly, otherwise it would simply spread and spread until it reached the advanced stage of runaway neglect which I saw before me now. '*Por Dios!*' he exclaimed. 'If those trees were children, they could only be described as *gamberros* – hooligans!'

'Old Paco didn't bring them up too well, eh?' I offered, sotto voce.

But Pepe was quick to jump to the defence of the former *dueño* of Ca's Mayoral. 'No, no,' he protested, not bothering to lower his voice this time, 'Paco would have kept *los higos* in check, never fear – until his health and motivation declined in later years, that is. And that would have been it. *Oye!* Never turn your back on a fig tree, as the old proverb goes, or its twigs will pick your pockets while its roots pull down your house!' Pepe gazed up into the confusion of drooping, upward-curved branches of one particularly unruly-looking specimen. '*Sí, señor*, the fingers *and* the toes of these *chicos* will have to be given a good manicure.' He whistled through his teeth. '*Vaya! Mucho, mucho trabajo!*'

So when would he be making a start on them? I asked, not particularly relishing the prospect of even more heaps of tree remains to sort out.

Ah, but unfortunately that would now have to wait until next year, Pepe disclosed. The pressure to attend to the needs of other waiting *clientes* was now very great, as I would appreciate from the time he had already spent on our orchards. Also, he had his own farm work to see to – so much work that it was well nigh impossible for him and his son to cope with it at this time of year, when their mornings were taken up pruning the trees of others.

'Oh, right – I see. You're a farmer in your own right, too,' I said, with a feeling of guilt about perhaps appearing to take his valuable time somewhat for granted. 'I mean, in addition to being a professional tree maestro, that is. Sorry, Pepe, I didn't realise…'

'*No problema*,' Pepe assured me, patting my shoulder, the merest hint of a proud little smile on his face as he confessed that he was well used to this way of life, having spent all his days working the same farm, while supplementing his family's income by hiring himself out to tend other farmers' trees when required. 'Es Pou my home is called, a *finca* of many hectares – or *cuarteradas*, to use the Mallorcan measurement of area. *Sí, sí, señor*,' he declared, his normal air of modesty dispensed with for the moment, 'I am the farmer of one of the biggest *fincas* in the whole of Andratx district – with thousands of almond trees and a very large herd of sheep!'

Naturally, I didn't want to insult this gentle little man by questioning what he'd just told me, but it did seem more than a little strange all the same. Because I'd seen it for myself – Pepe worked like a beaver, *all* of the time. Not for him the laid-back Mallorcan way of downing tools for a prolonged chat whenever the opportunity arose, so why push himself so hard to earn extra cash if he had such a profitable-sounding spread of his own? For even in Mallorca, the general agricultural maxim of 'the bigger the farm, the more viable' surely also applied. Still, the apparent anomaly that Pepe portrayed was his business, and it wasn't for me to pry.

'I would consider it an honour if you would come to visit my home, Señor Peter,' he said, loading his tools into the back of his ancient little Seat 600 car back at the Ca's Mayoral farmyard. 'The house of Es Pou is very old, very large – a *senyoríu* we call such a house here – with many traditional things to see. The farm and the animals, too. You will find it all very interesting.'

Whether Pepe had sensed that I'd taken with a pinch of salt his claim to be a 'big time' farmer and had merely invited me to his *finca* to prove me wrong, I didn't know. But his invitation had been made in the most cordial way, and I had no hesitation in accepting.

'*La Señora de Escocia*, also. Please bring her with you when you come. My wife and I will be pleased to welcome you to our home.'

And so a date was set, when Pepe assured me that he would be at home just after midday as usual. I was genuinely looking forward to it: to seeing first-hand the old Mallorcan features of his farm that he had briefly described. And, of course, I could hardly wait to decipher the enigma of this industrious, unaffected little man who quietly boasted such valuable material assets. Who knows? Maybe he would turn out to be more of a magpie than a blue tit!

- Three -

PASEOS, PEASANTS AND DINING WITH DEMONS

The arrival of the longer spring days also heralds the start of the *paseo* season proper in Spain. What's a *paseo*? Well, the literal translation is a stroll, but to Spaniards a *paseo* is much more than that. It's a stroll certainly, but also a display ritual, a social occasion, and a fashion parade all rolled into one. And the *paseo* is for all ages; a mandatory happening which takes place every evening, when the inhabitants of a town or village appear in the central *plaza* or a popular *avenida*. Dressed in their best, they saunter casually back and forth, exchanging polite greetings with neighbours in passing, then keenly talking about each other when out of earshot.

It's also an ideal opportunity for unattached young folk to strut their stuff and eye one another up. Groups of girls giggle coyly as they cross the paths of their male targets, who in turn swap pseudo-nonchalant comments while glancing over shoulders to check out the rear view of their fancied *chicas*. But the more elderly matrons are invariably the stars of the show, their hair always immaculately coiffured, delicate lace shawls draped stylishly over shoulders, and, whether the temperature warrants it or not, intricately-filigreed fans flicked open at regular intervals to cool the cheeks or, dare I say it, to hide gossiping mouths from the eyes of would-be lip-readers.

The *paseo* is, they say, a tradition which has been around since time immemorial, no doubt replicated in other Mediterranean countries, albeit under different names. But the Spanish have developed it into something special – a genteel affair in which even the most humble citizen can participate on equal terms with others, no matter how much better-heeled. Yet perhaps it's a Spanish custom which should be left exclusively for the Spanish to uphold. Not that the *extranjeros* of so many nationalities who now visit and live in their country would be spurned for joining in. On the contrary – after all, it would give the local folk something new to talk about. No, it's simply that only the Spanish have that graceful air of quiet poise so essential to the atmosphere of the event.

Spaniards 'give' a *paseo*, as they put it. Others merely take a stroll.

Until we went to live at Ca's Mayoral, the *paseos* which I remembered most were those observed while on holiday on Mallorca's neighbouring island of Menorca. Mahon, the pretty little city which is Menorca's capital, boasts a square known as the Explanada, where on still summer evenings the townsfolk gather to 'promenade' in the time-honoured way, while tourists like ourselves look on, fascinated and more than a little envious. For, a more pleasant situation for a *paseo* would be hard to find – a spacious, tree-shaded *plaza*, enclosed by green-shuttered buildings, where white doves flutter down to pick up sunflower seeds thrown to them by laughing children, and peckish natives and visitors alike mingle around kiosks selling sizzling *bunyol* doughnuts, or crusty *bocadillo* sandwiches daubed with *sobrasada* sausage. How unforgettable the spectacle, cloaked in the glow of a Mediterranean sunset.

We were looking forward to savouring the atmosphere again in our new island home, but, to our growing disappointment, the long hours of essential farm work had so far prevented us from doing so.

And then the *paseo* came to us! Not the full Plaza de España procession from Andratx town, of course, but a version much smaller and more modest, yet to us equally attractive in its own way. It happened one sunny evening towards the end of March, when the valley was basking in aromatic calm following one of the spectacular rainstorms that can be a feature of the spring and autumn season changes in Mallorca.

First it was one old woman ambling along the lane hand-in-hand with what we took to be her granddaughter; next an elderly man hobbling along with the aid of a stick; then two arm-in-arm teenage girls who looked like sisters (or maybe it was just their identical over-the-top make-up). Soon, upwards of twenty people, some in groups, others alone, had passed by at random intervals, each nodding a tentative, '*Buenos tardes*' to us as they glanced through our field gate, surprised, perhaps, to see us still working, and all of them proceeding at the leisurely pace essential to the true *paseo*.

We recognised them as people from the hamlet about half a mile away at the top of the lane – many of whom, until now, we had only ever seen looking out shyly from the doorways of their houses as we drove by on our way to Andratx. Most were clearly folk of modest means, as witness the unassuming terraced homes that flank the one street which constitutes all there is of their little village. And, somehow, they didn't look like Mallorcans. They lacked that easy, contented air so typical of the islanders – or certainly some of the older ones did.

'*Españoles*,' Jordi had explained when I'd mentioned this to him one day. 'Madrid government been send them over from the mainland. *Sí*, it makes many years ago, oh yes. They been bring the men for the making of the road round the mountains, man – up the bloody coast, far away to Estellencs, Banyalbufar, Deià as well also. Many danger working for the men,' he'd added, shaking his head gravely.

When pressed for more details, Jordi had said that the administration had 'exported' such families from poorer areas of mainland Spain, ostensibly to provide cheap labour to upgrade the tortuous road that clings, hundreds of metres above the sea, to the precipitous northern flank of the Tramuntana Mountains. And that was indeed what the menfolk had been used for, risking life and limb in what must have been extremely perilous conditions.

Yet many local folk had believed, and some still suspect, that the real reason behind the national government's settling of these families in Mallorca was to 'dilute' the fiercely independent native population with *españoles*. Because, although Mallorca is geographically and politically part of Spain, most Mallorcans devoutly think of themselves as Mallorcan first and foremost, and Spanish (in some cases, very reluctantly) only second.

But even if there had been a master plan to subjugate the Mallorcan people and suppress their *mallorquín* language by stealthily 'colonising' the island with mainlanders, the scheme had got no further, in this instance, than to create a somewhat solitary community of folk, not wholly welcomed by at least some of the local populace. Had there been an element of xenophobia on the part of certain Mallorcans, or were their suspicions justified? Memories of the Spanish Civil War, perhaps? Who knows? But time, the great healer, had eventually softened attitudes, at least among the younger generations of Mallorcans. They, for the most part, had come to accept their contemporaries, the incomers' children born on the island, as their equals and compatriots.

'For me,' Jordi had shrugged, 'I been taking one man as I finding him. I been being in Spain, France, Germany, England. Everywhere is Jordi been being. And I tell you this, man – there be being good ones and bad ones everywhere. Bloody 'ell! Life be being too baster short for making no welcomes to the good ones!'

A fair enough philosophy, and one which, in our position as grade one *extranjeros*, we were glad that all the Mallorcans we had met appeared to share. And that was how we, in turn, treated our ex-mainland neighbours from the village, in the hope that the feeling would be reciprocated.

After that rather furtive encounter during their opening *paseo* of the season, first one villager then another would pause in passing to exchange brief pleasantries and, we guessed, to have a closer look at these odd, fair-skinned loonies from the north who had arrived on the island actually to toil in the fields – even, as had been our enforced recent habit, during the sacrosanct *siesta*.

'Don't fancy your one much,' Charlie remarked to his older brother.

Sandy didn't even bother to look up from the irrigation trench which he was laboriously drawing round a tree, using a short-handled triangular hoe, the favoured hand implement in Spain for jobs as diverse as mixing concrete to... well, to digging irrigation trenches.

'I wonder what they call this in Spanish,' I said, taking the concave-bladed tool from Sandy to give him a breather.

'Bloody stupid, that's what *I* call it,' Sandy muttered. He rolled his shoulders and arched his aching back. 'Five hundred plus trees to go. God, there must be an easier way.'

'I said, I don't fancy your one much,' Charlie persisted.

I watched Sandy grimace as his eyes followed Charlie's repeated sideways head-jerking towards the gate opening through the lane-side wall.

'Oh, no,' Sandy groaned, 'not the dreaded Frightening Sisters again.'

They were a good thirty metres from where we were working, but even at that distance, I could see that the two over-made-up girls, who had featured in that first little *paseo* past Ca's Mayoral a couple of weeks earlier, were going through their now-familiar routine. It had become a habit, not just at conventional *paseo* times, but at any time of day when they happened to have time off from whatever they did for a living. They would amble along the lane feigning nonchalance, and if they noticed Sandy working in the fields, would stop at the gate and smile coyly at him with a come-hither batting of eyelashes heavy with mascara.

'I think my one has the edge class-wise,' Charlie teased.

'The voice of experience!' Sandy muttered, while pretending to have his attention drawn to something in the opposite direction to his two admirers.

'Go over and have a chat with them, Sandy,' I suggested, discreetly winking at Charlie. 'Good practice for your Spanish.'

Without turning round, Sandy began fiddling with a lower branch on an adjacent almond tree. 'Nah,' he mumbled, 'not really my type. A bit too B&Q for me.'

'B&Q?'

'Yeah, too much Polyfilla and Dulux vinyl matt.'

It was a crude way of putting it, but I knew what he meant. The first time I'd seen the girls strolling past, I'd thought at first glance that they were probably in their thirties, tarting themselves up in a forlorn effort to look younger. But since then I'd seen them close up a couple of times when passing them in the car, and had come to the conclusion that they were probably no more than seventeen or eighteen – pretty, raven-haired *señoritas* of obvious southern Spanish extraction, who, for reasons best known to themselves, had buried their natural facial attributes under a thick coating of foundation creams, blusher, crimson lipstick and over-applied eye shadow.

They looked as if they'd just come off the set of a Buster Keaton film, and although Sandy's sobriquet of 'Frightening Sisters' was perhaps a mite *too* uncomplimentary, the girls, in full warpaint, could certainly have given you a nasty turn if you'd suddenly come face-to-face with them on a dark night.

'It's their brothers who've put the wind up him,' Charlie confided as Sandy strode off through the trees towards our *castita de aperos*, the little stone shack which housed our tractor and various implements and tools. 'Two of them. They're usually hanging about in the distance when the Frighteners are on the prowl.'

'Chaperones, Charlie. Old Spanish tradition.'

'Minders – that's what I call 'em. I mean, how can you chat up chicks if you've got a coupla heavies breathing down your neck?'

The profound musings of a twelve-year-old.

But Charlie had clearly started to take an active interest in the opposite sex himself, and I had a hunch that his attitude to the game would not be so cautious as his older brother's appeared to be, at least on today's showing.

In any case, the enigmatic Frightening Sisters' long-distance overtures to Sandy gradually diminished in the cool breeze that blows from the figurative cold shoulder. The frequency of their appearances in the lane fell away little by little, and within a few weeks they were to be seen of an evening in Andratx town, having graduated from the rustic Ca's Mayoral stroll-past to the full-on Plaza de España *paseo* – still in over-the-top facial camouflage, still ambling arm-in-arm, still with their brothers in the background, and still, tellingly, without even one beau in tow.

But their day would come. Romance, as it always does in the enchanting warmth of Mediterranean evenings, would eventually seek them out; but only, I suspected, when they had removed the plaster and paint from their faces to reveal whatever unblemished charms lay hidden beneath. In the name of modernity (if that isn't too obvious a euphemism for what the enchanting warmth of Mediterranean evenings inevitably excites), the chaperoning brothers would then be conveniently ditched. And, doubtless, it was ever thus.

In the meantime, Ellie's 'secret' wish that Sandy would soon find a *novia*, a nice local lass who would steal his heart and so encourage him to put down permanent roots on the island, would have to remain on hold for a while yet. Although she *had* seen a glimmer of hope with the arrival at the gate of a certain village matron one morning...

She was one of the regular *paseo*-givers, a slim, grey-haired woman of about seventy who had always been the most outgoing of the bypassing villagers, ever flashing us a broad grin and unselfconsciously calling out a cheery greeting, in marked contrast to the more reserved ways of her neighbours. We had come to refer to her as Señora Bread Teeth, simply because that broad grin of hers invariably revealed a generous deposit of white *pan* clinging determinedly to the spaces between the immaculately formed teeth of her upper denture – a denture of which the *señora* was clearly, and justly, proud.

She knew it was very late in the season, she'd admitted as Ellie opened the gate for her, but she had noticed that there were still a few oranges on some of our trees, and would it be possible to buy some?

Indeed there were still some oranges on those trees that Pepe had spared from his most severe pruning, but they were well past their best, and certainly no longer in the fresh, plump condition which would have rendered them saleable to Señor Jeronimo. In fact, rather than see them go to waste, we had resorted to squeezing as many as we possibly could to make juice for our own daily consumption, to the point that Charlie swore that our skins were beginning to take on a distinctly Oriental hue. We were overdosing on vitamin C – bad for a kid his age, he reckoned – and if he never saw another orange in his whole life, it would be too soon!

Thus, relieved that someone else was willing to help save the oranges from eventually rotting on the ground, Ellie had welcomed the *señora* with open arms and had indicated to her in her customary blend of Spanish-spattered English that she was free to take, without charge, as many oranges as she liked – particularly if she didn't mind picking them herself. With a nod of appreciation, the *señora* had then dipped into her copious shopping bag to produce a pair of ancient but well-honed secateurs.

'*Siempre preparada*. Ever ready,' she declared, giving Ellie a close-up of the remains of a recent sandwich in her delighted smile. The *señora* was obviously no stranger to the 'God helps those who help themselves' maxim at the tail end of the orange-growing season. '*Ven aquí*,' she'd then called, going back through the gate to beckon someone standing round the corner of the high stone wall. 'Come here, Carmen, *pequeñita mía!*'

Carmen was her granddaughter, a pretty, shy girl of about seventeen, whose face blossomed into a beguiling smile as she shook hands with Ellie and gave a polite little curtsy.

'Oh, no need to be so formal,' Ellie had laughed, curtsying back as a reciprocal gesture of respect. 'I'm not the queen – and even if I was, I'd soon put a stop to all that subservient malarkey.'

'*Sí, señora*,' Carmen had then smiled back, curtsying again.

I joined Ellie in the yard after Carmen and her grandmother had wandered off towards the orange groves, Ellie gazing after them with a dreamy look in her eyes. The situation didn't take much assessing.

'You're wasting your time trying to wish up romantic attachments for Sandy, you know, Ellie.'

'No, I'm not.'

'Believe me, if Sandy's not a hundred per cent sure about whether or not his future lies here in Mallorca, getting a local girlfriend isn't going to simplify matters for him. Quite the reverse.'

Sighing, Ellie nodded her head in reluctant agreement. All she wanted, after all, was for the family to remain united in what many people 'back home' had regarded as the somewhat reckless adventure that we'd embarked upon. When we'd first broken the news to the boys that we were thinking of turning our backs on the familiarity and relative security of our homeland to go and be rookie fruit farmers in Mallorca, it was Sandy who had been brimful of enthusiasm at the prospect, and young Charlie who'd appeared, at best, indifferent. But now their positions had become almost totally reversed, it seemed.

Charlie, despite intense initial disinclination, had taken rapidly to the informal atmosphere of his new school on the island; an international English-language school, where the closest you got to a school uniform was T-shirt, sneakers and jeans. Also, the prevalence of American kids (many domiciled on the island with their mothers while their fathers worked in the oil fields of the Middle East) soon lent a mid-Atlantic drawl to the accents of all new pupils, no matter what their nationality. And Charlie was already right in there drawling with the best of them.

But while he was now revelling in the daily company of a plethora of new chums, new sunshine-bathed sports and a new, more laid-back approach to education than the one he'd been used to in Scotland, his older brother was stuck for most of the time in the valley, working on the farm in an environment where even his parents were youngsters compared to most of the immediate neighbours. Certainly, he had been signed by a Mallorcan junior football club whose ground was located over to the north of Palma. But that club was about twenty miles away, and although Sandy had integrated well and had become good friends with the mainly Mallorcan team members, none of them lived on our part of the island. So, local social contacts had to be made – not an easy task for an eighteen-year-old foreigner, still learning the language, in a quiet rural community populated mainly by people old enough to be his grandparents.

Hence Ellie's well intentioned but, in reality, ill-considered desire to find him a 'nice young *señorita* girl' who lived in the vicinity. And any notion she'd had that Señora Bread Teeth shared her matchmaking instincts was firmly quashed when said *señora* returned to the farmhouse, her shopping bag brimful of newly-picked oranges. Her visit, as it transpired, had indeed been intended, at least in part, to promote something on behalf of young Carmen, but that something turned out to be distinctly unromantic in nature.

'Carmen here is a good girl,' she stressed to Ellie and I. 'Honest, quiet and strong. A good worker – very clean in her habits. I tell you, *señores*, you could leave her in your house alone without fear of your *cosas privadas* being molested.'

Ellie looked at me blankly and muttered out of the corner of her mouth, 'What's my *cosas privadas?* Sounds painful.'

'Personal bits and bobs.' I smiled at the elderly woman while still speaking to Ellie in English. 'I think the *señora* is on a jobs-opportunity mission.'

And, sure enough, while Carmen stood silently staring at her feet and looking embarrassed, her grandmother continued to reel off her *nieta's* many work abilities, and to give her personal guarantee of the youngster's trustworthiness. Finally getting to the point, she said that she'd heard that the *Señora de Escocia* did not have a housemaid, and no woman could possibly be expected to look after such a big house herself. Carmen, she emphasised, would be just the girl to fit the bill. '*Hombre*, she will even live in!... Uhm, for the inclusion of her meals in addition to her wages, of course.'

Feeling unsure of how to respond to this genuinely made, if totally unexpected offer of assistance without creating offence, I hesitantly started to reply. But the old lady was on a roll.

'*Ah, sí, señor!* Another thing!' she butted in, turning to point a wrinkled finger at the orchards. 'There is also too much work on such a farm as this for a *caballero* like yourself. Here in Spain, the *señor* does not do the fieldwork himself.' She glanced at Ellie, smiled sweetly, then cast me a reproving look. 'And certainly the *señora* should never be expected to labour on the land. Never! *Nunca! Nunca!* No, *señor*, you need *labradores*, farm workers, to do the work for you. It is the way here. *Sí*... especially with the *extranjeros*.'

I was about to try to explain that we were a bit different from wealthy, retired, or vacationing foreigners who had bought farms in Spain purely to savour the charms of an old stone house, but the *señora* got in first again. She went on to inform us, as I somehow guessed she would, that she had three fine grandsons – strong, strapping *chicos*, well accustomed to the ferocity of the Mallorcan sun – who would make ideal farmhands for us. Then, noticing my uneasy expression, she appended with a hopeful smile, 'Ehm, on a rota basis, perhaps, *sí*?'

There was no point in my beating about the bush, so I proceeded, in as understanding a way as I could, to explain to the *señora* and her granddaughter that, where we came from, a small farmer is, by necessity, his own *labrador* – assisted in the fields, whenever required, by his wife (well, you have to have someone to shout at when things go wrong!), and, if he had them, by his sons. Financial realities made such a practice essential. Similarly, there just wasn't enough money to be made out of a *finca* like Ca's Mayoral to support anyone in addition to our immediate family members... and even that, I mused, was going to prove a struggle.

The elderly woman's previous enthusiastic mien descended into one of obvious disappointment for a moment. But she quickly perked up again, flashing us another doughy grin. 'But the house,' she enquired optimistically, '*la Señora de Escocia* will still be needing help in the house, no?' Then, reading my negative expression, she meekly ventured, 'Perhaps for only one or two days per week, *sí*?'

I slowly shook my head, apologising profusely for not being able to take up her kind offer, while re-stating my position clearly. Unlike other foreigners she may have encountered in rural Mallorca, we were not 'good life' hobby farmers who could afford to swan about enjoying the ambience of the countryside while paying others to do all the work. We were very much hands-on folk, doing our own chores for ourselves, and extremely happy to do so. That's what we were used to, Ellie also preferring to be her own Mrs Mop, chief cook and bottle-washer, the mistress of her own home in every way.

There followed some moments of pregnant silence, during which Señora Bread Teeth scrutinised Ellie and I in turn, a look of fading expectation in her eyes. '*Entonces*,' she ultimately sighed, clearly disillusioned, her image of us in tatters, '*ustedes... ustedes son nada mas que campesinos tambien?*'

I'd then been obliged to nod my head, raising my shoulders in a resigned shrug. 'That's absolutely correct, *señora*,' I confessed. 'I'm afraid we're really only peasants as well.'

The reason for Sandy's sudden dash to the *casita de aperos* turned out to be more practical than merely to escape the long-distance attentions of the Frightening Sisters. Yet, hearing the distinctive diesel clunk of our little Barbieri tractor coming from the direction of the implement shed did surprise me. Normally, Sandy almost had to be dragged screaming and kicking to the mini machine if I needed him to do some work with it, so why was he now steering it in my direction of his own free will? And why had he attached the plough when all the land had already been turned over and cultivated?

'Painless irrigation,' was his answer.

'I don't get it,' was my reply.

'I do,' Charlie breezed. 'Hey, good idea, big brother!'

'I still don't get it.'

The boys shared a private laugh.

'How's your back after ten minutes of shifting dirt with that hoe thing?' Sandy enquired.

'Damned sore, as a matter of fact.' I looked down at the little tool's curved shaft. 'Seems to me us northern Europeans are more suited to pushing hoes than pulling them. 'Anyway, why the sudden attraction to the wee tractor?'

'Easy,' the boys chanted in unison. 'No more sore backs.'

'Nah, nah,' I pooh-poohed. 'Pepe Suau said the irrigation canals have to circle each tree about a couple of metres from the trunk.'

'Why?' said Sandy.

'Because he says that's where the tree drinks – not at the trunk, but through the fine roots under the outermost tips of the branches.'

'You miss the point, Dad,' Charlie opined, a self-satisfied smirk on his face.

'No I don't, Charlie! You two smart Alecs reckon you can dig the irrigation channels with the plough. Right?'

'Right.'

'Wrong. Ploughs are designed to cut straight lines. Just try ploughing a circle with only a two-metre radius. No chance.'

The boys looked at one another, swapping cryptic winks now.

'But who said the channels had to be circular?' Sandy probed.

'Well... you know... well, that's the way...' I was toiling for an answer. 'I mean, yes, that's the way a tree's built. Look at it from above – bird's eye view – it's circular.'

'Pretty smart tree that can figure that its drink of water's coming from a square ditch instead of a round one,' Charlie sniggered.

The penny finally dropped. The boys were dead right, of course. Instead of digging a circular channel round every individual tree on the farm by hand, simply aim the tractor in a straight line, dropping the plough momentarily into the soil alongside each tree in every row. Then repeat the process in the other three directions until all the trees were surrounded by deep, water-holding furrows – albeit square ones. The lazy genes in my offspring had just come up with a labour-saving alternative to a backbreaking task that I hadn't been looking forward to one bit.

'Brilliant,' said Ellie, arriving on the scene to remind us that it was almost lunchtime. 'So brilliant that I think we should treat the boys to a celebration feed... out!'

It never took much to convince Ellie that a visit to a restaurant was called for – particularly on a Sunday, the day of the obligatory extended lunch for the typically extended Spanish family.

'Thanks all the same, but count me out,' Sandy said. 'Football, remember? We've got a home game today.'

'Yeah,' Charlie agreed mid-Atlantically, 'I think I'll give lunch a swerve too. Check out the ball game with Sandy instead.' He paused to join his brother in delivering me an expectant look, then added, 'Maybe we could pick up a coupla Big Macs on the way, though?'

'Done!' I replied, and gladly handed the boys the required amount of burger-buying pesetas, which, thankfully, amounted to considerably less than the price of what they'd have been likely to scoff in a more 'conventional' restaurant with us.

So, our family extending only to two in number on this particular occasion, Ellie and I donned our stepping-out clothes, jumped in the little Ford Fiesta and headed for Palma, unaware that the restaurant where we were destined to lunch today would turn out to be *far* from conventional...

The streamlined bulk of a cruise liner, berthed in the harbour of Porto Pi, towered above the roadway ahead as we approached the western outskirts of Palma, and stood as a pillar of affluence guarding the stunning array of craft moored in seemingly endless ranks along the wide curve of the city's bay. Elegant yachts swayed keel-by-hull with wave-skimming powerboats, each a bold statement of its owner's prosperity, but all eclipsed in turn by the sheer opulence of sleek, ocean-going motor cruisers, many with exotic Eastern names coiling along their flanks, and helicopters squatting on stern-mounted pads like giant metallic dragonflies.

'Obviously not orange farmers,' Ellie commented. 'We couldn't even afford to buy a tender for one of those things.'

'Hmm, just a few oil wells short at the moment,' I conceded. 'Truth to tell, we probably couldn't even stretch to a tender for one of the tenders.'

We pondered that thought in silence, while marvelling at the stunning beauty of Palma's palm-fringed seafront. Although less than twenty miles from our valley home, this popular face of Mallorca could hardly present more of a contrast. This is the hotel-studded jewel in the crown of a burgeoning tourist realm. Only the sight of a few small fishing boats, with oversized lanterns strategically placed for the nocturnal attraction of shoals of sardines, serves to remind you of an ongoing way of traditional island life, now obliged to share crowded quaysides with a growing influx of leisure-seeking wealth.

'Where are we going anyway?' Ellie asked.

'Out to the Manacor road on the other side of the city.'

'So why didn't we just take the *Vía de Cintura* ring route – the motorway? We could've been there by now.'

'Sure, but would you really swap the passing vista of concrete fly-overs for this?' I gestured through a forest of yacht masts towards the imposing outline of Palma Cathedral at the far end of the bay, dominating the city and its waterfront. 'This still has to be one of the most spectacular views in the Med. Enjoy it.'

Ellie offered no further objection.

Lying at anchor about a mile out to sea, we couldn't fail but notice the vast profile of a visiting American aircraft carrier, its brooding presence strangely at odds with the easy air of amity for which Mallorca is renowned. A sobering reminder, nonetheless, of the unrest which still haunts some lands bordering this beautiful sea, known in antiquity as the centre of the world, but policed now by the ships of a distant and comparatively youthful state, elevated to power by those very natural riches so coveted by Spanish adventurers of old.

We stopped at traffic lights to allow some groups of young American sailors to cross over from the dock area, where a shuttle service of motor launches was delivering them from the chaste confines of their floating fortress. Dressed in pristine white, faces aglow with shore-leave anticipation, many of the young mariners appeared to be heading straight towards the old trade exchange building called La Lonja on the other side of the carriageway. But, I suspected, it was not the artefacts of the island's maritime history displayed in La Lonja's fine museum that was attracting those seafaring sons of Uncle Sam. It was more likely to be the labyrinth of narrow streets and sunless alleys in the old town behind, where long-craved female company could be sought and bought for a fistful of Yankee dollars.

'Well, you know what sailors are,' I said to Ellie, who was watching this near stampede of bell-bottomed excitement with a frown of fascination on her forehead.

'Yes,' she muttered, 'a bunch of randy gits!'

The road to the bustling inland town of Manacor bisects Mallorca eastwards from Palma, leading eventually to a rash of popular holiday resorts fringing the cove-indented coast from Cala Ratjada south to the fishing village of Porto Cristo, some thirty miles from the capital. Not that I was intending travelling that far today. But, although we had set out in what we thought was enough time to beat the rush, the regular Sunday lunch exodus from Palma was already well under way. A steady stream of family cars was decanting from the city, carrying their occupants towards the tempting selection of large restaurants which pepper the ten or so miles of roadside between Palma and the country village of Algaida. We'd have to look sharp if we were to find a table at one of the more popular ones.

Beyond the city, the landscape that we were now passing through was the very antithesis of the dramatic mountain scenery that surrounded our home back in the south-west corner of the island. Es Pla, Mallorca's wide, central plain, stretched away from us in an infinite panorama of small, flat fields. Sandstone farmsteads, the colour of old almond shells, appeared like scattered flotillas of houseboats floating out on a vast patchwork of greens and browns. And the gap-toothed blades of a hundred windmills stood out like tattered sails against the blue horizon of distant hills.

Two hobbled cows, grazing an unfenced pasture, chewed the cud under the shade of a tall palm and gazed dreamily at a perspiring farmer wrestling with a mule-drawn plough as he prepared his land for a new crop – perhaps of fodder for those same contented cattle. Meanwhile, a huge passenger jet, crammed, no doubt, with early-season tourists, screamed low overhead on its final approach to Palma Airport. Es Pla was revealing two aspects of Mallorca, one almost terminally old, the other rapaciously new, caught for a fleeting moment in a snapshot of inescapable change. The brow-wiping farmer cursed the aeroplane and swore at his mule.

One of the island's greatest charms, though, is its enduring ability to surprise. After a few kilometres the road began to rise slowly from the plain, entering a softly undulating land of pinewoods and *monte bajo*, the maquis of Mallorca. Dwarf trees of evergreen oak and silvery olive lift their heads above a tangled undergrowth of buckthorn and broom, all breathing the mingled scents of juniper, rosemary and heather.

Typically, however, this gentle wilderness gave way before long to a cultivated landscape once more. But here was a landscape contrasting sharply with the manicured symmetry of Es Pla, where intensively-grown vegetables and soft fruit flourish on abundant supplies of underground water pumped up by those ubiquitous windmills. The gradient had levelled out again, and we were passing along a fast, straight road bounded on either side by pinewood copses screening groves of almond and olive. Platoons of those dependable trees of the Mediterranean, whose water needs are satisfied by the region's modest rainfall, stood easy in dusty soil, from which straw-coloured stones had been cleared over the centuries and built into walls enclosing each randomly-shaped field.

A large yellow bird swooped over the road ahead and disappeared into the matching whorls of a mimosa tree by the gateway to a farmhouse.

'Wow!' gasped Ellie. 'Some canary!'

'Golden oriole,' I chuckled.

'Come again?'

'I think you'll find it was a golden oriole.'

Out of the corner of my eye I caught Ellie staring incredulously at me. 'Since when did you become the expert ornithologist?'

'Well, I wouldn't have had a clue what it was,' I admitted, 'except Pepe Suau pointed one out to me when he was pruning our trees one day. Very rare to catch a glimpse of one, he said. Supposed to bring you good luck, though.'

'Well, I hope it brings me enough luck to make you stop at a restaurant soon. I mean, we've passed about half a dozen already. Why, for goodness sake?'

'Just because I haven't seen one with a car park that's busy enough. Always look for a well-patronised eating place – sign of quality, value for money.'

'That's all very well, but at this rate we'll never get in *any*where. Look at the traffic!'

But on the outskirts of Algaida village I eventually spotted what I was looking for, a roadside restaurant so popular that finding an available space in its teeming car park proved almost impossible. 'CA'L DIMONI', the sign said, 'Enter by the bar', which turned out to be an unpretentious watering hole, in which three unflappable barmaids were dispensing drinks to the noisy mass of humanity already crammed within its confines.

'You stay put by the door here,' I shouted in Ellie's ear, motioning towards an opening which led to the restaurant proper, already filled to capacity, from what we could see. 'I'll go to the bar and try to book a table.'

Ellie shook her head and yelled, 'No, you needn't bother. Look, there's a –'

Waving Ellie's objections aside, I started to wedge a way through the crush, shouting back to her, 'OK, it doesn't look too hopeful, I know, but I'm not giving up *that* easily.'

Ellie closed her eyes and continued to shake her head dejectedly.

'Defeatist,' I muttered to myself, squeezing my way between two pint-sized Mallorcan ladies with ten-gallon bosoms. '*Perdón, señoras,*' I puffed, raising my arms in an attempt to reduce my girth, but in the process accidentally brushing my thumb against what I instantly prayed was nothing more sensitive than a cardigan button on the gravity-defying chest of the *señora* facing me.

'*Oo-oo-ooh, la-la!*' she shrieked, lifting her own hands in automatic response, unmindful of the fact that she was holding a shopping basket containing, amongst other things but most significantly, a long baguette loaf.

I bit my bottom lip, smothering the bellow of pain that escaped in the form of a muted yelp down my flaring nostrils.

The baguette woman looked down to where her loaf had ended its rapid upward trajectory, then slowly raised her eyes to mine. '*Lo siento, señor,*' she apologised coquettishly, trying, but failing, to suppress a smirk.

Her companion sniggered. 'They say a good loaf always rises quickly, *señor,*' she remarked, directing a suggestive glance at my injured parts, 'but perhaps the baker put too much yeast in that one, no?'

'*No problema, señoras,*' I lied in a soprano yodel, blinking back the tears. 'My… my fault entirely.'

Proceeding more carefully now, I eventually made it to within a few feet of the bar. '*Una mesa para dos, por favor*,' I mouthed to one of the barmaids through the surrounding uproar of conversation. 'A table for two, please.' I held up two confirmatory fingers.

Without interrupting her rhythm of simultaneous coffee machine operating, draft beer pulling, bottle opening, glass filling, till punching, change giving, bar wiping and ongoing gossiping with her fellow barmaids, the girl raised one finger and pointed it towards the end of the bar, where one of Mallorca's characteristic little black-clad granny figures was standing grinning at me and waving a book of raffle tickets.

I mimed back to her over a sea of heads that I didn't want to buy a ticket. I was here to eat! The *anciana* smiled a weary smile and fluttered the raffle book again, gesturing vaguely towards Ellie, who was still standing where I'd left her, only a few feet from the ticket-toting granny. Ellie jubilantly held up a raffle ticket and summoned me back with an impatient wave of her hand.

'I haven't fixed a table yet,' I yelled at her through the babble. 'Just have some patience, OK!'

Ellie clearly couldn't make out a word of this. She beckoned me again, knotting her brows into a demanding scowl, yet barely concealing her delight as she pretended to eat the raffle ticket.

Taking a calming lungful of the smoke-tainted air that filled the room, I began to edge my way back between the same crush of bodies that I'd become moderately intimate with on my outward shuffle. 'Ehm, *perdón*,' I repeated, gently tapping on now-familiar shoulders and smiling sheepishly into puzzled Mallorcan frowns. Who was this *loco* foreign pansy, I could sense them thinking, who'd forced his way to within an arm's length of the bar, and was now returning... without even buying a drink?

'Nice one, Ellie!' I barked when I finally made it back to the door. 'I get battered, bruised and semi-eunuched trying to fix us a table for lunch, then you suddenly decide you'd rather eat a raffle ticket! Brilliant!'

Ellie allowed herself a smug smile. 'If you'd listened to me instead of barging off in such a mad rush, you'd have saved yourself all that hassle.'

'Uh-huh? How come?'

'Because the nice old lady in black there was trying to attract your attention when we came in.'

'Yes, well,' I mumbled, 'you can't move in bars in this country without somebody trying to flog you a ticket for some lottery or other. We came in here to eat, not to –'

'But the old lady isn't selling anything to anyone.'

'So why the tickets?'

'It's the system. If you want a table, she gives you a ticket with a number on it. And when your number's called out from the restaurant, she lets you through. A busy place like this, they can't have everyone bulldozing their way to the bar to book a table the way you tried to do, can they?' She gave a superior little laugh. 'I mean, if everyone did that, nobody would ever get a drink from the bar, would they?'

'Exactly,' I muttered, attempting to hide my shamefaced expression from the tittering old ticket dispenser, 'and that's precisely what I've got to show for my troubles – no bloody drink from the bar!'

Ellie leaned towards me and said in a gloating stage whisper, 'Well then, maybe you shouldn't have passed all those places that didn't look busy enough for you!'

Perhaps she had a point there, but we'd find out soon enough.

We grabbed a couple of just-vacated seats by the window, and sat down to take in the scene. I immediately began to wonder just why so many people were attracted to this place. It couldn't have been the premises – bare floor, bare tables and chairs, a couple of ceiling fans (static), taped musak fighting a losing battle against the din of shouted *mallorquín* conversation, kids screaming, and a wall-mounted TV with a news reader uttering the latest words of doom to the tops of a hundred unconcerned heads. A pair of squawking parakeets were apathetically picking their toes in a cage just above us, while a leather-lunged canary sang his heart out somewhere on the far side of the fug-filled room. Bedlam. In essence, this joint had all the allure of the stock Spanish drinking pit – and then some.

Indeed, I ultimately decided, it was really quite wonderful...

Except, that is, for the miniature devil dolls!

It was the sudden look of unease on Ellie's face that drew my attention to them. She was staring into the restaurant through a connecting hatchway behind the bar, her eyes fixed on a shelf on which a gang of the little fellows was standing, red eyes glaring from horned heads, arrow-tipped tails pointing down towards cloven feet.

'*Ca'l Dimoni!*' I told her, nodding towards a man-size satanic effigy holding a red-and-yellow trident just outside the window where we were sitting. 'I suppose it must mean "The House of the Demon" in *mallorquín*.'

Noticing Ellie's perplexed expression, the old ticket lady came over and explained that demons were a feature of the island's folklore, dating back to pagan times. Their image had ultimately been adopted by the Christians, and for centuries men and boys disguised as demons had played an important part in Mallorcan fiestas throughout the year. They were harmless figures, though, she reassured Ellie – not associated with the occult or anything nasty like that – just jesters entertaining the crowds with their mischievous pranks during festive parades. Why, the worst that these pretend demons did, the old woman laughed, was to smash clay pots and try to lift girls' skirts with their tridents. But even that was all part of festive tradition, and, despite their screams, the girls loved it! The Demons did *not* represent Satan, however, but were meant to be a harmless portrayal of the bad side of the human character while inspiring fear and fun at the same time. Also, it was a great honour to play the head demon in your village – one they called *Dimoni Cucarell*, whose role often remained within the same family for generations.

Judging by her pat delivery, the old woman had obviously related all this to many bemused strangers at Ca'l Dimoni over the years, and she returned to her post by the restaurant doorway with an air of quiet self-satisfaction.

But Ellie still didn't look too happy. 'I find this place a bit eerie,' she muttered. 'A bit spooky. It's, well… weird.'

'Don't be daft. The demon thing's only a gimmick – a crowd-puller.' I had a quiet chuckle to myself. 'Spooky, indeed. What nonsense.'

Just then, a flash lit up the greying sky, the lights behind the bar flickered, and a peal of thunder rumbled in the distance.

Poor Ellie. She really was terrified of thunder and lightning. And her predilection for creepy books and horror films didn't help. One thunderclap and her imagination went haywire. Left to her own devices, I'm sure she would have exited Ca'l Dimoni and taken flight there and then, but some gentle persuasion from me and the irresistible aromas of food drifting into the bar helped common sense prevail. And, as it happened, we didn't have as long as we'd feared to have our number called out.

We were fortunate to have been given a table so quickly, the *anciana* of the tickets told us as she ushered us past her into the restaurant, adding that there wasn't much demand for tables for two on Sundays. '*Las familias extendidas españoles, eh!*' She cackled a cronely chortle and wished us an enjoyable meal by calling after us, '*Bon profit!*' – the *mallorquín* version of the Spanish '*Buen provecho!*' – both expressions meaning literally 'Good profit!'

Odd, perhaps, but who are we to question such peculiarities in others' languages, when our own pre-prandial cordiality usually depends on borrowing a phrase from the French? A reflection, maybe, on what has been, until comparatively recently, the all-too-typical British attitude to eating as merely a bland necessity of life, as opposed to the cherished Mediterranean ritual of enjoying good company and animated discourse during a lengthy and relaxed celebration of the pleasures of kitchen and cellar.

And that was exactly the mood which pervaded this restaurant as we were shown to our table by one of a squad of white-aproned waiters, each one a credit to the professional dedication of the Spanish *camarero*, still smiling freely amid the turmoil of their afternoon's labours.

It always felt good to be out for Sunday lunch in Mallorca, and I had a hunch that Ca'l Dimoni wasn't going to disappoint. The look and ambience of the capacious dining hall appealed to me. Not because of its sumptuous furnishings or swanky décor, for rustic-leaning-towards-basic was the predominant theme in those departments, but because the place simply oozed good, old-fashioned Mallorcan charm. Two sturdy stone columns supported a pitched roof of round timber beams, the spaces between infilled with cane lath, and all glowing with the tawny patina of wood smoke drifting up from a huge open fire. Hanging horizontally from the ceiling were rows of long, rough-hewn poles, bowed by the weight of home-made sausages of strange shapes and many sizes, all dangling over shallow wooden troughs strategically suspended to catch any savoury juices which might otherwise drip onto the clamour of clients below.

According to the menu, the house specialities were *Carnes a la Brasa* – meats cooked on the grill – or in this case, meats cooked on something that could have doubled as a cattle grid. It was positioned over a giant brazier, fuelled by hot ashes raked from under smouldering olive wood logs the size of tree trunks. This culinary forge occupied one whole corner of the hall and was manned by a pair of brawny cooks, whose outlines of perpetual motion were just visible through fountains of sparks that spat from the embers with each turn of the barbecuing meat.

Our waiter laid before us the customary bowl of farm-pickled olives, a basket of crusty brown bread, and a *platito* of little mild peppers, returning a few moments later with an earthenware jug of the house *vino tinto* and a bottle of mineral water, the latter labelled with a thirst-sharpening picture of a snow-capped Mallorcan mountain.

Around us, while they awaited their first courses proper, large Mallorcan families – some obviously spanning four generations – were sharing 'picks' of stewed snails or spicy *butifarra* black pudding, while others were dipping into familial bowls of *callos* (bite-size nuggets of tripe), or delving their forks into communal *fritos* of chopped lambs' liver fried in olive oil with diced peppers and potatoes.

I poured myself a glass of wine and sat back to savour the ambience.

'I still think there's something strange about this place,' Ellie said, her gaze flitting nervously round the room.

The demonic theme had certainly been exploited to the full, with devil masks adorning the walls and, on a shelf in a dark corner by the bar, a metre-high demon carved out of black wood. It really was a *very* lifelike effigy. His cloven feet were prancing in a devilish dance, spidery hands raised as if playing an invisible pipe, the back of his pot-bellied body sprouting a dragon's tail and a huge pair of bat's wings. Horns thrust out from his head, and the grotesque leer on his face was caught in the eerie glow of a craftily placed light bulb.

Ellie was transfixed by it.

'Relax,' I laughed. 'Just a bit of folklore.'

'And take a look at that fretwork mural over there,' she gasped. 'All back-lit and everything.'

'Mm-m-m, the old Mallorcan pig-killing party,' I observed with minimal interest. 'Quite well done, isn't it?'

'It's gruesome! Two men with knives, ready to murder a pig tied to a trestle. And look – a woman standing by with a bucket to catch the blood.' Ellie shook her head and shuddered. 'It's enough to put you off eating meat forever.'

'Nonsense! It's only depicting the *matances*. Used to be a great end-of-year occasion on farms here. Still is on a few of them, according to old Maria Bauzá. All the neighbours mucking in to cut up the family pig and make the sausages and things. Then having a good feed, followed by a sing-song and a knees-up at night. Great fun.'

'Not for the poor pig, it isn't. Just look at the expression on that one's face. Absolutely grim.'

'Well, let's face it,' I laughed, 'you'd look a bit grim yourself if you were about to have your throat cut.' I gave Ellie a comforting pat on the hand. 'Anyway, it's only a decoration – like the demons. Here, have an olive.'

Ellie appeared too preoccupied to even notice what I was saying. 'Devils and death,' she mumbled. 'I don't like the evil in here.'

'Rubbish!' I scoffed. 'This place is about as evil as Disneyland!'

The gathering clouds of the approaching storm suddenly dimmed everything into semi-darkness, intensifying the macabre effect of the diffused lighting behind the demon masks and *matances* mural. In this murky light, the dancing devil looked even more realistic, standing poised and ready to leap into a wild, satanic jig at any moment. This all added up to an extremely unlikely theme for a restaurant, without doubt, but rather than scaring them, the deliberate creepiness of it all clearly delighted even the youngest members of the surrounding families.

I scanned the menu and, as expected, noted that the bill of fare certainly hadn't been assembled to attract vegetarians. As in most Mallorcan country restaurants, pork and, in this case, lamb dishes predominated.

The interesting thing about the native breed of lanky Mallorcan sheep is that the ewe hardly ever produces that golden goal of sheep farmers in cooler climes – twin lambs. In fact, nature has dictated that she wouldn't want to. One hungry youngster at a time's enough to rear when you have to exist on drought-parched grazings for much of the year. But the Mallorcan ewe does have a trick up her Mediterranean fleece, nonetheless. Unlike her cold-conditioned cousins in the north, she lambs twice a year instead of just once. Horses for courses, you might say in parallel livestock circles, and one plus one still makes two.

Anyway, those same frugal fodder supplies, combined with the value put on ewes' milk by their human masters, has decreed that many Mallorcan lambs can expect their journey to the plate to start at a very early age – often at just a few weeks young. A hard fact of ovine life, but resulting, nevertheless, in the most tender, delicately flavoured lamb to bear the name. In truth, it's a different meat entirely from that of the 'fat' lambs traditionally reared in Britain, for example, and one to which the Mallorcan people are proudly addicted.

It didn't come as a surprise, therefore, to see deliciously lean and succulent *costillas de cordero*, baby lamb chops, being served up at the next table. They were for the youngsters. Some of the adults had opted for leg of lamb – slender shanks of tender young meat on the bone, roasted to crackling-crisp perfection. Others had chosen another speciality of the Spanish country kitchen, *lechona asada*, roast suckling pig, the best of which, it's said, should be tender enough to be cut with the edge of a plate. It all looked and smelled irresistible.

Ellie, reading my thoughts, shook her head. The pig-killing mural had obviously blown it for me. This was going to be a meatless meal – unless, I presumed, I wanted to wait for another table and go and eat on my own.

Yielding to the immovable, I ordered *sopas mallorquinas* for two.

'And to follow?' the waiter enquired, clearly assuming that we would be adhering to local custom by having this particular dish as a starter.

'No, *gracias*,' Ellie swiftly piped up. 'The *sopas* will do us just fine, *gracias*.'

The waiter's consequent facial shrug left me in little doubt that, in his considered opinion, he was serving a couple who were just a few burgers short of the full barbecue pack. *Hombre*, come to Ca'l Dimoni and don't order meat? his expression seemed to say. *Ay-y-y, caramba!*

And at that moment, when I looked about at table after table of jubilant meat-eaters, I couldn't help but share his dismay. But Mallorca's deceptively simple rural cuisine, like the island's landscape, has a way of producing the most unexpected of surprises. For, while the menu's description of the *sopas* as 'a substantial cabbage stew' didn't exactly conjure up visions of a mouth-watering culinary classic, the reality proved otherwise.

As our waiter took the trouble of explaining when he laid two steaming earthenware *greixoneras* before us, the *sopas* word prompted the uninitiated to assume that he was ordering soup. Whereas, the name is actually a distortion of *sopes*, the fawn-coloured country bread of Mallorca which, he assured us, we would find had been used to line the bases of our dishes. Then a well-seasoned broth of shredded cabbage, tomatoes and onions had been added, and the whole left to simmer until all the liquid had been absorbed by the bread, leaving the still-moist vegetables on top.

The waiter made a circle of middle finger and thumb, which he directed at me as if throwing a dart. '*Fabuloso!*'

And he was right. This certainly was no soup, but a concoction so thick that it could have been cut into slices, and with a toothsome flavour which must have derived from a skilfully prepared stock, made, it seemed certain from its savoury taste, with a liberal quantity of meat in the recipe. I said nothing, and neither, more significantly, did Ellie – not until she had scooped up and wolfed down every last scrap of the *sopas* from her bowl.

'There,' she triumphantly announced, dabbing her lips with her napkin. 'Who says you have to eat murdered animals to have a delicious meal?'

I nodded my head in diplomatic agreement. It would be interesting, I pondered, to see who would break their virtuous resolutions first – Ellie the sudden vegetarian, or Jordi the trainee teetotaller.

Outside, the sky had become leaden and rain was starting to fall, but at least the threatened thunderstorm appeared to have receded, contributing to what I noticed was Ellie's considerably more relaxed demeanour now. And the continued intake of the robust house wine was having a similar effect on me.

'You know, Ellie,' I said with a little laugh of bravado, 'you almost had me going too – I mean with all that demons-and-death stuff you were prattling on about. Believe it or not, I was actually beginning to feel a bit uncomfortable in here too.' I laughed again and took a slug of wine. 'Silly fairy tale stuff. I should be ashamed of myself.'

'It's not silly at all,' Ellie retorted.

'Yeah, yeah – all those far-fetched fantasy yarns you fill your head with. Own up – writers of books like that have made fortunes out of gullible folk like you.' I gave a dismissive snort. 'Loada rubbish.'

A little smile was playing at the corner of Ellie's lips, the glow from the back-lit devil masks reflected in her eyes as a mischievous twinkle. 'So,' she probed, 'you don't believe in the Prince of Darkness, then?'

'Oh-h-h, but I do, my dear,' I droned in a poor take-off of Vincent Price. 'Yes, about as much as I believe in Santa Claus.'

Ellie was looking past me now, the smile abruptly wiped from her face. She was staring, hypnotised, at someone, some*thing*, behind my back. Out of my line of vision, a child let out a blood-curdling scream, and a ghoulish guffaw resounded round the suddenly hushed hall. I felt the hairs rise on the back of my neck, as a dazzling streak of lightning struck earth outside the restaurant, so close that the resultant explosion of thunder was almost instantaneous. The lights guttered and died, plunging the room into near darkness.

Then, out of an eerie silence, something touched my shoulder. Something sharp, something cold, something… sinister. An icy shiver ran down my spine, scuttling over my goose-pimpled skin like the feet of a wet sewer rat. Instinctively, I leapt to my feet, wheeling round heart-in-mouth to confront whoever, *what*ever had touched me.

'WA-A-A-H!' I roared, hardly recognising the sound of my own shocked voice.

It was *HIM!* He was standing there right before me, the horned outline of his huge head etched in stark silhouette against the backdrop of flames from the grill. All was deathly quiet, except for the rasping of his breath and the angry hissing and sparking of the fire. I saw the burning gleam of his eyes staring directly into mine.

Behind me, Ellie whimpered as another thunderbolt shook the building. In its stuttering flash, I caught a glimpse of what had touched my shoulder – a vicious-looking trident, gripped in this living demon's hairy right hand, and aimed now at my chest. My brain was telling me to be rational, not to let Ellie's absurd imaginings get to me, but my feet knew better and took a reflex sideways lunge. I tripped over my chair leg, staggered over the floor and, as the lights came on again, found myself sitting in the lap of the top-heavy *señora* whose 'button' I had inadvertently tweaked back in the bar.

The demon led the howls of laughter which rose from the surrounding tables, and I could see that Ellie was joining in the merriment, wiping tears of glee from her eyes, and all to the delight of an audience of little children who had gathered round to see the fun at close quarters. It was only then that I noticed the wad of lottery tickets hanging from a prong on this fancy-dress demon's trident.

'*Oo-oo-ooh-la-la!*' the eyelash-batting baguette woman breathed seductively in my ear, while I struggled red-faced and apologising from her arms.

'*Lo siento, señora*,' I repeated. 'I really am dreadfully sorry.'

'*El gusto es mío*,' she cooed, giving my bum a playful pat as I finally broke free. The pleasure, she assured me, had been all hers... again!

- Four -

NOBLESSE OF THIEVES

By the time we finally took our well-sated leave of Ca'l Dimoni, the mass return to Palma was already well under way. Food-and-wine-mellowed city motorists were conveying their families homeward in a steady and speedy stream, many trying to outdo the driving prowess of others with matador-like machismo. And unless you fancy the odds of your survival while jousting with four-wheeled metal bulls determinedly overtaking one another – preferably on blind corners – get off the Mallorcan main roads as quickly as you can on those post-lunch Sunday afternoons! Which is what we were relieved to do just a few hundred metres after leaving the restaurant.

Turning north into a quiet country lane bounded by dry-stone walls, we passed between well-tended fields where little herds of sheep and goats grazed between row upon neat row of almond trees, all freshly in leaf now after shedding their covering of 'snowflake' blossom a month or so earlier. The storm had died away to a far-off rumble, and ahead of us the stone houses of the sleepy village of Santa Eugenia once again reflected the spring sunshine in soft honey tones. As the road swung gently westward, the 'mountain' of Marron rose on our left, its modest slopes cloaked in pinewoods, its lower flanks concealing caves where it's said pirates once secreted their booty, far inland from the covetous eyes of rival sea-bandits.

But today there is no sign of such a dark past in this most gentle example of Mallorca's ever-changing landscape, where there is nothing more threatening than the Mickey Mouse-eared heads of a prickly pear cactus peeping at you over a garden wall. This is a countryside exuding a beguiling tranquillity which you feel has remained unchanged for centuries. Until, that is, a jet airliner whines loudly overhead, either landing or taking off from Palma airport. For we were now back on the island's central plain, albeit some miles farther north than where we had left it earlier.

Fallow fields, already sprouting buds of poppies and wild marigold, which by summer would paint the land in the vibrant colours of the Spanish flag, soon yielded to mile after mile of manicured vineyards, extending all the way to the picturesque old bodega town of Santa Maria. Away to the south, the high-rise façade of Palma's bustling outskirts shone brightly in the afternoon sunlight – a sprawling cubist sculpture, only a few miles distant, yet a world apart from the rural idyll through which we were still passing.

La Real is typical of many towns and villages that border the splayed hand of arterial roads fanning out from Palma. This one is a fairly humdrum example of past ribbon development skirting the northbound highway to Valldemossa, the historic mountain town where composer Chopin and his novelist paramour George Sand (aka Madame Aurore Dupin, Baronne Dudevant) once spent an illicit, but well-documented, winter. But no such cultural or romantic matters were the order of today. Just football – a subject far more important to the average Sunday-afternoon male of the Spanish species.

Homing in on the mingled sounds of cheering and cat-calling, we found La Real's ground tucked away behind the buildings lining one side of the road, a 'cosy' little stadium enclosed within breeze block walls, almost but not quite high enough, we noticed, to dissuade local boys from clambering to a free entry. The home team was playing a side from the neighbouring island of Ibiza, and the terracing was reasonably full of fans shouting encouragement and abuse at their respective heroes-cum-whipping boys. It was clearly all good-natured stuff, however, with neither section of supporters taking things *too* seriously.

'I don't see Sandy on the pitch,' Ellie remarked, a tad concerned. 'I hope he hasn't been injured! I mean, look at that playing surface – no grass, just hard-packed shale or something! God, you'd rip your skin off falling on that!'

'That's how it is with all these minor league pitches here,' I said. 'Stay on your feet, that's the answer.'

A moment later, one of the home team lunged into a kamikaze sliding tackle, leaving, just as Ellie predicted, about an acre of skin from his left leg smeared on the deck. To add insult to injury, the referee promptly booked him for a foul, much to the delight of the visiting support.

'*Hijo de puta!*' they yelled at him. 'Son of a whore!'

The home crowd showered him with praise.

'*El chico tiene cojones!*' they shouted. 'The kid's got balls!' And, of course, the universal: '*El árbitro es un pito tonto!*' 'The referee's a stupid prick!'

The little stadium positively bubbled with soccer bonhomie.

We were soon found by Charlie, burger money gone and 'desperate for a Coke'.

I dipped into my pocket and lobbed him a few coins.

Charlie glanced at the handout. 'Gee, thanks,' he muttered, then gave me a hearty slap on the shoulder. 'Tell you what,' he grinned, 'double that up and I'll stand you a Bud.'

'Don't push it, Charlie! Anyway, where's Sandy? Been shown the red card or something, has he?'

'Nah, didn't make the team. Three of La Real's top guys are back after injury, so...' He motioned towards a small, open-fronted shack tucked away in a corner by the entrance. 'Sandy's on the subs' bench.'

I did a double take at where Charlie had gestured. 'But – but, that's the bar!'

'Bar, subs' bench, gents' toilet,' Charlie shrugged. 'You name it – that's where it's at.'

'This I've got to see!'

Sandy was standing in the midst of a gaggle of middle-aged Mallorcan men, all obviously more interested in having a good chinwag and laugh at the bar than paying too much heed to the proceedings on the field of play. The second half of the match was already well under way, but by the flushed and merry looks on the faces of Sandy's companions, they had been studying the bottoms of their glasses a bit more than they'd been watching the football for the past hour or so. The jovial barman, I was intrigued to note, was dressed in the dark blue uniform of the *Policía Local* – the nearest Spanish equivalent you'll get to the old-style village bobby in Britain. Interesting.

Sandy introduced us to his chums in a jumble of Gabriels, Tomeus, Paus and Peres, all punctuated with firm handshakes, backslaps and, for Ellie, polite little bows which, in addition to being a mark of Latin courtesy, also provided the opportunity for the customary Latin appraisal of all points south of the female neckline.

'*Mucho gusto, señora,*' was the general response. '*Mm-m-m, sí, muy encantadora!*' Ellie had met with their approval.

'I – I hope you aren't drinking alcohol, Sandy,' she stammered, trying to cover her embarrassment, as the babble of *mallorquín* banter started up again all around us.

'Just 7-Up,' Sandy grinned, holding up his bottle. 'I'm driving, remember?'

One of the clutch of Gabriels or Peres thrust a beer into my hand, with a manly thump on the bicep and the accompanying Mallorcan wish of, '*Salud, pesetas y amor!*' – 'Health, wealth and love!'

Ellie, having been ritually appraised, was now ritually ignored by her appraisers, while their shouted conversation returned to football, politics and other subjects (presently at least) more worthy of men's attention.

'Something to drink?' I asked her, knowing that this incursion into a typical Spanish male chauvinist lair wasn't her cup of tea.

Wincing at a deafening howl of insult suddenly bellowed at the referee by nearby La Real supporters, she opted, without much enthusiasm, for a coffee. 'Oh, and earplugs, if they've got them!'

Another roar went up from the home fans around us, prompting even Sandy's coterie of ostensibly disinterested associates to look towards the pitch and throw their hands in the air with yells of delight. One of the Gabriels – or was it a Pau? – grabbed me by the elbow and bundled me towards the bar in the bosom of his scrummage of chums. Ellie was left to her own womanly devices.

'It's standard form with these blokes,' a beaming Sandy shouted at me through the ensuing mêlée. 'They're the players' dads – or uncles – family, anyway. You know what it's like in these villages – all related somehow or other.'

'But why the sudden stampede for the bar?'

'All part of the gang rules. Every time the La Real team gets a goal, the old boys here treat themselves to a celebratory *coñac*. Happens every game.'

I glanced over at the scoreboard. Just as I'd thought. '*Cero – Cero*.' No score. I looked quizzically at Sandy. 'Judging by the relaxed state the dads and uncles here are in, I'd have expected their lads to be at least seven or eight goals up by now.'

Sandy raised a resigned shoulder. 'Yes, well, it's been one of those games, I suppose. The goals just haven't been happening.'

'Uh-huh? So?'

'So the chaps here implemented what they refer to as the second protocol. They started having a *coñac* every time there was a corner kick in La Real's favour instead.'

'But, listen, I was watching, and unless my eyes deceive me, there wasn't a corner just now. Only a throw-in!'

Sandy pulled a wry smile. 'Like I said – one of those games.'

'Hmm, a day for the *third* protocol, right?'

Sandy gave a you-got-it-in-one nod of the head.

Someone nudged me right up to the bar counter, and the laughing policeman on duty behind it closed my fingers round a bulbous glass, then glugged in a generous measure from a Fundador brandy bottle. He then poured himself an identical celebratory nip and clinked glasses with me.

'*Salud, amigo!*' he toasted amicably.

'Ehm, yes,' I hesitantly responded, caught off guard at being called 'friend' by a policeman I didn't know – especially one drinking *and* selling hard liquor while in uniform. 'Yes, *salud*, uhm… *amigo!*' I turned to Sandy and muttered out of the corner of my mouth, 'What's the deal with him?'

'Oh, only taking his turn behind the bar like all the other dads and uncles, that's all.'

'So he's off duty, then? Ah, well, that's a different story.' I raised my glass to the officer and flashed him a warm smile. 'Your good health, *amigo!*'

But Sandy was quick to correct my naïve misreading of the situation. 'No, no, he *is* still on duty, all right. But it's just that, well, there's never any real police work to do at these games.' He was quite adamant, adding, 'You know, none of that football hooliganism stuff like back in the UK.'

Right on cue, a fracas broke out in the crowd on the other side of the pitch, the sudden excitement heightened by the referee's manic blowing of his whistle. It appeared that the same home-team player who'd been booked earlier had just committed another foul, and a particularly vociferous pack of teenage girls in the visiting crowd were giving him a really hard time for his sins.

'*Animal sucio!*' they screamed, chucking a couple of well-sucked orange wedges. 'Dirty animal! *Fuera! Fuera! Fuera!* Off! Off! Off!'

At which, the gallant young recipient of their gibes promptly made the ultra-insulting sign of the goat, dropped his shorts, then bent over and treated them to an unobstructed view of his naked backside. As uproarious hilarity erupted on the terraces, out came the referee's yellow card again, followed automatically by a red one. La Real's mooning miscreant was sentenced to treat his bare bum – and his *cojones* – to an early bath.

The barbs which his delighted female tormentors then hurled at him sounded to me as if they were being delivered mainly in the Ibizan patois. But, through the pervading din, I did just manage to recognise the words for 'lovely', 'arse' and (I *think* I've got this right) the poetic 'tight as the cheeks of a frost-bitten clam!'. Whatever, the *cojones* kid responded with the expected phallic gesture, pulled up his shorts and swaggered off bath-wards under a mixed hail of boos, hisses, wolf whistles and cheers.

The bar brigade, without recourse to discussion, cheerfully progressed to the fourth protocol.

'But of course!' beamed their uniformed drinks purveyor. 'Y *viva el fútbol, eh!*'

Ellie was first to notice the open gates.

'You did lock them when we left, didn't you?' she asked me.

'Well, I could have sworn that I did.'

'No, you *def*initely did. I watched you.'

A feeling of apprehension gripped me as we drove into the yard behind the Ca's Mayoral farmhouse. And then we saw it. One of the double doors to the *almacén*, the big storeroom that took up much of the ground floor of the house, was slightly ajar, the wood near its lock crudely splintered. Ellie was out of the car and making a beeline for the house even before I'd pulled the handbrake on.

'Wait!' I shouted after her. 'Wait, Ellie! They could still be in there!'

The boys, who had driven home behind us from the football game, arrived in the yard just in time to see their mother rushing into the house. Without exchanging a word, the three of us dashed after her, adrenalin surging. Instinctively, we grabbed makeshift weapons from hooks on the *almacén* wall – Sandy the broken shaft of a garden spade, Charlie and I a hammer each. Ellie was nowhere to be seen, but I recognised her footsteps running from room to room over the tiled floor upstairs. There was still every chance that the robbers were still in the house, and I genuinely feared for her safety.

It was the first time that any of us had been in such a situation, and it was strange how wc all acted in the same impulsive, or – with the benefit of hindsight – foolhardy way. I suppose that most of us tend to assume that, faced with potential danger such as that, we would act rationally, fully aware that the housebreakers could be armed and would take whatever desperate measures were necessary to make good their escape. Extreme caution would be your byword – phone the police, summon help, do anything except risk life and limb by confronting the intruders.

Well, that isn't how it works in practice. Rational thinking doesn't come into it. It hadn't with Ellie, and it didn't with the boys and me either. Ellie's automatic reaction when seeing the forced door had been to find out immediately what had happened inside the house, *her* house, *her* family's home. The boys and I simply wanted to save her from whatever personal danger her precipitate action might now be exposing her to.

In the brief seconds it took me to see that every cupboard and drawer in the downstairs living area had been opened and rifled through, Sandy and Charlie were already clambering up the stairs, yelling to their mother to come back. I was right behind them, the initial shock of realising that we had been the victims of a break-in replaced now by a curious mixture of hurt and outrage. Who were these people who had dared to force their way into our home, who had had the effrontery to rake through our personal belongings as if it was their right? Looking back, I dread to think what would have happened had any of us actually come face-to-face with our robbers just then.

Again, rational thinking would not have come into it, and the outcome would most probably have been bloody. And this for a normal, peaceable family for whom violence would never usually be an option.

But – fortunately, as I now realise – such an appalling scenario did not come about. While the boys checked the other upstairs rooms, I found Ellie in our bedroom at the far end of the hallway, standing staring down at the bed, her face a study in stunned disbelief.

'They've taken it all,' she said, her voice trembling. 'All except these.'

I looked down at the three pieces of jewellery that had been left, almost perversely, in a neat line on the bedspread.

'Cheap trinkets. Just fun stuff,' Ellie explained, still transfixed, 'but they've stolen every single thing of any value.' She shook her head, then looked at me, tears welling in her eyes. 'Imagine,' she said, forcing a smile and showing me her left hand, 'of all the days to go out wearing only my wedding ring, I had to pick today.' She motioned towards the wardrobe and two chests of drawers, all open, their contents ransacked. 'They knew what they were after and where to look. Experts.'

'It's the same throughout the house,' Sandy informed us, stumbling breathless into the room.

'Yeah, they've been through everything,' Charlie puffed. 'Even that box of old Disney videos from when I was a kid!'

The four of us stood silently for several moments, the gravity of what had happened finally sinking in. The original adrenalin rush, which had stimulated us into taking such impulsive action, quickly subsiding now, leaving a cold realisation that this wasn't a bad dream. It was real, and it had happened to us. That initial feeling of vengeful rage steadily changed to one of injury, to one of vilification, driven bluntly home by the inescapable truth that strangers' hands had violated the sanctity of our home and had groped contemptuously through our personal things.

'It makes you feel strange – almost unclean in an odd sort of way,' Ellie murmured.

And I doubt if there could have been a more succinct way of expressing how we all felt at that moment.

'They, ehm, they've gone, by the way, Dad,' Sandy said quietly. 'Charlie and I checked the whole house.'

God! In my preoccupation with Ellie's safety, I'd allowed myself to ignore that the boys had taken it upon themselves to run the risk of confronting the burglars on their own. With mixed emotions of remorse and relief, I patted their backs and thanked them, the fact that we had been extremely fortunate finally crystallising in my hitherto alarm-fuddled mind. The house had been broken into and sacked, jewellery and maybe other items stolen, and there was nothing we could do to change that now. But the important point was that we were all unharmed. The loss of material things, when compared to this, suddenly paled into insignificance – at least for the moment.

Putting on a brave face for the boys, Ellie made to start tidying up the contents of a drawer that was spilling crumpled-up articles of clothing.

I grabbed her arm. 'No, Ellie! Don't touch it! Don't touch *any*thing else until the police have been!'

It was then, I think, that the full impact of what we were now enmeshed in hit Ellie like a sledgehammer. The shock of discovering what had happened had been bad enough, but that would only be the start of further invasions of our privacy, and the realisation that she wasn't even free within her own four walls to follow her instinctive urge to clear up the mess was clearly a bitter pill to swallow.

'OK, I'll, uhm – I'll just go and have a look in the other rooms, then,' she said, somehow managing to summon up a little dewy-eyed smile as she passed the boys. 'I'll just, you know, try to see what's missing.'

'Look,' I said, 'you lads go and keep your Mum company. She'll need a bit of moral support. I'll, ehm, I'll look up the Guardia Civil's number – report this whole bloody awful business.'

Then it struck me just how inadequate my command of the Spanish language was. All right, I could get by pretty well now as long as the required vocabulary revolved around things agricultural. But, hell, I didn't even know the word for robbery, never mind the ones for jewellery and necklaces and so on. And it would be a waste of valuable time looking them up. At traumatic moments like this, it's good to have a friend to call, and that's precisely what I did. I rang a friend who spoke Spanish *and* Mallorcan like a native.

'Dinnae worry, son,' Jock Burns calmly said on the other end of the line. 'I'll phone the Guardia Civil station in Andratx right away, and I'll be wi' ye *rápidamente*. Nae bother. Just stay cool till I get there, right?'

Stay cool! OK, good advice and well intended, but easier said than done. I replaced the phone, noticing for the first time how my hands were shaking. The mellowing effects of the Ca'l Dimoni wine and football-match *coñac* had been well and truly wiped out. Yet a nerve-steadying drink was the last thing on my mind right now. Keeping a clear head to cope with what lay ahead *was* the only priority, and I knew that only too well.

Although it took Jock little more than twenty minutes to drive almost as many miles to Ca's Mayoral, it gave us time enough to assess the full extent of the robbery. Ellie had established within seconds of entering our bedroom that the thieves had found what they were looking for, and they had zeroed in on it like guided missiles. This, despite the fact that the ever-cautious Ellie had hidden all the valuables in several unlikely places, like inside her leather knee boots in the wardrobe. Unlikely places, that is, to anyone but the expert jewellery thief, as we now knew to our cost.

Having found what they came for, it appeared that they had then taken the time to spread all the items out on the bed and separate the sellable from the rest. Why hadn't they just bundled the whole lot into a bag, made a rapid exit and worried about sifting through the loot later? The cool minds of seasoned criminals, perhaps? Or maybe just swaggering over-confidence? We hoped we'd soon find out.

One thing was already certain, however. As Ellie had quickly realised, every single piece of valuable jewellery had been taken – her rings, necklaces, bracelets, brooches, everything. And although they hadn't amounted to all that much in quantity, they were things which she'd carefully scrimped and saved for over the years, and they *were* of good quality. But worse than the adverse monetary implications was the sickening thought that items of irreplaceable sentimental value were gone, perhaps forever. Items like Ellie's engagement ring, a locket containing a picture of another of our sons who had died when only five years old, and (my one purely personal treasure) a gold watch and chain that had been given to me by my grandfather, including a little medal which he'd won in a horse-ploughing contest when a young lad back in Orkney, over three generations ago. Those were the things that we were already praying would be recovered, even if the rest never was.

'Tidy job,' said Jock, doing a quick tour of the house with me while we waited for the arrival of the police. 'Aye, I'll say that for them, they could've left the place in a bigger mess, if that's any consolation.'

Well, it wasn't any consolation at the time, of course. But I saw what Jock meant. Although no nook or cranny had been left unexplored by the intruders, nothing had been wantonly defaced or destroyed. And even the contents of the drawers and cupboards hadn't been gratuitously disturbed – until the robbers had reached the master bedroom, that's to say, when a frenzy of rummaging seemed to have overcome them as they closed in on their plunder.

'Anything else nicked,' Jock asked, '– apart from the jewellery, that is?'

I shook my head. 'Not as far as we can make out. The telly's still there – video too – music centre – pictures – clocks – all present and correct. No, it looks as if they've been after one thing and one thing only.'

'Could've been worse then, son. Mind, don't get me wrong – this is a right disaster for ye all, and no mistake. But, know what I mean? Well, could've been worse, eh?'

I could tell that Jock was trying, as best he could, to lighten the ordeal he knew we were going through. A self-conscious, almost clumsy attempt for someone normally so extrovert, no doubt, but a genuine show of concern, nonetheless, and an insight into a side of his nature which Jock had hitherto kept concealed.

I gave him a reassuring smile. 'Could've been worse, right enough, Jock. Come on – let's go and see if there's any sign of that police guy you phoned.'

It was almost an hour later and already getting dark when the little Renault 4, painted in the distinctive two-tone livery of the Guardia Civil, pulled into the yard. We had been expecting a full team of detectives and forensic experts, but only one officer was in the car, dressed, not in the imposing dark-green uniform of his august corps, but in a baggy tracksuit and old white sneakers. And he didn't look too pleased to be here either.

He was officially off duty, that was the first thing he said, pausing to take an almost casual glance at the splintered edge of the *almacén* door as he sauntered into the house. He'd been playing tennis with his wife and children, he dryly informed us – the first Sunday he'd been able to spend with them in over two months. But as he was the domestic robbery officer for this area, he had been summoned to investigate this one. '*Mi día libre o no,*' he added bluntly. 'My day off or not.'

'*Habla inglés?*' I asked him. Did he speak English?

My question went unanswered, but the look he gave me left us in no doubt that, as this was Spain and as he was an officer of the Spanish Civil Guard, there was only one language to be spoken, and we'd have to make the best of it. And that was fair enough, I silently conceded. After all, if we'd been a Spanish family in similar unfortunate circumstances in Britain, the chances of our being sent a Spanish-speaking bobby to look into our plight would have been remote, to say the least.

'Arrogant bugger!' Jock opined for my benefit, while simultaneously flashing his own charm-loaded smile at the officer. 'Mainland Spanish, like a lot o' his ilk on this island. Far south, most likely. Jumped-up fandango merchant.'

The policeman's expression remained inscrutable. We had been hanging about helplessly awaiting the arrival of the law for the best part of two hours now, all of us frustrated to the point of distraction by the thought of how much of a head start our robbers were being given. But, for all that, the Civil Guard officer seemed in no hurry. He impassively asked Jock and I to accompany him on an inspection of the house. The *señora* and our two *hijos* would not be required... for the present.

'Is this it?' I hissed at Jock, scarcely able to believe what was now becoming increasingly apparent. 'One copper! I mean, where's the finger print guys? And who's contacting the neighbours and going round the village asking questions? *Some*body must have seen something! At this rate, the culprits are going to be off the island before the investigation even starts!'

Jock duly relayed these points on my behalf in Spanish, and was given in response a series of take-it-or-leave-it shrugs. The policeman, meanwhile, seemed to take only the most superficial interest in anything he saw in the way of evidence, until we reached the master bedroom, where he had already been informed the valuables had been hidden. Taking what I, in my impatient state, took to be an inordinately protracted amount of time doing a detailed inspection of Ellie's leather boots (was that a slightly kinky smirk twitching at the corner of his mouth?), he eventually looked up, smiled woodenly, and said the investigation was over.

'He must be bloody joking!' I snapped at Jock. 'The robbers! Ask him who the hell's been going after the robbers while he's been farting about here!'

He would require to see the property's insurance policy, was the lawman's only response to Jock's translation. Then he would have a final word with the *señor* and his family back down in the *almacén*.

If I was knocked speechless by this, I was totally flabbergasted by the announcement he made to us prior to his eventual departure, barely fifteen minutes after his arrival.

'I am pleased to inform you, lady and gentlemen,' he declared in perfect English, 'that I am satisfied that there has indeed been a robbery here.' Then, turning to Jock, he smiled a charm-loaded smile and said, 'Not bad for a jumped-up fandango merchant, Mister Burns. Correct?'

Now Jock was knocked speechless too – the first time I'd ever witnessed such a phenomenon. And woe betide Jock if he ever got on the wrong side of the Andratx branch of the Guardia Civil from now on!

The officer then addressed me again, saying: 'If you would be good enough to bring your family to my office in one hour – it will take me that time to write my report – we can then conclude this entire matter to everyone's satisfaction.' As my jaw dropped, he shook my hand, then Ellie's, and added: 'Please accept my sympathies for this unfortunate occurrence, *señores*.' He casually gestured towards a workbench where the boys and I had deposited our makeshift self-defence weapons. 'And may I say,' he pronounced in officious tones, 'that you can think yourselves lucky that you did not cause your intruders any physical harm. If you had, *you* would be heading for prison at this moment, not them.' He then clicked the heels of his sneakers and, with a salute and a polite '*Hasta luego*', was gone.

'Fuck me!' Jock blurted out. 'Eh, pardon the ethnic vernacular, Ellie darlin', but that Guardia bloke takes the biscuit! There *has* indeed been a robbery here, he says! The bandits headin' for prison? Come on, do me a favour! Like you said, Pedro, nobody's even tryin' to find out where the hell they are, for Christ's sake!'

'Not to mention *who* they are,' Sandy put in.

'Hey, maybe the cops were in on the heist!' Charlie immediately speculated, with more than a hint of enthusiasm for the possibility.

I was tempted to say that the same suspicion had also crossed my mind, but I'd noticed that Ellie had been ominously quiet for a while. 'You all right?' I asked her, then immediately realised the stupidity of the question. Of course she wasn't all right. None of us were. Even the normally garrulous Jock had nothing to say as a little cloud of gloom gathered over our heads. We all just stood there for a while, staring at the broken wood of the *almacén* door, silently thinking our own thoughts.

The local Guardia Civil post is situated in a fairly featureless block in a backstreet of Andratx. We were shown to a dingy little room, spartanly furnished with a wooden table and a scattering of spindly-legged stacking chairs. One naked light bulb dangled from the ceiling, casting a dismal light on bare walls stained brown by years of cigarette and cigar smoke. It was too easy to visualise some poor wretch of a suspect cringing at that table for hour upon hour at the hands of a succession of merciless interrogators. The room radiated an atmosphere of foreboding and despair.

After endless minutes, during which none of us said a word, a bored-looking duty corporal came in and blandly informed us that we would have to wait until the report on the robbery had been typed up, then studied by his chief. The *señores*, he grunted, should make themselves comfortable in the meantime.

'Comfortable?' Jock gasped after the *cabo* had gone. 'Comfortable! A bit bloody ambitious that, eh!'

There was no answer to that, so silence descended upon our little group once again.

Without having to ask, I could tell by the expressions on Ellie's and the boys' faces that they would rather have been anywhere but in that gloomy room just then. Anywhere at all, but preferably, I suspected, back 'home' in Scotland, surrounded by friends, family and things familiar. And I knew exactly how they felt. Certainly, we had had our share of setbacks since starting our new life on the island, but nothing had really prompted a feeling akin to homesickness until now. Although the robbery and subsequent events were no different for us than they would have been for a Mallorcan family, we still couldn't help but feel a sense of not belonging. We were gullible dreamers who had finally found themselves in a nightmare... but in someone else's land.

And as Ellie admitted when eventually she broke the depressing silence, it wasn't just the feelings of hurt and degradation which had overwhelmed us originally, but the subsequent chilling realisation that we had been watched leaving the house, our movements monitored by persons unknown, who had been waiting their chance to strike on a rare occasion when we had all been away from the farm at the same time.

Then unhealthy suspicions started to creep into our thoughts. Could one of our neighbours have been involved? No, there was no way that old Maria, or Pep or Jaume would have stooped to such a thing; they had all gone too far out of their way to show us kindness and to help us settle into their community for that. Not even the crafty Ferrers deserved to come into the reckoning, grasping as they may have been in other ways.

So who, then? Who knew that a foreign family (and all foreigners are rich in some people's minds) had recently moved into Ca's Mayoral? Who would have had sufficient knowledge of us and the house to have planned such a neatly executed robbery? The answer to those questions was 'anyone'. Anyone in the village at the top of the lane, for example – one of the regular *paseo* people, perhaps – or one of the tradesmen who had done work in the house – or the log man, the postman, the baker's vanman – any one of a hundred local folk. Or could it have been people from another area entirely – well-organised, city crooks who learn about their remotely situated prey by eavesdropping on conversations in country bars, for instance? There was no way of telling. All we knew was that the longer we sat in that little room with no apparent investigation under way, the slimmer would be the chances of ever finding out.

Half an hour later, the immaculately uniformed *comandante* of the post strode in, carrying some sheets of paper. Without ceremony, he drew a chair up to the table and informed us that this was the investigating officer's report, in Spanish and in triplicate – one copy for the Guardia Civil's own files, one for our insurance company, and one for ourselves. We would have to sign all three. But first, he was required to read us the findings of the report, during which time it would be necessary for us to make drawings of all the stolen items.

'How in heaven's name do you draw a flat-link chain and make it look any different from a round-link chain?' Ellie asked me, a look of incredulity on her face. 'Or make one diamond ring look any different from a thousand other diamond rings? Honestly, this is ridiculous!'

The *comandante* gave her an admonishing scowl. 'What is ridiculous, *señora*,' he countered in English, 'is that you had such a valuable collection of jewellery in your possession without taking the precaution of photographing every item for identification purposes in such circumstances as this.' He turned to Jock. 'Now, sir, I understand that you will translate my reading of this report as I go along.' Then, before I could yield to my urge to ask why he didn't just read it in English himself, he pronounced to us all that he was obliged to relate the contents of the report in the language of the land, and it was up to us to satisfy ourselves that we had understood every detail of it before signing.

Suitably cautioned, we nodded our humble acquiescence, and Ellie started to draw circles, some interlocking, some not. At least she knew how to make a chain look different from a ring!

The fine details noted in the report removed any notion we may have been harbouring that the tracksuited officer who wrote it had been as cursory in his inspection of the house as had appeared. He hadn't missed a thing, right down to a detailed description of the security precautions which we had taken – or rather *hadn't* taken. Firstly, the little Yale-type lock on the *almacén* door was totally inadequate, a point proved by the minimal amount of damage done to the door by the intruders, who had clearly gained access to the property without much difficulty at all. A list of other security oversights on our part followed, ending with particularly harsh criticism of Ellie having hidden valuables in such an 'obvious' location as the toe of a boot – the first place even the most amateur of thieves would look!

And we could argue with none of this. Now that it had been pointed out to us, we had to admit to having been a bit naïve, to say the least. It was the old story – until it happens to you, you simply don't think of such things. So there we were, a sense of guilt now compounding our existing feelings of loss and victimisation.

'But why wasn't a search for the thieves put into motion as soon as the robbery was reported?' I asked the *comandante* when he'd finally finished reading the report.

'Because, sir, we had no idea what stolen items we were looking for.' He glanced at Ellie's valiant but glaringly inadequate attempt at drawing those very items, smiled disarmingly and added, 'Until now, that is.'

Even Ellie couldn't resist a reciprocal smile at this. She was only too aware of the total futility of her artistic efforts, but then we *should* have had photographs available. Guilty again.

But why, I enquired, feeling slightly peeved, had the investigating officer made the flippant remark at the end of his inspection of the house that he was satisfied that a robbery had, in fact, taken place? 'That was a bit uncalled-for, wasn't it?'

The *comandante* held up one copy of the report. 'This is for your insurers, sir. And they will most certainly not regard my officer's findings as flippant.'

The penny dropped like a lead weight. 'You – you mean he had actually suspected that we'd faked the break-in just to –'

'Just to fool your insurance company? Precisely. From experience, that has to be our first priority in these cases. Domestic insurance fraud, sir – a very common practice indeed.'

For the second time in the space of a few hours, I was dumbstruck. While the actual culprits had been making their getaway, we ourselves had been the prime suspects of having committed our own robbery!

'Aye, well, this is Spain, son,' Jock pointed out once we had finally taken our leave of the Guardia Civil, 'and that's how it is. Oh, and don't forget, like the *comandante* said, it's the incomers, *extranjeros* like you and me, that are the main baddies in these insurance rip-offs.' He gave me one of his near-Masonic winks. 'Been tempted to have a go at it masel' a coupla times – get the old mits on some easy *dinero*, know what I mean?'

We were standing in a huddle under the dim glow of a solitary street lamp outside the police station, exhausted, punch-drunk and not really up to Jock's well-meaning attempt at lightening up the prevailing mood of despondency. Ellie was looking particularly down in the dumps.

'Being absolutely honest,' she said to Jock, 'do you think there's any chance at all of the police getting our stuff back?'

'Everything's possible in Mallorca, darlin',' he shrugged. 'Everything's possible in Mallorca.'

But deep down, I think we all knew that we'd never see the stolen things again. Even the Guardia Civil *comandante* had warned us that there was every likelihood that, as in most crimes of this type, the jewellery would have been fenced, melted down or even spirited off the island before the break-in had even been discovered. It seemed a somewhat defeatist attitude to us at the time, but on reflection, the man was only admitting the truth. Hundreds of thousands of people arrive in and leave Mallorca every day by air and sea, so the chances of apprehending sneak thieves, unless actually caught in the act, would often be in the needle-in-a-haystack category. But his officers would do their best, he'd assured us, and we would be invited to inspect displays of recovered valuables in the Palma police headquarters at regular intervals.

We were left with the distinct impression, though, that, had we not been insured, a more visible attempt might have been made to investigate our case. But as we *did* have insurance cover, the tacit police attitude appeared to be that the robbery was more a matter to be settled between ourselves and our insurers than one to put further strain on the force's 'already-overstretched manpower resources'.

We had learned a few lessons the hard way. For a start, don't make it easy for housebreakers by having inadequate locks on doors. And install a safe. That was the insurance company's instruction when, after putting up a determined struggle, they eventually coughed up some compensation. Thereafter, because of our 'bad security record', they would cover jewellery only when locked in the safe. But the moment it was removed for wearing, our insurance would cease to be valid. A loopy state of affairs, no doubt, but one which we were obliged to live with from then on.

Naturally, word of the robbery spread round the immediate vicinity like wildfire, and our near neighbours all paid us visits to offer their heart-felt commiserations... and to see the evidence of the forced door first-hand, tutting in disgust as they inspected the splintered wood. Like the honest country folk they were, they seemed almost ashamed that what they regarded as such a terrible thing could have happened, particularly to people who had chosen to come from so far away to live in their valley.

'*Basuras!*' was how old Pep described the robbers. 'Trash!' And they would have been mainland *españoles* too! Of that he was in no doubt. Drug-taking trash that would be garrotted, if he was in charge of the country! Too soft with criminals these days, that was the trouble with these modern governments. '*Basuras!*' Why, in his day, you never even *thought* of locking a door. But now? '*Coño*, don't get me started!'

'You need a dog,' was old Maria's concise advice.

And for once, I agreed with her. I'd see to that as soon as I could, I assured her. And I meant it.

A day or so later, Ellie and I were enjoying a budget *menú del día* lunch at the Bar El Piano in Peguera after a visit to the supermarket. On hearing our tale of woe about the break-in, Señora Esperanza, El Piano's genial hostess, threw her arms in the air in horror, showering us with apologies on behalf of the whole Spanish nation. How could this have happened to such kind and generous *señores?* she wanted to know, her voice rising to a treble pipe. She had intended giving us today's meal without charge in any case, she said (referring discreetly to the crate of Valencia oranges I had previously gifted her), but in the light of this awful news, a much more comforting gesture would have to be made.

'*Tío!*' she shouted to a waiter who was serving coffees at the bar. '*Champán para Señor Pedro!*'

Well, a bottle of expensive Spanish *cava* to wash down an economy lunch did seem a touch incongruous, but

I realised that Esperanza was genuinely trying, in her own way, to atone for a wrong that, simply by being Spanish, she felt somehow remotely responsible for. So, to the sound of cheers from the nearby tables of lunching workmen, the cork was duly popped and the comforting liquid sipped.

'*Un asunto triste,*' the waiter said a while later as he poured the last of the sparkling *vino* into our glasses. 'A sad affair.' He himself had been the victim of a robbery once, he gravely confided – back in his native Murcia on the mainland, so he knew the horror of such an experience. '*Sí, es un asunto muy triste, señores.*'

'Ah, well, not so bad in our case,' I expansively assured him, the mid-afternoon intake of champers having the predictably benevolent effect on my disposition. 'OK, having our stuff stolen was a bit of a shame, I suppose, but as my friend Jock Burns said, it could have been worse.'

Both Ellie and the waiter gave me enquiring looks, clearly nonplussed by the surprisingly blasé attitude that I'd adopted all of a sudden.

'Worse, *señor?*' said the waiter.

'Yes. I mean, the thieves could have done a lot more damage. Only broke the door a little bit, that was all.'

The waiter still looked puzzled.

I leaned towards him, laid my hand on his arm and said confidentially, 'You see, where I come from back in the UK, housebreakers often smash the place up, daub paint on the walls and, well, relieve themselves on the floor, things like that. So that's what I mean, no wanton damage done in this case. See what I mean?'

The waiter's face lit up. He saw what I meant now, all right. 'Aha,' he smiled, his chest expanding proudly, 'but that, *señor*, is because we Spanish are a noble people!'

I nodded sagely. Ellie choked on the dregs of her bubbly.

- Five -

IT TAKES TWO TO TANGO

It's surprising how quickly you get over a nasty experience like a housebreaking. You don't forget, but you soon pick up the pieces and get back to normal. You have to. No point in moping about feeling sorry for yourself. And in our case, we were helped by the urgency shown by the local tradesmen who had come to our aid promptly after the event. Maybe they could be as prone to the *mañana* syndrome as the next person when it suited, but in response to our request for emergency assistance, they couldn't have been more on the ball.

Juan Juan the carpenter had been the first on site – on the very morning after the break-in, turning up in his little van to make good the damage to the *almacén* door. Then came Pablo Mir the blacksmith, to measure up for removable metal bars inside the doors and for lockable steel security gates outside them. He even brought a portable welder in order to fix a row of harrow teeth to act as anti-scaling spikes on top of the double gates leading from the lane. All of this may have seemed something of an overkill to him (it certainly did to us), but these Fort Knox security measures had been dictated by our insurance company, and we had been warned that we would ignore putting them in place at our peril. No such precautions, no insurance cover – as simple as that. Dramas and crises? Never!

I called at Pablo's Andratx workshop a couple of mornings later to pick the things up, only to find Pablo gone and the smithy work being done by his wife. She was in her late thirties, pretty, petite and the very antithesis of the brawny hulk you expect to see operating heavy metalworking gear. When I walked in, she was stooped over the anvil, hammering the finishing touches to the fixings for our door bars, dressed in an oversize boiler suit, sweat dripping from the end of her grime-smudged nose.

'Ah, Señor Peter,' she beamed, plunging a red-hot bracket hissing and spitting into a tub of cold water. 'Just in time! Everything is ready for you.'

I took one look at the weighty wrought-steel security gates propped against the wall and said, 'Look, no hurry, *señora*. I can call back a bit later, when Pablo's around to give me a hand to lift all the stuff out to the car.'

She laughed at that. 'Ha! If Pablo were here, he'd expect *me* to help him lift it anyway, so I may as well help you. Same difference, *sí*?'

'Well… if you're really sure. But be careful. You don't want to strain a muscle or something.'

She laughed again, and I found out why soon enough, because I was the one who did all the grunting and huffing and gasping as I struggled at one end of the bulky gates, while she whistled merrily at the other, bearing the dead weight as if it were a bag of groceries.

'Appearances can be deceptive,' I panted when everything was finally loaded onto the car.

'I'm used to it, *señor*,' she smiled. 'Being married to a blacksmith, you have to be.'

And I thought I'd given Ellie a rough time over the years, expecting her to shovel tons of grain at harvest time, to help hand-lift acres of turnips from frost-frozen fields in the middle of Scottish winters, and even to wrestle with temperamental bullcalves that didn't fancy being separated from their testicles. I felt a lot better now!

'How much do I owe you, Señora Mir?' I puffed, clutching my aching back while fumbling for a chequebook in the car's glove box.

This question induced yet another laugh, this one tinged with a touch of irony. 'No, no, you must see Pablo about that,' she insisted. 'Toiling in the forge is one thing for a woman, but getting involved in the financial affairs of the business is quite another.'

I allowed myself a wry smile at that gibe, because, only the week before, a similar situation had arisen for Ellie – albeit in reverse – when an electrician had refused to accept a cheque she'd made out to him. It would have to come from the pen of the *señor*, he had indignantly decreed, looking at Ellie as if she'd just escaped from a lunatic asylum. Some things are slow to change in Spain. But little did the misguided fellow realise that writing cheques was, in fact, one of this emancipated foreign woman's chief talents – even in Spanish, although actually *speaking* the language didn't yet rate as a comparable priority.

'So, when will Pablo be back?' I said to his wife.

She checked her watch. 'It's almost eleven o'clock, so just call into his office on your way home. He should be there by now.'

'Office?'

'Yes, it's known as the Bar Nuevo – in the Plaza de España. Know it?'

As I say, some things in Spain are slow to change.

However, now that we had the security gates, Toni Ensenyat, the local builder, was quickly on hand to fit them for us. Toni was frequently to be found at the old mill down the lane which Francisca and Tomàs Ferrer, the former owners of Ca's Mayoral, had hired him to convert into a weekend *casita*... of ever larger proportions, we couldn't fail to notice! The machinations of that particular matter, and how they would affect us, were to become all too apparent in the fullness of time. But for the present, we were just grateful that Toni had put the Ferrers' work aside for a couple of hours in order to help us out.

He was a quiet and kindly man, and an excellent craftsman who took pride in his work, and didn't believe in overcharging for it, either. Not the type of character you encounter too often anywhere in his cowboy-infested trade. And Mallorca does have its fair share of such chancers too – most of them fly-by-night foreigners who specialise in expensively conning fellow ex-pats who are shy of trying to converse with the native artisans in their own language.

In the days following the robbery, a brighter, more contented atmosphere than before had somehow settled on Ca's Mayoral. Not that we hadn't been very happy there prior to the traumatic event, but that sinking feeling of not belonging which had hit us in the Guardia Civil office had steadily been superseded by a renewed sense of purpose, a greater determination than ever to make a success of what we had set out to do when buying the farm. Any self-pitying thoughts of quitting which may have crept into our minds at that low moment had been banished quickly enough by the support unselfishly given, not only by our old friend Jock, but also by our close neighbours in the valley, and now by local tradesmen who had hardly known us previously. Our aspiring sense of community had not only been restored, but firmly reinforced as well. Unwelcome things happen everywhere, after all – even on idyllic Mediterranean islands. That's life, and we'd learned that not even the rosiest of rose-coloured specs will hide the fact.

Ellie had been busy varnishing the inside of the repaired *almacén* door.

'Like a cuppa tea, Toni?' she chirpily asked, swinging open the security gate which he'd just cemented into place outside the front door.

Señor Ensenyat, gathering up his tools, his back to the doorway, jumped a clear foot off the ground as the heavy metal gate came crashing down beside him.

'*No, gracias, señora*,' he said, smiling patiently at Ellie, who was standing with her hand to her mouth, gazing pop-eyed at the now-empty fixing holes which Toni had laboriously cut into the stone of the door opening, 'I've brought my own coffee.'

And it was to the eternal credit of this true gentleman that, instead of drawing Ellie's attention to his flattened Thermos flask and maybe suggesting where she could shove it, he simply hoisted up the offending gate and proceeded to re-fit it without fuss. And little did our tight-fisted and dictatorial insurance company know how close their over-the-top security requirements (with a little unintended assistance from Ellie) had taken them to a public liability claim for death by misadventure!

'*Edward And Elizabeth Invite You To Take Luncheon*', the gilt-edged card said.

The Smythes had called at Ca's Mayoral a couple of weeks after our arrival on the island, having been told by a local estate agent, they said, that a British family had recently settled in the area and would probably be able to tell them about the pros and cons of such a move. For they, too, were looking for a 'little place' to buy in the Mallorcan countryside, both having just retired from their posts in the British Foreign Office. Despite their mature years, they had only recently married (the first time for both), had sold Edward's 'little place' in the Cotswolds to a rich Arab businessman, and therefore had sufficient funds to invest in a modest property on the island.

'Too many damned foreigners in England these days,' was Edward's candid view. 'Piss-poor show, don't you think?'

What could we in our inexperience tell them about living in Mallorca, other than a rather trite, 'If it appeals to you, do it'? And evidently they had, although the posted invitation to lunch was the first that we knew of it.

Not surprisingly, the boys elected to send their regrets, so Ellie and I drove off by ourselves, over the mountains towards the sleepy inland town of Calviá. Calviá is an unpretentious place, where the only evidence of the local authority's stunning wealth is the palatial new town hall and council offices, in which the rates and taxes from one of the most lucrative stretches of holiday coastline in Spain are collected.

Smaller, certainly, but just as splendid in its own way, was 'Chez Smythe', a lavishly restored, traditional Mallorcan farmhouse, tucked quietly away along a little lane on the outskirts of town. Standing in its own walled grounds of about an acre, the newly-whitewashed house overlooked an avenue of tall palms, which led to a magnificent heated swimming pool. The palm trees, we were to learn later, had been specially shipped over from Alicante, and the swimming pool built by a company from London. 'Coals to Newcastle' would have been an apt summing-up of the latter extravagance, Mallorca being not exactly short of swimming pool builders itself. But then, Edward was not a man to trust anything to the 'foreign Johnny', if it could be helped.

We were met at the remotely-controlled, eight-foot-high gates by two snarling Rottweilers.

'That's the end of the luncheon date,' I said to Ellie. 'I'm not going in there to be on the menu for that pair of man-eaters!'

'You're not getting out of it that easily,' said Ellie, knowing full well that I was about as keen on this social visit as the boys had confessed to being. 'This looks interesting!'

At that, a diminutive Filipino man, dressed in white trousers, white button-to-the-throat 'bum-freezer' jacket, white shoes and gloves, came trotting down the drive shouting at the dogs in what we took to be his native Tagalog tongue. The growling brutes slunk reluctantly away, leaving us in no doubt that we were *not* welcome. The Filipino servant smiled, chattered incomprehensibly and bowed incessantly as he ushered us through the gates and on to the house. Elizabeth, dressed in a flowing pink chiffon gown, was standing regally beside an opulently set dining table that had been placed in the shade of the open *porche*.

'I think I could be a bit under-dressed for this,' I muttered to Ellie, looking down at my casual shirt and trousers. 'Maybe I should've hired a tuxedo!'

'Ah, Peter and Ellie!' Elizabeth gushed. 'How absolutely wonderful of you to come!'

'Our pleasure,' said Ellie, and I could have sworn that there was the hint of a curtsy there.

'Edward has just popped into the village for some cigars,' Elizabeth informed us, while picking up and ringing a little crystal bell. 'Shan't be long. Drinks?'

'Yes… well, yes please,' I replied. 'Ellie doesn't usually, but a beer would be fine for me, if you've –'

Elizabeth delivered a carefully enunciated command – in what I again took to be Tagalog – to a cowering little Filipina woman, also dressed from head to toe in white, who appeared from within the house in response to the call of the crystal bell. Her male compatriot, still smiling and bowing, wasn't far behind.

Elizabeth reiterated the command, then barked, 'Schnell!'

I recognised the latter word as meaning 'Make it quick!' in German. And so, apparently, did the white-uniformed pair, who swiftly disappeared back inside the house.

'Anthony and Cleopatra, we call them,' Elizabeth informed us through a courtly smile. 'Can't speak a word of English, of course. But Filipinos, they're the only servants you can hire at an affordable price these days, don't you find?'

'Quite,' I said authoritatively, not wishing to appear ignorant of such an essential fact of life.

Anthony and Cleopatra reappeared, Cleopatra balancing a silver tray of fine champagne flutes, Anthony carrying a silver ice bucket containing a magnum of Bollinger. 'When it comes to bubbly, I always say that you can't beat the real thing,' said Elizabeth. 'Can't be doing with that Spanish *çà va* stuff, or whatever they call it.'

'Seems like I'm not getting that beer,' I whispered to Ellie as Elizabeth assiduously instructed her man and maidservant on how correctly to pour the champers.

A car horn sounded out in the lane, and Anthony automatically rushed into the house to press the gate-opening button. A huge vintage Bentley coupé swept in, soft top down, Edward at the wheel, something akin to a tobacco-coloured Exocet missile protruding from his mouth.

'Jolly nice of you both to come along,' he breezed, climbing out of the car. He strode over to Ellie and enveloped her in what could only be described as an exploratory bear hug. 'Absolutely marvellous to see you again, my dear!'

I'd noticed that he was still wearing the same navy blue blazer, complete with regimental badge on the pocket, that he'd been wearing the day they'd called at Ca's Mayoral. And this despite the fact that it was a very warm Saturday afternoon in April, when anything other than shirtsleeve order would have been, *should* have been, uncomfortable. But Edward was made of sterner stuff, and to prove it, he was wearing a cravat as well.

He snapped a military-style order at the ever-smiling Anthony, then threw him the car keys. 'Can't speak a word of English, of course,' he grinned at me, grabbing my hand in a wholesome handshake. 'Same goes for those chaps at the filling station down the road. I mean, they've been dealing with me for almost three months now, and they still can't understand the simple phrase, "Fill 'er up". Damned poor show, don't you think?'

The 'Old Colonial' image was maintained by our host and hostess as they took us on a leisurely stroll round their sumptuous gardens, for which, Edward was at pains to point out, even indigenous Mediterranean plants and shrubs had been imported from specialist growers in England.

'Can't beat your jolly old Blighty nurseryman,' was Edward's opinion. 'Damned sight more reliable than any of those Spanish bods trying their hand at the game hereabouts, *I* can tell you! Had to buy the palm trees in Spain, of course,' he added, almost apologetically. 'But took no chances – flew over a couple of expert chaps from Kew to supervise the planting of 'em.'

I was suddenly reminded of one of Edward's ilk whom I'd stood behind in a grocery shop on the Spanish island of Menorca on one occasion. He was trying to buy, in shouted English, a bottle of what he referred to as mayonnaise, and was becoming increasingly irate as the long-suffering girl behind the counter persisted in offering him just that – a bottle of mayonnaise, a sauce invented in and named after Menorca's capital, Mahon, the very town we happened to be in. 'Dammit all, you silly woman,' he eventually spluttered, his eyes lighting on a bottle of Heinz Salad Cream on a shelf behind the counter, *'that's* what I want – a jar of genuine *English* mayonnaise!'

India had been Edward's first overseas posting on joining the Foreign Office from the Army, he told us between rows of aromatic rosemary hedging and sips of chilled champagne. 'Mountbatten's staff, y'know. Pukka chap, Mountbatten. German lineage, y'know. Just the ticket for the Raj. Could handle the vindaloo-wallahs like no one else. Damned fine fellow.' Edward had eventually found himself in France. 'PS to a jolly important British chap who shall remain nameless.' He tapped the side of his nose. 'FO – Official Secrets Act and all that.' But the years spent in France had also involved lengthy spells in Germany, a country close to the heart of his important charge, and a country that Edward himself was to become besotted with too. The detail that it was also in Germany that he had met Elizabeth was appended as a somewhat throwaway afterthought. 'Damned fine chap, your average Jerry,' Edward opined.

'You do *sprech Deutsch*, I take it?' Elizabeth asked us.

'*Ein bier, bitte*, is about my strength,' I confessed, 'but Ellie can handle it quite well. She was born there, actually.'

'Ah, excellent! You'll get on famously with our other guests, then. Somehow I just knew you would. How absolutely *wunderbar!*'

Elizabeth then insisted that we see something of the inside of the house. As with the grounds, it was instantly obvious that no expense had been spared in its transformation from basic old country dwelling to a place that could now grace the glossy pages of *Homes & Gardens*. Our hosts were unashamedly proud of what had been created, and in such a short time, too. It made the redecoration and 'improvements' which we had so far managed to do at Ca's Mayoral seem distinctly modest by comparison. At the same time, there was something a bit bizarre about the accomplished effect inside 'Chez Smythe', which had clearly been achieved according to Edward's and Elizabeth's taste.

Gone were the traditional characteristics that almost certainly existed when they bought the house – genuine Mallorcan features like an inglenook fireplace in the kitchen, exposed wooden beams and plain whitewashed walls. Instead, the ceilings had been plasterboarded over and now sported intricate cornicing, and roses from which hung gilt chandeliers. The fireplace surround was mahogany, and of a Georgian style more suited to the drawing room of a British mansion of that era. And not even the rough old walls had escaped the Anglicising attentions of the tradesmen who, Edward confirmed, had been brought over especially from 'home'. Smoothly replastered, the walls were now covered by velvet-embossed wallpaper, blending perfectly with the fireplace and ceilings, no doubt, but glaringly out of place in what, until recently, had been a typical Mallorcan farmhouse.

The furnishings also reflected the Smythe's background – a curious mix of Cotswolds chintz and officers' mess leather, with the former *almacén* having been turned into a formal dining room, complete with Victorian furniture straight out of a gentleman's club in Mayfair. And everywhere was evidence of foreign lands served in. There were memories of India in the form of carved ivory ornaments, French lace and paintings of Paris, Mexican pottery, and even an enormous German beer stein decorated with frolicking fräuleins.

It was easy to forget that we were in the Mallorcan countryside. But this was the Smythe's new home, and although the way they had reformed it seemed a tad strange to us, they had clearly recreated an atmosphere in which they felt happy – in which they felt 'at home'. In their retirement, they were merely holding onto the now-defunct ways of colonialism that they had become accustomed to throughout their working lives. And in so doing they were harming no one, the only potential victim of their ostentatious ways being their own image in the eyes of more down-to-earth local folk. But that was a situation that they would have created, albeit unwittingly, many times before, and one which obviously didn't concern them one iota now. This was their one little acre of Empire on which the sun still hadn't set – and wasn't about to, either!

Outmoded though this attitude was, however, Edward and Elizabeth came over as genuine people, a likeable elderly couple comfortable with the privileges which they could afford to enjoy and which, apparently, were happy to share when entertaining.

Helmut and Hilde arrived in a gleaming new BMW. We hadn't met them before, but we did know of them. Their son was in Charlie's class at school, and rumour was rife among the other parents that Helmut, who maintained an extravagant lifestyle with no visible means of support, was at best an arms dealer, or at worst a drugs trafficker. They could both speak a bit of English. That we knew. But on this occasion they chose to converse mainly in German – as did our hosts from now on. And fair enough too, I reckoned. After all, Mallorca is a cosmopolitan place, so you have to try to cope as best you can with whatever language you happen to encounter.

I tried a meet-you-halfway question to Helmut in Spanish, but that was greeted with a look that seemed to say, 'Where in *himmel's* name do you think you are – Spain?' I got the same reaction from Edward.

Partridge would be the main dish today, Elizabeth informed us, as we took our places at the table in the *porche*. They had been cooked Bavarian-style, *natürlich* – wrapped in bacon and served on a bed of sauerkraut with bread dumplings on the side. And quite excellent the combination was, too.

Edward was delighted to be told so. 'Used to shoot the little buggers in the Black Forest with the Duke, y'know. Oops! Almost let it slip there.' He gave a nervous little laugh, then went on, composure swiftly restored, 'Had to have these chappies shipped out from Fortnum & Mason's, however. Can't get 'em too easily here. Natives have shot everything to bloody extinction except butterflies, and I wouldn't give much for *their* chances of survival either. Let's face it – never know what you're eating in that rice stuff. What do they call it? "Payola" or suchlike, isn't it?'

And so the meal progressed and the afternoon wore on, Helmut and Edward guffawing heartily at German jokes, every one of which, in keeping with his impeccable manners, Edward repeated to me in English. I, in turn, laughed politely on the delivery of each punch line, although, in all honesty, I felt that the humour must have been losing something in the translation. Then again, maybe it was just me... or how Edward told 'em. Either way, I was finding it all a bit hard going.

A welcome diversion eventually came about in the form of a plump brown hen, which suddenly appeared in the *porche* and flapped up onto Edward's shoulder.

'Ah, there you are, my dear!' he beamed, tickling the bird's wattle with a fingertip. 'Her name's Mrs Wallsy,' he informed me, apparently unaware that he had probably just let another one slip. 'Rhode Island Red, y'know. True blue American. Used to have a playmate, too, actually.' He became reflective for a brief moment. 'Hmm, the dogs helped themselves to him for lunch one day, though. Damned pity, really.'

Next, Edward tore a piece of crust from a bread roll and placed it in the pet hen's beak. Whereupon she clucked her appreciation, squirted (unknown to him) a dropping of many colours down the sleeve of his blazer, fluttered back to terra firma, and stepped primly away. Mission accomplished.

'Ma-a-a-arvellous,' Edward grinned as he watched the hen depart. 'Damned sight more intelligent than we give 'em credit for.' He then signalled the diligently hovering Anthony to replenish the wine glasses, and resumed the recitation of Teutonic funnies.

Ellie, meantime, was chatting away quite efficiently in German with Hilde and Elizabeth, although, as time passed, I noticed that our hostess was getting more and more preoccupied by and uptight about Cleopatra's table-serving performance. To Elizabeth's oft-voiced annoyance, Cleo just couldn't seem to grasp simple points of etiquette, like how 'absolutely essential' it was to serve the food while standing to the left of each guest, for example.

'One simply can*not* get the quality of staff these days, can one?' I heard her exclaim to Ellie. 'You wouldn't bel*ieve* how many hours I've spent showing her how the place settings should be laid out, and *still* I have to come after her and sort out the mess of cutlery!'

But the politically-correct excrement finally hit the fan when the hapless little Filipina – who, I suspect, had been tippling away at the Liebfraumilch on her frequent visits to the kitchen – stumbled and emptied the entire contents of a large dish of apple strudel and cream onto her mistress's expensively-draped lap. Elizabeth exited the scene in a furious swirl of chiffon.

'Not to worry, chaps,' Edward grinned reassuringly, indicating to Anthony with a snap of his fingers that the chaps needed some service. 'The old gal will soon clean herself up. Worse things happen in China, huh?'

The chicken shit on his blazer had now dried to an elongated crust, its shape closely resembling, curiously enough, the map of jolly old Blighty. No doubt the old boy would clean himself up in the fullness of time as well, but for the moment, there were more important matters to attend to. Anthony was instructed, in English, to bring coffee, schnapps – 'Make it *Steinhäger*' – and cigars. 'Oh, and, uhm, see what the memsahibs want too, will you? Mints and suchlike, no doubt.' He shooed the totally confused Anthony away. 'Carry on. There's a good chap.'

Helmut, already at least one more sheet to the wind than our rapidly mellowing host, broke wind loudly. Edward guffawed and quoted what I took to be an old German farting proverb. Veneers were beginning to crack, and I thanked my guardian drinking angel that the cloying sweetness of the Liebfraumilch wine had prompted me to consume considerably less of it than my two table companions during the afternoon. I resolved to do likewise schnapps-wise.

Elizabeth soon returned, soiled frock replaced by an equally elegant number, regal poise restored. I followed Edward's chivalrous lead in standing up when she approached the table. Helmut sat tight, hiccuped and tried to focus.

'At ease, old boy,' Edward told me. 'I'm just off to point Percy at porcelain. Know where the latrines are if you need 'em, do you?' He swayed off houseward without waiting for a reply.

I decided to make a second attempt at conversing with Helmut, this time in English. 'Lived in Mallorca long, have you?'

He fixed me with half-shut eyes, shrugged his shoulders in a what's-the-difference? sort of way. 'I come... I go.'

'Ah, business, eh?' My curiosity was getting the better of me. 'What, ehm – what line of business would that be, Helmut?'

He made a sideways throwaway gesture with his hand. 'I buy, I sell. I import, I export. *Ja*, I come, I go.'

That particular line of questioning had evidently come to a quick and abrupt end. I'd try another tack.

'So, uhm, known Edward and Elizabeth long, have you?'

'*Nein.*'

He started to drum his fingers on the table, quietly humming what could have been a Strauss waltz, whilst looking calculatingly at each of the chattering ladies in turn.

I aborted my futile attempts at striking up a conversation and sat pondering the situation instead. Helmut and his wife were odd friends for the Smythes to have, it struck me. Apart from the German connection, they didn't seem to have much in common at all. Edward and Elizabeth were undeniably at the upper end of the middle-class social ladder, while Helmut and Hilde were… well, let's say members of a distinctly lower order, despite (or emphasised by) their surfeit of bodily gold.

Still, it takes all types, and, in spite of their stiff-upper-lip air, the Smythes were probably just lonely and trying to establish a circle of new friends in a new country. You have to start somewhere, after all, and any likelihood of their even contemplating integration with the local Mallorcan community was clearly a non-starter.

'Your wife,' Helmut grunted, jolting me out of my musings, 'she speaks *Deutsch gut, ja?*'

'Yes, she gets by very well.' Breakthrough. Now I could get that conversation going by telling him about Ellie's German background. 'Yes, she was actually born in –'

'*Ein* very attractive woman,' Helmut cut in, eyeing up Ellie through bleary eyes. 'She likes to dancing, *ja?*'

What the blazes was this all about? 'Ehm, well, I can't really –'

'*Ich*, I like to dancing!' Helmut proclaimed. '*Und meine* Hilde likes to dancing!' He then thumped the table and began bellowing out the waltz melody, waving time with his wine glass in true *bierkeller* fashion.

'This is all going rapidly downhill,' I said guardedly to Ellie, while Elizabeth continued the womanly conversation with Hilde, now looking distinctly pink about the gills herself. 'I sense negative developments.'

It was then that we heard the tango music. The staccato accordion strains of 'Jealousy' blasted out from within the house.

'Ah!' smiled Elizabeth, noticing my confused expression. 'Only Edward indulging his passion for Latin American dance music records. Give him good food, good wine and, most of all,' – she paused to wink conspiratorially at Ellie – 'charming new female company, and out comes his Edmundo Ros.'

Ellie froze in her seat.

Then Edward re-emerged, a red rose gripped in his teeth, and a female dressmaking dummy clasped to his breast. The dummy was wearing his blazer. He tangoed forth, knees seductively bent, left arm and empty blazer sleeve held rigidly out in the direction of travel.

'Soon we shall have the pleasure, my dear,' he informed the cringing Ellie, hesitating mid-tango by her chair to arch his torso over his inanimate dancing partner, then chasséing unsteadily off with it down the colonnade of tall palms.

'Once spent a few months in our Buenos Aires embassy,' Elizabeth explained matter-of-factly, lighting up a cigarette in a foot-long bamboo holder. 'Learned to do it like a gaucho.'

If that didn't do it for Ellie, Helmut's leering proposal to her certainly did.

'You like to dancing *mit* me, *meine liebling?*'

She got to her feet, glancing frantically at her watch. 'Oh dear! Is that the time already?' she flustered. 'Almost forgot, Elizabeth. Have to pick up a friend at the airport in half an hour. Sorry. It's been a super lunch, but we really do have to rush. We'll return the compliment at our place sometime. Looking forward to it.'

She shepherded me urgently towards the car. 'Let's get away from here fast!' she warbled, clearly panic-stricken. 'I'm not having that lecherous old geezer and his mate trying their Ricky Martin stuff on me!'

With that, the music blaring from the house changed to the aptly-titled 'Blue Tango', and the sound of a loud splash, accompanied by a strangulated yell, drifted through the palms from the swimming pool area.

'Maybe that'll cool his ardour,' Ellie muttered, slamming the car door behind her.

I turned the ignition key. 'If not,' I answered, 'it'll certainly save him having his blazer cleaned.'

That was the last we ever saw of Edward and Elizabeth. Nice people, if a touch eccentric, and prime examples of an essentially British stereotype, still clinging defiantly to a 'superior' way of life in their own little corner of a foreign field.

'And long may they reign over it,' said Ellie. 'Give me a slice of bread rubbed with tomato and a no-nonsense chinwag outside old Maria's *casita* any day.'

I said amen to that.

- Six -

CONUNDRUMS OF CRUEL COMPASSION

'Found one!' Sandy called out. 'Here, in the classified ads of the *Majorca Daily Bulletin*!'

Charlie sprang up from his seat at the breakfast table to look over his brother's shoulder. 'Yeah! How about it, Dad?'

I took a deliberately unhurried sip of coffee. 'Better tell me what the ad says first, don't you think?'

But Ellie had already deserted the cooker and was also eagerly peering over Sandy's shoulder at the open newspaper. 'Boxer pups!' she gasped, unable to hide her excitement.

'Pet shop in Palma,' Sandy said, a twinkle of anticipation in his eyes too.

'Good pedigree! Brindle! Fully vaccinated!' Ellie twittered.

'Last two, though,' Sandy cautioned, with a little glance of concern in my direction. 'And this is yesterday's paper. Could be too late.'

'But there's a phone number here!' Charlie urgently advised. 'I'll call them up right now, OK?'

I raised a subduing hand. 'Just have patience, OK? This is the first ad we've seen for boxers, but there'll be plenty more pups for sale soon enough, even if these ones are gone. I mean, there's more to choosing a decent dog than falling over yourself to buy the first one you see, you know. Plus, pet shops can be dodgy. Better to go straight to the breeder.' Grim-faced, I shook my head. 'I think we should wait.'

Through the icy silence that followed, three pairs of eyes glared at me, willing me to change my mind, daring me not to.

I still found speaking Spanish on the phone a lot harder than carrying on a conversation face-to-face. Something about not being able to see who you're speaking to, I suppose, about not having the help of reading the other person's lips, no matter how unconsciously. But in this instance, I managed to put my query to the woman in the pet shop without too much trouble, and her reply wasn't difficult to follow.

'What did they say?' three voices chanted in unison the second I put the phone down.

'Only one pup left,' I said. 'A bitch. And the woman promised to hold it for us until we've seen it and made up our minds one way or the other.'

'Magic!' Charlie declared. 'We'll all go! School won't miss me for *one* day, and –'

'And you can forget it, Charlie. Your mother and I have to go into Palma this morning anyway. Papers to sign at the lawyers. We'll drop you off at school on our way there. And Sandy –'

'I know, I know,' he sighed, 'I promised to take the tractor over to old Pep's today and rotovate some land for him. Don't worry, I'm on my way.' He sloped reluctantly to the door, then turned and said in solemn tones, 'I hope you get that pup, though. I've a hunch it'll be a good one.'

We'd had boxers before, and like most fans of the breed, tended to think of them as being more human than canine, particularly if you're lucky enough to get one with more than average smarts, combined with a trusty nature. Not a blend of qualities all that common in dogs *or* humans, but we'd usually been fortunate before (at least with dogs!), and we could only hope our luck would hold again.

'Mind you,' I said to Ellie after we'd deposited Charlie at school, 'I wasn't totally kidding with all that "being-cautious" malarkey about buying a pup – particularly from a pet shop. So, you know, don't go getting all slushy and soppy when we go into this place. I know what you're like. Just remember, all pups are cute; even badly-bred little tykes that are going to grow into four-legged nightmares.' I paused for breath while negotiating a particularly hair-raising left turn through the impatient Palma traffic. 'And don't forget,' I continued, 'this isn't Scotland, and we don't know anything about Mallorcan pedigrees and so on. The price too. I mean, we'll have to watch it. Could be ripped off dead easily if we're not *really* careful. Last pup to sell, as well. Probably the runt of the litter.'

Ellie maintained her practised diplomatic silence, accompanied, I noticed out of the corner of my eye, by a resolute little smile. I was obviously wasting my breath – as usual.

The pet shop, situated on the far side of Palma near the Plaça Pere Garau, had the usual pet shop smell – a unique blend of sawdust, disinfectant and mouse droppings. But it was scrupulously clean, and the owner a very pleasant woman with a gentle disposition.

'Mother-humpin' faggot!' a raucous voice behind me shouted out. I spun round to be confronted by a very large and colourful macaw parrot. He was trudging back and forth along an open rail, his head bobbing up and down impatiently, one beady eye fixed unblinkingly on me. It was instant animosity, and I was very relieved to note that he had a chain on one leg securing him to his perch. That beak could do serious damage.

He had belonged to a sailor from the American aircraft carrier that had visited Palma recently, the shop's owner explained. A new captain had recently taken command of the ship, had taken a dim view of one of his crew having a pet on board and had ordered him to get rid of it immediately. That was why he was for sale now at such a bargain price. The bird was an excellent talker, too, she was keen to point out – although she couldn't understand any of what he said, being unable to speak English herself. But perhaps he would make an entertaining companion for the *señor*, she suggested, throwing me a hopeful look.

I declined politely but firmly.

'Scum-suckin' sonofabitch!' the parrot squawked.

End of conversation.

Ellie was already crouching down by a small dog cage in the corner of the shop, cooing baby talk, her forefinger poked through the wire to tickle the chin of the eagerly-licking little bundle inside.

'Ah, the *señora* likes my little *bambina*,' the shop owner smiled, sensing a better chance of a sale here. She opened the cage and lifted the wriggling puppy out. '*Sí*, and my little *bambina* likes the *señora* also!' she observed, shrewdly handing her to Ellie.

'Mm-m-m, you're lovely,' Ellie crooned, and the pup's tongue washed her face while its little docked tail wagged its body in the way that only boxer's tails can do. 'Yes, you're a lovely girl, aren't you?'

Just the reaction I'd anticipated. Love at first sight. However, I had to admit to myself that it was indeed a good-looking pup, and certainly not stunted in growth, as I'd feared. It was, in fact, a beautifully proportioned little animal, dark brindle all over, with big brown eyes looking out of a cute face that, without need for words, was begging to be taken home. I was about to ask the shopkeeper why such a fine puppy had been the last of the litter remaining unsold when I noticed the reason for myself – an ugly-looking scab on top of its head. I pointed it out to Ellie.

'*Ah, sí*,' the owner said, quick to spot my look of concern, 'a little blemish – a little wound sustained when playing with her brothers and sisters. Nothing to worry about, *señor*. It will soon be gone.'

Maybe she was right, but I didn't want to take any chances. It could just as easily have been some form of skin disease. The start of ringworm, perhaps. I had encountered that problem often enough in cattle and, although curable, it was a highly infectious and unsightly scourge and one which you wouldn't want to introduce into your own house. I explained this as best I could to the shopkeeper and, to her credit, she accepted what I said without trying to push for a sale. Other people had had the same concerns about this particular puppy, she admitted, taking the tiny dog from Ellie and placing it back in its cage. '*No problema, señores.*'

The expression of utter despair on that little creature's face was enough to break the hardest of hearts. Gone was the sheer joy of being held and petted by kind hands, gone were the fleeting moments of hope of being taken at last from her lonely prison. She just sat down on her litter of shredded newspaper and gazed pathetically up at us, shivering, a squeaky little whimper her final appeal for a loving home.

'Poor little thing,' Ellie whispered, bending down again to stroke the puppy's velvety black muzzle. 'We could take her to a vet – get it checked,' she said, looking at me through misty eyes.

I already felt a complete louse, and this scene of near-Dickensian pathos wasn't helping. 'It'd only be cruel,' I said, in a pretty feeble attempt at making Ellie feel better. 'If the vet gave her the thumbs down, she'd only have to be brought back here.'

'But she's so unhappy now,' she replied. 'Look at her – poor little thing – and such a beautiful puppy, too.' She cupped the forlorn little coconut face in her hand.

The shopkeeper looked at me, raised a shoulder and pulled one of those typically-Spanish what-are-you-gonna-do-now? facial shrugs.

'The breeder of this puppy,' I said, suddenly inspired, '– would you know if they'll have another litter available soon?'

'But I am the breeder, *señor*,' she smiled. 'And, *sí*, there will be another litter of boxers ready in three weeks. Different mother, but same father.'

'Same strain, then?'

'*Sí, sí – exactamente!*' And all her dogs were from the best-bred lines of boxers in Spain, she was proud to say. '*Muchos campeones! Pedigrís excelentes!*'

'There you are, then, Ellie!' I enthused. 'That's what we'll do, eh? Come back in three weeks and you can have the pick of the litter! What do you say?'

Ellie continued to pet the puppy through the mesh of its cage, saying nothing, but making no secret of the fact that *this* was the one she really wanted.

'Look – tell you what,' I said, feeling rotten, but still convinced that I'd made the right decision, 'I'll buy you a canary to keep you company in the meantime. It'll, ehm, you know, help cheer the house up with all its whistling and everything. Great wee singers, canaries!'

If I had convinced myself, I certainly hadn't convinced Ellie. She was still looking back at the puppy, exchanging doting glances with it, when we finally headed for the door of the shop – me with a caged canary, Ellie with a heavy heart.

'Fuck off, asshole!' croaked the parrot as I passed his perch.

'Touché!' I muttered, head bowed, suitably humbled.

Even the canary was silent during the long drive back towards Andratx, and not even the offer of a *menú del día* lunch at one of our favourite country eateries was enough to lift Ellie's mood of despondency. I'd have to think of *some*thing to cheer her up.

'Mario Lanzarote, we'll call him!' I breezed at length. 'Mario Lanza, because he's a singer, right? And the "rote" bit on the end, because he's a canary! Get it?' I forced out a laugh. 'Lanzarote – you know, one of the Canary Islands, right?'

Ellie was singularly unamused. 'Better get him home and out of the car,' she mumbled. 'You know what canaries are like. Wouldn't want any nasty petrol fumes snuffing him out, I'm sure.'

The sound of silence prevailed once more.

'Look, Ellie,' I said after a while, 'you know that buying that pup with the scab on its head would have been a mistake.' I was trying to be sympathetic, while at the same time appealing to her sense of better judgement. 'I mean, what's the point of buying a dog and then having to take it straight to the vet? We'd be mugs. I mean, be fair – even the woman in the shop seemed to think that.'

Ellie heaved a sigh. 'Yes, you're right, absolutely right. We'll just have to wait for another three weeks, that's all.'

'*That's* more like it! Yeah, you'll get a nice pup then, all right.' I patted her knee. 'Nice pup with no scabby bit on its head, eh? Pick of the litter and all! You'll see – it'll be worth the wait.'

'Yes,' Ellie conceded through a sad smile, 'and that lovely little puppy *will* find a good home... eventually.'

We arrived back at the pet shop just as the owner was preparing to close up for the afternoon *siesta*.

'Ah, *señores!*' she smiled. 'I was expecting you. And so was my little *bambina, sí?*' She motioned towards the counter, where the pup was patiently waiting inside a little plastic travelling crate. She perked up immediately she saw Ellie, standing up on rubbery legs, her tail wagging frantically.

'Tell the lady we won't be needing the crate,' said Ellie, lifting out her precious pooch and cuddling it. 'Just a nice cosy bed, a little collar and some puppy food.'

'Yes,' I admitted on the second homeward trip of the day, glancing down at the pup curled up and sleeping blissfully on Ellie's lap, 'she's a bonny wee thing, right enough.'

'That's what we'll call her, then,' said Ellie.

'Thing?'

'No, silly! Bonny! We'll call her Bonny!'

She was called several other things during the next few nights, when her howled attempts to make us let her sleep upstairs with the other humans kept us awake at bedtime. But she got used to the arrangement, as all pups do, and it wasn't long before the warm corner of the kitchen inglenook where we had placed her bed became her very own and much-cherished retreat. And her love affair with Ellie, which had started so poignantly under the hostile eye of a foul-mouthed parrot, instantly spread throughout the family. Bonny was special. We knew that. But, more to the point, so did she. And, like all little ladies blessed with that certain gift, she soon learned how to steal the heart of everyone who met her – with a couple of notable exceptions!

Just to be on the safe side, on the morning after we'd bought her, Ellie and I had taken Bonny along to Gabriel

Puigserver, the local vet, to have that little 'blemish' on her head looked at. And as the lady in the pet shop had said, it *was* only the aftermath of a playtime wound, which, Gabriel assured us, would disappear in a few days without any need of medical attention.

'You have a good one there,' said the vet, having given her a thorough examination. 'A healthy little *chica*, and pretty, too.' He stood back to take an appraising look at Bonny, who was standing proudly on his bench, clearly adoring all this attention. 'Nice conformation,' he adjudged. 'Well bred. *Sí*, you have a good one there.'

'I knew it all the time,' Ellie grinned, gathering up her little *bambina*. 'Come on, I'll take you back home and give you a nice saucer of warm milk for being so well-behaved at the doctor's.'

But Gabriel, who claimed not to speak English, clearly understood at least one word of what Ellie had just said. He waved a cautioning finger at her and warned that one should never give a puppy of that age milk. It would only upset its stomach and probably make it sick – diarrhoea, certainly. Boiled broken rice mixed with chopped scraps of cooked chicken and vegetables was all that Bonny needed for now – with water always available, of course. But milk? He waved that finger again. '*Nunca!*' Never!

Well, that was a new one on me, but you learn something every day, particularly as a rookie settler in a country with different practices from your own – and, no doubt, with excellent reasons for implementing them. And I was soon to be taught another lesson...

'*Weh-ep!*' came the greeting from the gate.

'*Weh-ep!*' I called back in response. I don't know what the salutation means. Nothing in particular, probably. It certainly isn't in the dictionary, but that's how Mallorcan country folk hail one another, and I'd fallen into the habit easily enough.

I was in the yard at Ca's Mayoral, knocking together a tiny wooden birdhouse in which Ellie hoped blue tits would be tempted to nest. She'd noticed one or two of the colourful little birds flitting about in the grove of pine trees at the side of the house, and reckoned that this would be a good time to entice them to stay, now that Francisca Ferrer's gang of mangy cats had finally ceased patrolling the immediate environs of their former home. I'd just finished making a bird table, too, and it was lying on the ground bedside me.

'There aren't enough birds around the place,' Ellie had said. 'Mario Lanzarote is going to need some company – poor little fellow, caged up all alone out on the balcony there.'

To be fair, I *had* been going to buy him a female companion that day in the pet shop, but the owner had advised me that, if you wanted a canary to sing, he had to be kept on his own. The things you learn in a new country! But the fact that Mario hadn't whistled up a single note since his arrival did make me wonder if there was more to this singing-canary lark than just keeping him in solitary.

'*Weh-ep!*' old Pep repeated, sauntering across the yard with that slow John Wayne swagger of his.

It was a beautifully warm April morning, the sun already clearing the highest ridges of the eastern mountains, the valley air humid and heavy with the evaporating moisture of the night. Even in a thin T-shirt, I had broken sweat after making just the first few cuts with my saw. But old Pep – Señor Cool personified, despite his advanced years – was wearing, as ever, his ancient leather bomber jacket, a red neckerchief knotted rakishly at his scrawny throat, his trusty black beret pulled forward to shade his all-seeing black beads of eyes. The habitual self-rolled cigarette jutted from the corner of his mouth, his lips contorted into a little lopsided smirk. It was obvious that he was intrigued by what I was up to. He stopped by my side, observing closely for a minute, but remaining ominously silent, the rattle of his chesty breathing and the accompanying crackle of his sparking *cigarrillo* melding with the rhythmic rasp of my saw.

'*Qué pasa?*' he finally barked. 'What's going on?'

I sensed I was in for a verbal hiding here. 'Birds,' I said, looking up and giving him a sheepish smile. 'They're, ehm... for birds.'

I was showered with a cascade of tobacco sparks as Pep let rip with one of his crepitus laughs – more a series of smoke-induced chokes, coughs and wheezes than a conventional laugh, but a laugh nonetheless.

'*Coño!*' he spluttered, flicking a tear from the corner of his eye while gasping for a fresh intake of breath. 'You will never catch a bird with those contraptions! *Cuarenta putas!*'

'Forty whores!' was the meaning of Pep's last exclamation, a curious curse, and one that he reserved for special occasions of derision.

A quick change of subject was worth a try, I reckoned. 'Did, uhm, did Sandy make a good job of the rotovating for you the other day?'

Pep poked a callused forefinger into the little hole I'd bored in the front of the blue tit nesting box. '*Sí*,' he grunted, more interested in the hole than my question, it seemed. '*Sí, sí… gracias.*'

But at least he had stopped laughing, puzzlement having taken over from derision now. That was a step in the right direction. I looked on as Pep inspected both of my little wooden creations in great detail.

'The tractor,' I ventured as a subject-changer again, '– I mean, you were quite happy to have Sandy tilling your soil with, well… with a tractor, were you?'

Pep continued to scrutinise the blue tit house. '*Sí*,' he croaked.

Our dour old neighbour had always made a point of stressing that he would never have a tractor polluting the air on his farm, never mind working the land, so it had struck me as strange when he'd asked Sandy to take our little Barbieri diesel machine over to his place to help out that day. But an explanation was about to be forthcoming at last – though in Pep's own good time.

'*Mi caballo*,' he muttered, referring to his mule as a horse, which – for reasons of image, I suspected – he always insisted upon doing. '*Mi caballo estaba cojo.*' His mule had been lame, he pronounced offhandedly.

Somehow, Pep's explanation didn't sound too convincing, but it was clearly all I was going to get. His inspection of my handiwork complete, he looked me squarely in the eye and told me that there was, perhaps, potential in these strange devices of mine after all. But they were both basically flawed in that the design of neither included any mechanism for actually working as an efficient trap.

'Ah, well, yes – but that's because they're not actually –'

Pep shut me up with a frosty glance. '*Mira!*' he commanded, instructing me to look first at the bird table. The theory was reasonably good, he grudgingly conceded, but I had failed to build in a quickly-removable support – to be remotely operated by a length of string, needless to say – which would allow the roof to drop down and capture the bird, or birds, which had been lured onto the deck. A commendable effort, but much too elaborate, was his final judgement. I should dismantle it and start again. Or, better still, scrap the damned thing completely and opt for the much more simple and efficient Mallorcan equivalent – a flat slab of stone, propped up with a stick, again with a length of string attached. Same principle as my Scottish design, but costing nothing, quicker to assemble, foolproof, tried and tested. '*Hombre*, just better! *Comprende?*'

I opened my mouth to make another attempt at explaining what these two objects really were, but Pep got in first.

'This one, *amigo*, is slightly more interesting,' he said with a lofty nod, taking the blue tit box in his hands in the manner of an antiques expert on TV. He could see that it was intended specifically to attract smaller birds, he affirmed, prodding his finger into the hole again. Robins, things like that. The hole was slightly too small, of course, but that was a fault easily enough remedied. However, we were still left with the fundamental question of how a bird entering the box was going to be trapped. A hinged flap fixed over the entrance hole would be the obvious solution – again remotely operated with a piece of string.

I tried yet again to get an edifying word in edgeways, but Pep promptly raised a silencing finger, a smug smile, indicative of the impending delivery of the *coup de grâce*, wrinkling his craggy features. How, he begged to inquire, was a bird to be enticed into this trap in the first place? Why, even the smartest of robins flying overhead would be pushed to see a maggot or a worm through a solid wooden roof like the one I had nailed onto the box! *'Correcto, amigo?'*

With a resigned shrug, I allowed Pep his moment of chortled triumph. May as well let him go the whole hog, I thought. There was obviously more to come, and – on the positive side – I might just learn something useful. I looked at him expectantly.

'En todo caso,' he continued, 'in any case, even if you got really lucky and caught one robin in this trap, how would you propose to catch *more* than one, eh?'

I raised a haven't-gotta-bloody-clue shrug this time.

Catching one robin was no use to anyone, he firmly stated. You needed at *least* a dozen to make a decent-sized pie – maybe even more if it was going to be a stew. Not that he ever ate robins himself, mind. *'Coño*, too many sharp little bones to get stuck between your teeth, no?' The tiny detail that Pep could have accommodated something akin to a brontosaurus humerus between most of his mouthful of well-spaced dental gravestones was conveniently, and perhaps revealingly, ignored.

'But do you want to know something, *vecino mío?*' he went on, warming ever more to his theme, an air of confidentiality creeping into his delivery now. 'Catching that first robin is the key to catching a dozen.' The robin, being a fiercely territorial and aggressive creature, he explained, would attack any other robin that dared enter his domain. A fight to the death would often follow. 'Tuneful and enchanting whistlers they may be, Don Pedro, but beneath all that, they are vicious, murderous little *bastardos!*' So – and this was the crux of the matter – you had to exploit that very same territorial trait of the robin in order to outsmart him.

Thus far in life, I hadn't had any need to outsmart a robin, but the more old Pep developed the subject, the more fascinated I became. I folded my arms, crossed my legs and paid attention.

Pep went on to disclose that there are only two things you need to catch that vital first robin – a tomato and some sticky birdlime; the former placed on top of the latter on an open piece of ground within the targeted robin's patch of woodland, or whatever. Seeing the red tomato, the flying robin, being both quick-tempered and stupid, would think it was an interloping robin and would dive down to attack, become stuck in the birdlime, and '*Oye!*', you had your first robin. After that, it was a simple matter of moving on to another robin's territory, sticking the first robin in a dollop of birdlime on the ground and waiting for a few minutes behind a convenient bush for your second robin to strike. This simple process would then be repeated throughout the wood until you had caught enough birds for your culinary needs.

Suddenly, my fascination had turned to revulsion. Yet, on reflection, what right did I have to be critical of this particular bird-hunting technique? After all, it wasn't all that different in principle from placing a wooden duck in an area of wetland, lying in hiding till a flock of the real thing glided in to land alongside the decoy, then blasting them out of the sky. Both practices had their roots in man's need to find food, but the latter, at least, was now followed in the name of sport. Yet, while I am fortunate enough, like most people nowadays, not to *have* to participate in either practice, I've eaten duck often enough without a second thought. And, when you get down to basics, in the eyes of the genuinely hungry, the only real difference between a duck and a robin, apart from size, is one of image. In other words, it's just the duck's bad luck that it doesn't feature on Christmas cards!

Whether or not Pep subscribed to the same philosophy, I don't know, but his reaction was one of absolute shock when I eventually got a chance to reveal that the purpose of my two little wooden structures was indeed to attract birds – not to eat, but just to enjoy watching. I learned a few more *mallorquín* oaths in the tirade that followed.

What in the name of all the harlots in hell did I think I was playing at? Was my head full of pig shit? Didn't I realise that keeping birds *away* from the orchards was the prime purpose of every fruit farmer in the valley? *Madre de Dios!* And why did I think that so many men went to the bother of netting millions of thrushes flying through the cols of the Mallorcan hills in the migrating season? Because they enjoyed sitting for hours at dusk up to their *cojones* in heather?

'I always thought it was because there was a big demand for thrushes in the butchers' shops,' I meekly offered.

Pep almost exploded. Selling them to eat was merely a by-product of the exercise, he snapped, the main reason for trapping the thrushes being that they would otherwise decimate the olive groves and ruin the livelihoods of countless families. *Hombre*, carry on with this *loco* plan to encourage more of the flying sons of whores into the valley, he warned, and I would be lynched *rápidamente!*'

Point plainly made, and lesson duly learned.

Just then, and for reasons known only to himself, our temperamental Mario Lanzarote started to sing at last.

Frowning, Pep looked up to where Mario's cage was hanging on the balcony. 'And,' he growled, prodding me in the chest, 'you should let that canary go free.'

'Really?' I said, totally taken aback. 'Why's that?'

'Because, in my opinion, *amigo*,' he declared, 'keeping a bird in a cage is the height of damned cruelty.'

It was truly amazing how quickly the trees were recovering from Pepe Suau's major surgery of just a few weeks earlier. There had been some heavy rainstorms in the intervening period, so we hadn't had to irrigate the trees yet, but we had started feeding them (the Spanish word for dung having entered our ever-extending vocabulary), and, under Pepe's tutelage, we'd been spraying any blotches or bugs which appeared on the bark or leaves. We were learning, *poco a poco*, little by little, about previously-unfamiliar potions like Bordeaux Mixture and White Oil, what arboreal ailments they were intended to cure, and where and when to apply them.

To people like ourselves, accustomed to the ways and pace of nature some fifteen hundred cooler miles to the north, the comparative speed of spring growth in this Mediterranean climate was a revelation. Even a row of what I'd taken to be some kind of big thistles, and which in my ignorance of 'exotic' plants I'd cut to the ground, had quickly re-sprouted and had flourished into what old Maria tactfully advised me were artichokes. As folk in the valley had told me often enough, the best friends of the Mallorcan farmer are '*el bon sol y agua*' – the good sun and water. The sun was nearly always there for everyone (sometimes too much of it!), but water was a different matter entirely. And, coming from a country where its abundance is taken for granted, you don't even begin to realise the value of the stuff until your very existence is governed by the lack or availability of it. Something else we had to learn.

During our first winter at Ca's Mayoral, all our domestic water requirements had been drawn from the *aljibe*, a big storage tank situated under the west terrace of the house. Rainwater from the roof was directed into it, and we'd topped it up occasionally with water piped from the well in the farthest field. Water was not a problem. In fact, it was so plentiful that we had even invited visiting friends, who normally had to buy their water, to fill up their five-litre plastic flagons from our bountiful source. Until Tomàs Ferrer saw me replenishing the *aljibe* with well water one day, that is.

'You cannot do that!' he gasped.

Then it dawned on me that it was a Saturday. The legal agreement made when we had bought the farm from the Ferrers was that we would have sole use of the well water on weekdays, but access to it at weekends would be theirs alone. This, we had been assured, was a common arrangement when a farm was sold and the seller retained some of the land, which, indeed, the Ferrers had done, just to have a field to work as a hobby during weekends spent away from their apartment in Palma. Even after a long and successful career as a local government official, Tomàs Ferrer hadn't forgotten his peasant roots, and he genuinely loved getting back to his little *finca* for those two days of farming every weekend.

'Sorry,' I said, quickly shutting off the hosepipe, 'I honestly forgot it was a Saturday.' Tomàs was clearly taking this incident very seriously – far too seriously, I thought – so I tried to make light of it. 'Once it's time to start irrigating your land, I'll, ehm, I'll pump some of my weekday water over to your place to make amends, OK?'

Tomàs was not amused. 'How long have you been putting the well water in the *aljibe*?'

'Well, all winter, I suppose – off and on. But this is the first time I've done it at the weekend – honest.' I was sounding like a schoolboy who'd been caught stealing apples. I knew that, and I realised how silly it was, but that was the effect that the domineering Tomàs Ferrer had on people.

'It is not the day of the week that is important, *señor*, it is the fact that you are doing it at all.' Drinking water from an open well like the one on Ca's Mayoral, he continued, was tantamount to committing suicide. That we had not been poisoned already was little short of a miracle, and it was lucky indeed that there had been sufficient winter rain to dilute the tainted water from the well. 'Just smell it!'

He turned on the hose and poured some water into my cupped hands. And, true enough, it did smell somewhat less than wholesome.

'Rats,' Tomàs said, 'mice, dead birds, rotten leaves, anything at all could be at the bottom of that well.'

Now I not only felt silly, but sick, too.

'You have two choices,' he went on, '– you either install an expensive filtration unit, although there won't be enough water to irrigate the trees *and* supply the house in the summer, or you do what we always did – buy your drinking water by the tanker load.'

Suddenly, the simple matter of water wasn't so straightforward any more.

Tomàs took me over to a downpipe that led from the roof guttering into the *aljibe*. 'You must block that pipe up from now until the start of the autumn storms. Any summer rain that falls will only pick up dust and other contaminants from the roof tiles. Pujol-Serra is the name of the water-trucking company in Andratx. I suggest you contact them immediately.'

With that, he left, leaving me to contemplate a little complication of life that I hadn't anticipated.

'Oh, *otra cosa*,' he said, pausing and turning at the corner of the terrace. 'Another thing – those fuzzy nests in the pines at the side of the house. *Procesionarios* – caterpillars of the processionary moth. They will strip the trees bare. I suggest you remove and burn the nests immediately.'

With that, he left again, leaving me to contemplate yet another little unexpected problem.

Now, the caterpillar of the pine processionary moth is an interesting and devious creature, though one that I hadn't known existed until then. It lives in large numbers in cocoons which could best be described as clusters of white candyfloss – innocuous enough looking puffs of fluff in which the little fellows sleep by day, emerging at night to march forth in long nose-to-tail lines to sate their voracious appetites on pine needles. Then, when it suits them, they descend from the trees, again in Indian file, and parade off in search of a suitable patch of earth in which to bury themselves, miraculously emerging some months later as moths. Since being accidentally introduced from the mainland in the 1950s, *procesionarios* had become a plague in Mallorca, second only to forest fires as a cause of the depletion of the pine woods which give the hills and mountains of the island their distinctive verdant beauty. We had to do our bit to fight the menace.

'How do we get them down from there?' I said to Sandy, staring up at the scattering of nests hanging from the higher branches of the tall pines.

'Only one way,' he replied. 'One of us is gonna have to climb up there and cut them down.'

'True. I'll hold the ladder.'

But the ladder didn't even reach halfway to the lowest of the cocoons, so Sandy had to resort to some daredevil tree climbing to get to them. He had taken a small pruning saw, the idea being to cut the branches containing the nests, so that they'd fall to the ground for burning. But, as so often happens, theory didn't quite match practice.

'It's no use,' he called down. 'The branches are far too thick for this little saw. I'll have to climb out and pull the nests off by hand.'

I didn't like the look of this. And, apparently, old Pep liked the look of it even less. Just as Sandy was about to take hold of the first nest, Pep ran in from the lane, shotgun in hand.

'Don't touch it, boy!' he yelled. '*Cuidado!* Out of the way!'

Sandy ducked behind the main trunk of the tree as Pep took aim, blasting first one cocoon from the branches, then another – pausing only after every second shot to re-load his gun. The nests lay on the ground, spewing their teeming contents of splattered caterpillars. I couldn't see any signs of surviving life, but Pep was taking no chances. He shot every fallen nest yet again, blitzing everything to smithereens.

'Why in the name of every wooden saint in Christendom did you let your boy do that?' he snapped at me. 'Don't you know how dangerous these *procesionarios* are?'

'Dangerous? Caterpillars? Come on, Pep – you must be joking.'

'Would I have fired off a whole box of cartridges if I was joking?' Pep was really outraged. '*Hombre*, think yourself lucky that I noticed what was going on here, or you would have had your conscience to live with!'

'I don't understand. I was just doing what Tomàs Ferrer told –'

'Ferrer! I should have known it! Did he not tell you what happens if you touch a *procesionario?*'

'No – well, no, he didn't.'

'Typical of the man! *Mira!*' Pep bent down and, using a twig, picked up the remains of a caterpillar. 'Do you see these fine hairs along its back? Well, touch those and you'll contract a very severe and painful eruption of the skin. *Coño*, it can prove fatal to people with a certain susceptibility to the poison of the *procesionario!*'

'Nice of Señor Ferrer to omit that little detail of information,' Sandy muttered.

'Ferrer? Never trust him!' Pep was right on his high horse now. 'But that's not all he should have told you. Worse than the skin rash, if your son had touched the *procesionarios* and then rubbed his eyes, *hombre*, he would almost certainly have been struck blind!'

I could see that Pep was in deadly earnest. I'd already been made very aware that he didn't think much of Tomàs Ferrer, and I could have been forgiven just then for coming round to his way of thinking. Not that I suspected for one moment that Tomàs had intentionally neglected to tell me about the danger of touching these caterpillars, but his oversight could have proved disastrous. Then again, if, as our old neighbour had now advised, the processionary moth problem in Mallorca was so common, Ferrer may simply have assumed that I knew all about the creatures. I said so to Pep, who responded with a derisory snort. Words were not necessary to express how he felt about *that* hypothesis.

'What do we do with all these dead ones now, Pep?' asked Sandy.

'You rake up every last one, pour petrol over them and burn them.'

'They won't just be eaten up by birds, then?' I enquired, the naïveté of my query eliciting another snort from Pep.

So venomous were the *procesionarios*' hairs, he said, that no bird would go near them. 'Except,' he added after a moment's contemplation, 'great tits.'

I was half expecting one of Pep's crude quips to follow. But no, he was still deadly serious. Not many people had witnessed the phenomenon, he disclosed, but he had been one of the fortunate few – right here under these very pine trees, when old Paco was still running the place.

'So, great tits are immune to the poison, is that it?' I said, still suspecting that a bawdy punchline was about to be delivered.

Pep shook his head emphatically. 'No, no – not immune, *amigo*. Just smart! For the great tit has the ability to turn the caterpillar outside-in before swallowing him. So,' he raised his shoulders, '– no stinging hairs, *no problema*.'

Neither Sandy nor I could resist a little chuckle at that, but Pep, clearly offended by our appearing to doubt his word, berated us with a string of *mallorquín* oaths, shouldered his shotgun and proceeded, in high dudgeon, homewards across the lane. And, as implausible as Pep's tale of the great tits may have seemed at the time, I was subsequently assured by a much-respected authority on Balearic wildlife that it is, in fact, true. Apologies, and a large slice of humble pie (without robins), have since been tendered to Pep, whose concern and quick thinking, when all's said and done, *had* saved Sandy from what could have been a very unpleasant experience.

And my discarded nesting box was eventually recovered from the rubbish heap and fixed to one of the pine trees in the hope that a pair of great tits would move in and raise a family of new *procesionario-*

eaters. None ever did, though – the clever little fellows presuming, no doubt, that the box was actually one of Pep's bird traps.

- Seven -

A PREDICAMENT FOR PEPE

The day which had been set for Ellie and I to take up Pepe Suau's invitation to see over his farm turned out to be a beauty, the brilliant late-spring sunshine already giving a foretaste of hot summer days to come. As we drove into the lane, a midday heat haze was rippling up from the valley floor, causing the craggy cliffs of the surrounding mountains to shimmer in an almost mirage-like dance. No more chill mists rolling down through the high clefts and gorges, no more shadows of passing clouds creeping darkly over the wooded slopes. The seasons were changing again.

Situated on the opposite side of Andratx from Ca's Mayoral, the farm of Es Pou occupies an elevated and privileged position overlooking a wide valley just a few kilometres beyond the outskirts of town. I'd noticed the fine house before on the couple of occasions I'd passed that way and I'd greatly admired it, though not suspecting for a moment that it belonged to Pepe. But this was where he had instructed us to come, all right, and the closer we got, the more impressive the farm looked.

The house could truly be described as a *senyoríu* in Mallorcan terms – more of a lesser mansion than a farmhouse – and it puzzled me again why Pepe, with a large property like this, would want to work so hard, constantly buzzing about in his little old Seat car, to do his tree magic on other people's smaller *fincas*.

Handsome and understated, rather than fussily-ornate, would be a fair enough way of describing many a typical Mallorcan *senyoríu*, and that was certainly how the façade of Es Pou house appeared to me. It stood solid, rectangular and white beneath a gently pitched roof of ochre tiles. Regularly-spaced green-shuttered windows were framed by painted surrounds, which I noticed echoed the soft biscuit colour of dry-stone walls retaining terrace upon terrace of cultivated *bancales* that stepped ever more steeply up the mountainside beyond. There was an air of serene dignity about the place. Fields on either side of the long driveway paraded orderly ranks of almond trees – meticulously cared for, as could be expected – the oatmeal soil between already all but hidden under leafy green drills of winter-sown cereals.

We could see that Pepe, still in his familiar working clothes, was waiting for us at the front of the house. Smiling that unassuming little smile of his, he beckoned me to drive through an archway which opened into a cobbled *clastra*, the spacious central courtyard so characteristic of those large old Mallorcan properties. And if we had been quietly impressed by the public face of Es Pou house, we were totally captivated by what we saw now.

A spreading palm tree shaded an old well taking pride of place within an enclosed quadrangle of two-storey farm buildings, none of which had been whitewashed like the front of the house, but which wore the patina of age comfortably on the beige of their mellow stone walls. Towards one corner, open forestairs ascended to a first-floor loft, while along the adjoining wall, old farm implements (still in use, by the look of them) peeped from within a row of arched cartsheds. This was like stepping back in time. We had seen similar places before when visiting the island on holiday: *clastras* like this which had been turned into rustically-stylish alfresco restaurants – old farmsteads in which things traditionally Mallorcan had been 'recreated' for the delectation of the tourist. One or two went so far as to feature costumed folk dancers and musicians, lace-makers and artisans of other 'olde worlde' country crafts, and sometimes even a selection of farm animals, including the mandatory drowsy donkey for the children to pet. And very interesting and entertaining such places can be, too – well worth a visit, in fact.

But the courtyard of Es Pou was the real thing. This was clearly still a working farm. Yet, for purely practical reasons, I'm sure, everything had been so carefully maintained that the place still looked as it must have done a century or more before. A dozen or so hens pecked for seeds and grubs between the cobblestones, their contented cawing and clucking the only sound to be heard within the almost reverential tranquillity of the yard, save for a soft breeze rustling through the drooping fronds of the palm tree. Pepe's old dog, which had looked up semi-interestedly from his sleeping position on our arrival, rolled over and resumed his nap against the warm backdrop of a sun-bleached barn door. The atmosphere was one of ageless calm, a comforting atmosphere exuding a feeling of security and seclusion, imparted, no doubt, by the encircling walls of the *clastra* – a cloister, albeit of a secular kind, indeed.

Pepe welcomed us with polite handshakes and the customary, '*Qué tal? Benvinguts!*' Then, when we remarked on how much we admired the courtyard and the immaculate order it was in, he confessed that he felt privileged to be the farmer of such a fine old place, and that he saw it as no more than his duty to carry on the tradition of looking after it in an appropriately respectful way.

It was certainly refreshing to hear someone in Pepe's fortunate position adopting such an appreciative attitude towards his legacy. I tried to think of how often I'd heard such sentiments expressed by similarly favoured farmers in Britain. It didn't take me long to do the count.

Guiding us across the *clastra* towards the house, Pepe paused beside the well and explained that this, the purest and most reliable source of water for kilometres around, was what the farm had been named after – '*pou*', as we would perhaps know, being the *mallorquín* word for 'well'. Siting a grand *senyoríu* like this round such a *font*, he continued, had always been the way in Mallorca; an absolute necessity, in fact, particularly on the many *possessiós*, the huge estates, that are situated in some of the highest and most remote valleys of the Tramuntana

Mountains. Unlike Es Pou, which was only a few minutes from town, many of those *possessiós* in the high sierras were so far off the beaten track that, even today, a few still could not be reached by motor vehicle.

'And people still live up there and work those farms?' I asked.

'*Pues, sí!*' Pepe emphasised. 'They rear sheep and goats and grow olives as they have always done.' He pondered that for a moment, then added, a wistful look in his eyes, 'But not so much as before. A small fortune could be made in one year from a good *possessió's* production of olive oil, even during my lifetime. But those days are gone. And the days of the estates making a fine profit from the timber and charcoal of the oak forests are gone forever, too. Few young people want to follow that way of life any more, so the many families of workers needed to capitalise on such large and difficult tracts of land are not there now. And, in some ways, who can blame them?' He raised a resigned shrug. 'It was never an easy way to make a living – just a way of life that you had to be born to. And the dangers of being in such isolated spots! Why, some of the most cut-off mountain *senyoríus* are built with battlements on top of the *clastra* walls to help fend off the bandits who used to plunder such lonely places.' He shook his head. 'No, no, *señores* – not an easy way to make a living.'

But, for all his stated acceptance of the situation, I suspected that Pepe hankered after those times long past, when, at least for the owners of such vast spreads, life would not have been without its material advantages. Remoteness, after all, would only be a drawback if you couldn't afford to escape from it to enjoy the fruits of your, or, more likely, your workers' labours when the fancy took you. And, like well-off estate owners everywhere, I had little doubt that the grand old *dueños* of the Mallorcan *possessiós* would have done precisely that. Yet our hard-working and modest friend Pepe just didn't seem to fit the image of a son of that advantaged ilk, no matter how privileged he was to have inherited a comparable property down here in the rolling foothills of the Tramuntanas. He was, indeed, something of a paradox.

Saying that he would show us the 'master' accommodation first, he guided us back through the archway to the house's front door, located to the right of the opening, with an uninterrupted view over the valley to the western outskirts of Andratx, and beyond to the soaring heights of the Costé de Na Mora ridge. In common with the exterior aspect of the house, the entrance and reception hall were impressive without being in any way ostentatious. And, as Pepe shepherded us from drawing room to dining hall, from library to billiards room, and from study to parlour, the collective impression was one of modesty, both of size and amenity. Also, most of the rooms seemed to lead directly from one to the next, corridors being virtually non-existent.

Sombre portraits of previous generations of the estate's *dueños* looked down from age-darkened canvases, their positions on the stark white walls interspersed with ornately-framed paintings with staunchly religious themes, and faded tapestries depicting hunting scenes from a bygone age. And the furniture, although antique and in typical Spanish style, was simple and functional rather than ornate. There were chunky tables and sideboards with wrought iron appendages, straight-backed dining chairs with seats of stiff leather, and equally uncomfortable-looking couches resembling upholstered church pews. Even a boudoir grand piano in the drawing room seemed to have been selected for its distinct lack of embellishment.

The ceilings also reflected this mood of simplicity in that, instead of flaunting the elaborate plasterwork that might have been expected in such a fine house, they were of the basic exposed-beam variety, in keeping with those of even the most humble Mallorcan cottage. Upstairs, too, the bedrooms, many also interconnected, owed little to extravagance. The furnishings, though of evident good quality, were of almost monastic austerity, with only the master bedroom giving way to anything approaching luxury in the form of a four-poster bed, though even that had the appearance of being somewhat less than eiderdown soft.

Like the courtyard, then, the interior of the house had an air of yesteryear about it, a feeling of a simpler, more frugal age, long before the advent of today's taken-for-granted creature comforts. But, while it was undoubtedly a splendid house, it *was* just that – a 'house', and more resembling a carefully preserved but rather lifeless memory of the past than a welcoming, lived-in 'home'.

Leading us back into the *clastra*, Pepe took us up the flight of stone stairs that I'd assumed led to a storage loft of some kind – perhaps for hay, or almonds even. And it *was* a loft, a very large one, but empty and not for storing produce in, as Pepe was about to explain.

When he was a boy, he said, the people who worked on the farm – as many as eleven families of them – lived in these basic *dormitorios* overlooking the courtyard. This was their home, though with few home comforts, but the only home that most would know in their entire lifetime. And despite the Spartan conditions, the families had been happy with their lot – provided always, of course, that the *dueño* of the farm had been a good and fair employer. We stood with Pepe for a minute or two, while he silently savoured his own memories of a way of life truly gone forever, of a time when this now silent farmstead must have been alive with activity from dawn to dusk.

'Come,' he said quietly at length, 'there is a very special place I want you to see.'

Taking us back across the yard, he led the way up a few steps to an arched doorway which, I now noticed for the first time, was situated beneath a little open bell tower. Pepe pushed the heavy oak door open, removed his cap, and beckoned us to follow him inside. It was a tiny chapel, simple in the extreme, yet perhaps the most spiritually moving place of worship I had ever been in. Pepe bowed his head to a small carved statue of the Virgin Mary looking benignly down on him from an alcove above the altar. We stood back and left him to his hushed moments of reverence.

His eyes were moist with tears when he finally looked up. 'Every morning,' he said, 'the bell would be rung and all the families on the farm, from the youngest baby to the oldest grandfather, would gather here for prayers with the *dueño* before the men went out to the fields to begin their day's work. The same in the evening. The bell would welcome the workers home, calling them here with their families to give their thanks for a safe return from the land.' He smiled and sighed, 'The simple pleasures of a simple life. And I do miss those days, *señores*, when this place and others like it were more than just farms or country estates. They were communities, where you were born, married, raised a family, spent your working days and finally died, having lived a life in an environment where everything and everybody was interdependent. *Sí* – hard days at times, but happy days mostly.'

Outwith the confines of the courtyard, Pepe proudly showed us some of the *dependencias de los animales*, outbuildings used for housing livestock, including a couple of sties of extremely well-fed and healthy-looking pigs, and a larger shed used as a shelter for his herd of sheep during the unbearably hot days of summer. He smiled reflectively again, as he recalled one old Es Pou shepherd who, when Pepe was still a small boy, used to follow the ancient tradition of also sleeping during the hottest hours of the day when the sheep slept, then stayed out in the fields with them all night, playing his *xiramías* (little Mallorcan bagpipes) to his charges as they grazed away through the relatively cooler hours of darkness.

Apart from a small grove of enviably lush-looking orange trees adjacent to the main farm buildings, I noted that all of the fields that we could see appeared to be devoted to almond production. There would certainly have been olive trees aplenty on the farm at one time, Pepe admitted, there being enough olives grown around Andratx back then to keep up to thirty oil-producing mills going. But that was something which time had changed, too, and now it was nearly all almonds, except in water-abundant valleys like our own, of course, where fruit growing had become the thing; oranges, lemons, peaches, apricots – all the varieties of fruit trees we had on Ca's Mayoral, in fact.

'But Ca's Mayoral is tiny compared to this place,' I said, 'and we're pushed to keep up with the work at times. So, I mean, I don't want to appear nosy, but how do you and your son manage to run a place of this size by yourselves, when it took the members of eleven families to do it before?'

'Oh, we manage somehow,' Pepe laughed. 'We don't try to produce as much as in those days, and mechanisation helps. Plus, we can always get casual labour to help out at the busy times – the almond harvest mainly.'

He led us back into the *clastra* and ushered us through a door on the opposite side of the archway from the principal rooms.

'And now you must meet my wife,' he said, introducing us to an amiable little woman in a floral overall. She was busy baking at a wood-burning stove in a fairly cramped kitchen-cum-sitting room which, in marked contrast to the grander apartments we had seen earlier, simply oozed warmth and cheer. Brushing flour off her hands, Señora Suau cordially invited us to sit at a scrubbed pinewood table, just big enough to accommodate four. Two well sat in, but comfortable, easychairs rested by an open fire within a snug inglenook, and an array of earthenware *greixonera* dishes sat neatly on shelves on either side. It was obvious that this homely refuge was what Pepe and his wife chose to use as a living room, forsaking the more elegant trappings of the main part of the house for the modest, everyday comforts of a working farmhouse kitchen.

His wife had prepared a special little treat for us, Pepe revealed, smiling in anticipation himself as she took a tray of biscuity fingers from the oven.

'"*Sospirs de Manacor*",' she smiled – '"Sighs of Manacor".' It was a classic titbit, she told us, based on a Moorish recipe of almonds, lemon rind and spices, which tradition held had originated in the town of Manacor away over in the east of the island. And the result of the creation, I had to admit, matched the romantic name. Melt-in-the-mouth seduction.

But, tasty sweetmeats aside, my curiosity was getting the better of me again. I was dying to ask Pepe why he chose to work so hard, why he opted to live in these comparatively cramped and humble quarters when unlimited living space was lying empty on the other side of the archway. I was now also itching to find out why his wife was doing her own menial kitchen tasks – though patently enjoying doing so – when a woman in her position might normally be expected to have domestic help. Pepe was about to spare me the inevitable embarrassment of asking such rude questions regarding their personal affairs.

'Do you like this farm of Es Pou, Señor Peter?' he enquired.

'Yes – magnificent. You're a lucky man, Pepe.'

'Would you like to buy it?' he asked, right out of the blue.

'Well, ehm, yes,' I stammered, totally taken aback. 'I mean no – that is, yes, of course. But, well, the price could be a bit beyond my means, I think.'

I looked carefully at Pepe, searching for a facial clue that would tell he was pulling my leg. But he clearly couldn't have been more serious. Nor could his wife, who, like him, was now scrutinising my expression expectantly.

I gave a self-conscious little laugh, telling them that I'd need to win the *lotería* before contemplating the purchase of a *senyoriu* as grand as this.

But Pepe wasn't going to be put off that easily. The house was fine, he said, but old and without central heating for the cold winter nights or air-conditioning for the summer. That would be reflected in the price, as would the value of the farmland – a large dryland farm never being nearly as expensive per hectare as an intensively cropped, irrigated *finca* like Ca's Mayoral.

'No,' I muttered, 'but when you multiply those cheaper hectares by the amount within the extensive boundaries of Es Pou, you'd still come up with a figure which would make my bank manager commit suicide... by laughing himself to death.'

'*Perdón?*' Pepe keenly probed, not having understood any of my English-language mumblings.

This was getting difficult. Pepe was obviously in earnest, but as much as I would have loved to buy a big Mallorcan agricultural property like Es Pou, it really was well out of our financial league. I explained this to Pepe and his wife, and I could see the disappointment in their eyes. I waited for a moment, then plucked up the courage to ask the obvious question – why had he decided to sell up?

Pepe continued to look at me, his expectant expression changing to one of incredulity. He exchanged glances with his wife.

'I'm sorry, *señor*,' he said after a moment. 'I hope you don't think us impolite, but your question showed that you misunderstand the situation. Es Pou, you see, is not mine to sell.'

'But – but you said that you were the farmer.'

Pepe raised his eyebrows and shook his head, the look of disappointment returning to his face. 'And I *am* the farmer of Es Pou,' he stressed, 'but here in Mallorca, the farmer, *el agricultor*, of a such a large property only farms the place on behalf of the owner, the *señor*. And very often, as here, the *señor* does not even live on the premises – perhaps having a profession or a business in the city, maybe even over on the mainland.'

Now, at last, the jigsaw pieces were beginning to fit.

Pepe went on to point out that it was normal practice in such situations for the farmer to undertake the entire running of the estate on the owner's behalf, for which he, the *agricultor*, would either be paid a modest wage or given an equivalent share of the enterprise's annual profit – if there was one. He would also be required, as Pepe did, to live permanently on site, in appropriate quarters provided free by the *señor*.

I was finally able to understand why Pepe and his son worked so hard at their extramural labours. And the broader predicament that he was now having to face was also becoming crystal clear.

Pepe picked up my train of thought. 'You see,' he said, 'if the present *señor* of Es Pou sells up to someone who doesn't want my services...'

'You'll be without a job?'

'*Claro*, but without a job *and* a home.'

I could now appreciate why Pepe had appeared so emotional at times during his guided tour of the farm, particularly when showing us the former working families' lowly *dormitorios*, and more especially the little chapel. Es Pou and the lifelong memories it held were clearly very dear to him, and I could see now that even the thought of having to leave the old place was almost breaking his heart.

'Pepe has told me about your sons,' Señora Suau piped up, trying very hard to put on a cheery, positive face. 'He has told me what good workers they are.' She nodded her head enthusiastically. 'Just like their *mamá y papá, sí*? Why, just think how good it would be for them to come to Es Pou! Plenty room in the big house for them when they marry and have children of their own! And it would be good for the farm, too! With your family working alongside Pepe and our son Miguel and his family – *hombre*, it would be almost like old times here!'

How I wished that we could have found a way to join in her dream. I truly would have liked nothing better. And the fact that we had been so flattered by Pepe and his wife made it all the harder to emphasise to them that, with the best will in the world, financial practicalities dictated that we really couldn't take advantage of the wonderful opportunity of which they'd so thoughtfully made us aware. Our hosts accepted what I said with grace and civility, wishing us well in our own lives and inviting us to visit them again at any time.

But, although we left the Suaus at the archway of Es Pou having exchanged hearty handshakes and jovial '*Hasta luegos*', we knew that such pleasantries did little to hide the pervading sense of sadness felt by us all. All Ellie and I could hope for was that their *señor* would find an understanding and worthy buyer for the property…

Or, that we might indeed win the lottery!

- Eight -

FISHY HAPPENINGS IN THE DRAGON'S LAIR

As it was a Saturday, Charlie had had a school basketball game to play in the morning – his class team versus one from the American School at Portals Nous, not far from where his own seat of learning was located, overlooking the bay to the west of Palma city. Sandy, ever keen to 'have a good laugh', as he put it, at his younger brother's sporting prowess, had agreed to drive him there, on the understanding that we'd all meet up for lunch later on. Being such a beautiful day, it had been agreed that an eatery somewhere by the sea would be best, so Ellie and I turned right at the bottom of the Es Pou driveway and headed, as arranged, for the fishing village of Sant Elm.

Whilst the original winding roads, leading to certain rapidly-growing coastal towns in this corner of south-west Mallorca, had been straightened and widened to cater for the ever-increasing volume of summer tourist traffic, the one to sleepy Sant Elm still presented something of a challenge to the unaccustomed driver. For, although well surfaced and maintained, it was still more a lane than a road, only just wide enough at some points for two vehicles to pass – and only then with great care. But we'd driven the route before and had been so bowled over by the sheer beauty of the surrounding landscape that any small traffic hazard that we might encounter on the way was deemed well worth the risk.

Leaving Andratx behind, the road soon runs out of valley and starts to twist steeply upwards through a rugged pass between Molins and Sa Font mountains. To meet an oncoming tour bus on one of the narrow hairpin bends, which lead blindly from one to another on this stretch of road, is a nightmare scenario to be prayed against. However, we'd reckoned the chances of such an encounter would be minimal this early in the season, and, fortunately, the hunch proved to be correct. Good luck also favoured us in the form of an old *campesino's* rickety Citroën 2CV van, gamely spluttering up the tortuous incline ahead of us, spewing petrol fumes while farting like a diesel, but struggling sufficiently to keep the pace down to a level which allowed me occasionally to take my eyes off the road for long enough to appreciate the scenery.

Although we were passing through an extension of the same Tramuntana range that dominated our valley, here the overwhelming grandeur of the mountains was so much closer that it was truly breathtaking. The pine and holm oak woods that commenced at the edge of the road reached their green fingers all the way up to the highest sierras, the trees miraculously clinging to great riven outcrops of dove-grey and salmon-pink rock as if rooted to the very stone itself. Opening the car window, the ever-present hint of juniper and thyme and a hundred other bewitching perfumes wafted in on the air, while the sound of birdsong trilled over the drowsy rhythm of crickets chirruping in clumps of wild fennel by the roadside. And as if to confirm that summer was on its way, little pomegranate trees, growing wild over the honeystone walls which held the mountain back from the road, were already spangled with a scattering of tiny scarlet flowers.

After clearing the pass and zigzagging down to S'Arraco, a village which basks in a wide, fertile basin evoking images of a Mallorcan 'Sleepy Hollow', the road continues on through a gully shaded by overhanging pine trees on one side. On the other, the ground falls away into a narrow glen that follows the course of a creek, unseen under lush copses of bamboo, and bordered by slivers of rich land fanning out from the little stream on its final approaches to the sea.

Although the village of Sant Elm hasn't been left totally unsullied by the rapacious advance of tourism, it is still, nevertheless, a haven of relative development restraint skirting a cove of stunning natural beauty. The bay sweeps out in a spectacular crescent from a deep wedge of golden sand at the entrance to the village. On the far side, the turquoise waters are shielded by a horseshoe of mountains, whose tumbling flanks finally descend to forelands of beige cliffs that plunge vertically into the sea. But it's only after passing along the narrow main street to a point near the 'harbour' that the most impressive views can be had of the dramatic scenery with which this fairly remote corner of the island is blessed.

We parked the car in a little back alley where the only signs of life outside the low white buildings were two unsociable-looking cats hissing and growling over the spilled contents of a plastic rubbish bag. But to our relief, the salty sea air was heavy with the appetising smell of sardines being grilled – a welcome clue that, although the tourist season hadn't really started yet, at least one of the nearby trio of waterfront bar–restaurants was likely to be open for business. We were a bit ahead of the time that had been set for meeting Sandy and Charlie, which suited us fine, because it gave us a chance to savour the soothing ambience of the place before being hustled indoors in the clutches of the boys' inevitable hunger frenzy.

At the end of the alley, a panoramic seascape opened up, ranging from the headland of the bay away to the left, right round to Sa Dragonera, a scrub-dappled island that dominates the skyline west of Sant Elm like a reclining colossus – or dragon, depending on your sense of imagination. A smudge of mist was hanging just below the island's summit, leaving the tiny hermitage of Dragonera floating magically in the clear sky. The image served as a reminder of the mystical aura of this area which, in former times, had prompted Trappist Monks to build their now-ruined Sa Trapa Monastery on a remote clifftop overlooking the sea, a difficult and rocky trek over the mountain to the north of the village.

In those days, and until not so long ago, the easiest way in and out of this still-secluded part of the island would have been by boat. And, not surprisingly, modern entrepreneurial minds hadn't been slow to recognise the commercial potential of the fact. Though this corner of the village was deserted today, in a few weeks, or even days, the first of the day-trip boats would arrive from Palma, loaded to the gunnels with scores of *sangría*-plied holidaymakers, who would be decanted ashore for just long enough to have lunch, before commencing a rollicking singalong return voyage back round the coast to their resort hotels. A daily culture shock for the people of sleepy Sant Elm, no doubt, but business is business, and this sporadic shattering of the peace had long been turned into a tidy profit – at least by two local families.

The Restaurante El Pescador could hardly have been more aptly named, because it is genuinely the lower half of an old fisherman's cottage, sitting snugly beside the similarly-converted Restaurante Vistamar. This brace of unassuming little eating places is located conveniently at the top of the sea-wall steps where hordes of hungry day-trippers just happen to climb in search of sustenance. All that stands between the two stone cabins and the sea is a small canopied esplanade, which both establishments ingeniously use as alfresco extensions to their limited indoor dining areas. Two summer goldmines. But for the independently-travelling visitor who can time his arrival to avoid those occasional mass invasions, a tempting selection of sea-fresh fish is usually available at either place, simply but well prepared, and served up unfussily in a location of priceless beauty.

I wandered across the empty esplanade and looked down to the small jetty and a few wooden, ladder-like slipways that connect the little boathouses beneath the terrace to the waters lapping at the rocky shore. This was how it must always have looked to the local fishermen setting out in search of the day's catch – before 'progress' brought bigger and more lucrative fish to fry for some, that is. Out in the bay, a few tall-masted yachts and little flare-bowed *llauds* swayed dreamily at their moorings, no sign of life aboard, their red-and-gold stern flags hanging limp in the placid air. A kind of expectant stillness pervaded. The lull before the tourist storm, some might well say.

'There they are now!' said Ellie, pointing up a gentle rise to a bend at the end of the main street where our little Seat Panda was pulling into the kerb.

Sandy, a broad smile on his face, was first out of the car, followed by a distinctly glum-looking Charlie. I signalled that we'd join them in the restaurant immediately adjacent to where they'd parked, and which appeared to be open.

El Restaurante Na Caragola – The Snail – has, from its favoured location above and to the side of the little 'harbour' area, an uninterrupted view of the entire mouth of Sant Elm Bay, looking out over the tiny islet of Es Pantaleu to the open sea. Although there were no day-trip boats today, a few small craft had started to appear round the headland, the good weather having tempted their owners to set out for a family lunch at just such a favourite haven as this.

In the couple of minutes it took us to join them, the boys had already organised a window table in the restaurant, a wonderfully bright and airy place, in which an interesting and unusual feature is the 'gallery' of paintings by local artists displayed (complete with price tags) on the rear wall. Not that the boys were interested in such artistic attractions. Food, as anticipated, was the name of their mission.

'A good basketball game, Charlie?' I leadingly asked.

'Yeah, not bad,' he mumbled, not even bothering to glance up from a particularly uncharacteristic scrutiny of his fingernails.

I looked at Sandy for a pointer, but all that came back was a shrug and a lop-sided smirk.

But Ellie, as ever, was right on the button. 'What happened to your new trainers?' she said, pointing accusingly at Charlie's feet, which he'd been trying very hard to conceal under the table. 'Look at them! Filthy – and all scraped! I thought I told you *not* to play in them, especially on that tarmac pitch!'

Now it was Charlie's turn to pull a shrug, but in his case accompanied by a dejectedly lowered head. 'Just thought I'd try them out,' he mumbled.

'May as well tell them,' Sandy grinned, obviously delighting in the pickle his brother had got himself into. 'The sports teacher's going to contact Dad about it anyway.'

The arrival of the waiter to take our order bought Charlie a two-minute reprieve.

Paella, universally considered to be Spain's national dish, can be at best a gastronomic delight or at worst a soggy disaster. For, although there are many variations of the fundamental rice-based recipe, most Spaniards would agree that there's only one correct method of cooking it, and the chef at Na Caragola had the reputation of being a master of the art. Of course, as well as being extremely filling, a good *paella* doesn't come particularly cheap nowadays – giving the boys two excellent reasons for ordering it. Not to be outdone, Ellie and I followed suit. The waiter then informed us that it would take up to thirty minutes for the dish to be prepared, usually a welcome sign that no culinary corners were going to be cut, but also meaning that Charlie was going to have plenty of time to do some explaining.

'Well?' I prompted, gesturing towards his scuffed training shoes, a grossly overpriced brand currently all the rage with his fashion-plate school peers.

'Stood on my toes,' he mumbled. 'German guy.'

'Only *one* German guy? It looks as if a whole panzer division trundled over your feet!'

Sandy started to chuckle.

'We're waiting, Charlie,' Ellie said.

He was given another moment's respite by the waiter returning to our table with a basket of crusty bread, a dish of garlicky *allioli* mayonnaise and a steaming little *greixonera* full of stewed snails.

'A speciality of the house,' he smiled. 'To keep the *señores* and *señoritos* busy until the *paella* is ready.' With that, he produced some wooden toothpicks for winkling the little gastropods out of their shells. '*Bon profit!*'

'You're on your own, gentlemen,' Ellie said once the waiter was out of earshot. 'Snails?' She gave a shudder. 'Yuck! Always remind me of bogeys!'

'Yeah, great!' Charlie enthused, wasting no time in getting his toothpick working. 'Wow, I'm ready for this!'

'And we're ready to hear what happened to your trainers,' I reminded him.

'Mm-m-m, right,' he droned, the old look of despondency swiftly wiping the food-induced grin off his face. 'Stood on my toes – on purpose – twice.' Charlie was now peering into an empty snail shell as if hoping to find a way of crawling inside.

'So?'

'So, I, ehm… well… decked him.'

'Oh, no,' I groaned. 'Don't tell me you actually floored one of the opposition.'

'Opposition?' Sandy spluttered. 'No way opposition! The German lad was on *Charlie's* team! Young Heinz. It was his parents you had that near-tango experience with, remember?'

Ellie and I sighed in unison. Heavily.

Marvelling at the limp, shapeless form of a shelled snail dangling dark brown and slimy on the end of his toothpick, Charlie added sotto voce, 'Anyway, nobody would've noticed… if Ben hadn't sunk the boot into Heinz when he was down, that is.'

'Ben?' I queried.

'Little Jewish guy.'

'On the American team, right?'

Charlie shook his head and removed the snail from his toothpick through puckered lips. 'Nope. Our team, too.'

Sandy took up the story now, gleefully revealing that the remaining two members of Charlie's team – an Argentinian boy and an Egyptian – had then become involved in the fracas, feet and fists flying everywhere, the American team scoring unopposed meanwhile. 'Then the ref blows his whistle and goes running across to sort the scrap out. Anyway,' he went on, 'Heinz spills the beans – tells the ref that Charlie belted him.'

'Yeah,' Charlie confirmed, umbrage patently taken, 'and Ben says that's right and tells the referee he never kicked Heinz, only tripped over him.'

'Referee?' I gasped. 'Sounds more like a job for a United Nations peace-keeping force!'

'You said it!' Sandy agreed. 'The next thing, Charlie's chum Ali, the Egyptian lad, steams into the squabble and swears blind to the ref that it was Ben and not Charlie that felled Heinz.'

'Hm-m-m,' Charlie lamented, 'a couple of the American team got the ref to take Ben's side, though. Grassed on me.'

'But you should have owned up anyway, Charlie,' Ellie rebuked. 'I mean, you started it, so you should've admitted it.'

'Yeah, but that would've made Ali look like a liar,' Charlie reasoned.

'But he is!'

'Still a good guy, though – coming to the aid of his pal and all. Anyway, Ben lied too.'

'This starts to sound more like a lesson in international politics than a report on a basketball game between twelve-year-olds,' I muttered.

'Well, Heinz shouldn't have messed up my good sneakers,' Charlie stated. 'And Ben shouldn't have been such a jerk.'

'And you shouldn't have worn your new trainers for games,' Ellie retorted. 'Then none of this would've happened.'

I was almost afraid to ask, but I took the plunge anyway: 'And what, Charlie, was the consequence of this schoolyard vignette of the start of World War Three?'

'Real bummer. Me and Ali were sent to the sin bin, and the Americans went on to thrash our team stupid. Well, you know – five against three...'

I resisted the temptation to draw any parallels between the realities of international affairs and this adolescent sporting drama. And the arrival of the *paella* saved Charlie from further immediate censure.

Two waiters were on the job this time, one toting a small, linen-draped table which he placed at the side of ours, the other carrying a *paëllera*, the traditional two-handled *paella*-cooking pan. This one was almost as big as a trash can lid, and it was laid on the little side table with due flourish. Before serving, both waiters stood back to allow us a moment or two to feast our eyes on their chef's creation.

I felt all thoughts of Charlie's basketball altercation and nagging worries about likely repercussions rapidly draining from my mind. This *paella* did look so good that it seemed almost a sacrilege to destroy its beautifully executed presentation. Pieces of rabbit, pork, monkfish and squid basked in the saffron-gold rice, jewelled with peas and sliced red peppers, and surrounded by a garland of prawns and mussels in their shells. And the aromas rising from this colourful fusion of ingredients were just as irresistible.

'*Es buena, sí?*' the waiter asked, his delighted expression revealing that he knew full well what our response would be.

He then presented us with little side dishes of fresh radishes, mild green peppers and wedges of lemon, before finally adorning our plates with the *paella*. And while the size of the *paëllera* may have seemed a bit daunting at first, it says everything about the quality of its contents that not one solitary morsel remained in it at the end of our meal.

A terrace, with a gnarled old pine tree to the side, runs all the way along the front of Na Caragola, looking out over that spectacular sea view, and providing the perfect spot to sit and relax with an after-lunch coffee.

'Look!' said Ellie, nudging my elbow. 'See – down there at the jetty! Somebody's waving to us from that boat!'

Sure enough, a bikini-clad young woman, whom I didn't recognise, was standing on the deck of a *llaud* fishing boat and appeared to be beckoning us to come down. Why, I couldn't imagine, but it had to be us she was waving to, since all the other tables on the terrace were unoccupied.

Then she shouted, 'Sandee-ee! Charlee-ee!'

'Have you guys been keeping something from us?' I asked, intrigued.

But before the boys could answer, the woman called out again. '*C'est moi* – Josephine! Come and join us, *non*? Your Mama and Papa, *aussi*! We go fishing, *oui*?'

Just then, a stocky, dark-haired young man appeared on deck beside her.

'I take it that'll be Napoleon,' I remarked.

'No, his name's Andreu,' said Sandy, grinning from ear to ear as he waved back. 'Andreu and Josephine – French couple. I met them at the school this morning. They were there booking one of their kids in, and they hung about for a few minutes to watch Charlie's basketball battle. Nice couple – just arrived on the island – interested in sharing the school run with you, they said.'

'Hurry, *s'il vous plaît!*' Josephine called out. 'Come with us to the catching of *les petits* fishes!'

'Nip down and thank them for the offer, Sandy,' I said, 'but tell them we've made other arrangements. Honestly, I'm too full of snails and *paella* to do anything too energetic.'

'Suit yourself,' Sandy replied, standing up and preparing to do my bidding, 'but I thought you'd be interested to know that Andreu's family have a fruit import–export business – France, England, mainland Spain and everywhere. Really big-time international stuff. Says they're opening a huge warehouse in Mallorca soon as well.'

My ears pricked up at that. 'Find your sea legs, family,' I said, succumbing to a sudden energy rush. 'We're going fishing!'

Although traditionally little open boats for fishing the inshore waters of the Balearic Islands, these days *llauds*, or rather their beautiful flowing lines, are being replicated in the construction of expensive pleasure boats. And many well-off Mallorcan folk choose their elegant though unpretentious style in preference to the flashy, speed-first craft more commonly the choice of many who can afford such terrific toys. As if to highlight the comparison, Andreu's *llaud*, I noted, was named '*Donzella del Mar*' – 'Maiden of The Sea' – whereas a phallic-prowed powerboat moored nearby boasted the subtle handle of 'Wet Dream'. I knew which I'd rather be stepping aboard.

Andreu and Josephine couldn't have been more
welcoming. An attractive young couple in their early
thirties, Gallic charm they had aplenty, as well as an
enviably well-appointed boat. There was a deceptively
roomy and comfortable cabin, complete with mini-galley
and toilet, and a fold-down table at which their two young
children – Michelle, who was about six, and her brother
Sasha, a year or so younger – were sitting contentedly
drawing with crayons.

We were going to be heading for the far side of
Dragonera Island, Andreu informed us while firing up
the reassuringly robust-sounding diesel motor. That was a
favourite spot of the local fishermen, he said, and he had
had many successful catches there himself over the years.
'Only 'obby fishing, of course,' he stressed. 'Nothing too
sérieux.' We would enjoy the experience. 'Bien sûr!'

Like the scenery of inland Mallorca, we were now
about to learn that the surrounding sea can be ever-
changing in aspect and disposition, too. And with very
little warning. A solitary dark cloud drifted over the
sun as we were casting off from the jetty. With the
resultant change of light, everything took on a clearer,
sharper look. Distant cliffs seemed closer than in the
bright sunlight, the previously turquoise sea reflecting
the darker colour of the sky in tones of inky blue.
The calm waters became uneasy, appearing to run
diagonally over the bay as if caught by a sudden tide.
Even above the throaty rumble of the llaud's diesel, we
could hear small, agitated waves splashing against the
rocky foreshore, caressed only moments before by the
gentlest of ripples. Moored boats now turned to face

the oncoming swell, while Josephine grabbed a wrap to protect her scantily-clad curves from the chill of a rising breeze – an obvious disappointment to Charlie, whose eyes returned reluctantly to their sockets.

Andreu seemed to sense the qualms that this deterioration in the weather had brought about in at least one or two of his guests. We shouldn't worry, he told us with a casual shrug. This was only a momentary *contretemps* – a little Mediterranean sneeze – the change of *les saisons, non?* Everything would return to normal *bientôt.* '*Pas de problème!*'

I hoped he was right, and I could see from Ellie's tense expression that she was praying that he was, too. Not being the best of sailors even in a stabilised, ocean-going ship, it would be interesting to see how she coped with anything rougher than millpond flat in this little vessel.

But Andreu appeared to know what he was about, exuding confidence as he eased open the throttle and steered seaward. He was obviously well accustomed to the task in hand. And this was reflected in the confidence of his children, who had rushed on deck as soon as we'd got underway, and were now sitting with their legs dangling over the front of the boat, holding on tightly to the rails and squealing in delight as the spray from the bow waves broke over them.

Then, no sooner had we cleared Es Pantaleu islet, leaving the shelter of the bay behind, than the sun emerged from its cloak of cloud and, as if by magic, the sea reverted once more to an almost flat calm.

'*Voilà!*' Andreu laughed, nudging the throttle further open. 'Like I tell you, it was only a little sneeze, *n'est pas?*'

And he was right. In contrast to the choppy seas of a moment ago, bright ribbons of reflected sunlight now snaked lazily over the smooth water, across which a zephyr-like breeze wafted up from the south – a balmy yet invigorating breath of the Mediterranean. Up ahead, the hulking mass of Dragonera Island seemed to hover above the sea on a shimmering cushion of light, while off to our right, a scattering of houses looked out from the pine-fringed coast like little boxes blown ashore by a winter storm.

While Ellie and Josephine joined the two young children up front, the boys and I stood by the helm with Andreu and listened to the story of his family background. He had been born and had spent most of his life in France. So, he astutely deduced, we would be wondering why he had such a typically *mallorquín* Christian name as Andreu, *non?*

'*Oui,*' we said.

D'accord, he continued, this was because, although his mother was French, his father was a Mallorcan, who had left the island when a penniless young man to seek work in the southern French Port of Marseilles. As we would know, there had been a healthy export trade in oranges from Mallorca to Marseilles for centuries, so there was nothing unusual in young *mallorquines* going there in search of a better living. Times were hard on the island back then in the thirties, we would understand, long before anyone even dreamed that there would ever be a booming tourist industry like today. *En tout cas,* his father had worked very hard for several years, lugging heavy crates of fruit about on the quayside for long hours every day, until the time came when he had finally saved enough money to return to Mallorca to fulfil his dream of buying a little orange grove of his own.

'A 'appy ending, *non?*' Andreu asked, arching an eyebrow in typically French-inquisitive fashion.

'*Oui,*' we said again.

'*Non!*' he replied flatly. What his father had carelessly forgotten, he pointed out, was that his fellow Spaniards had fought a bloody civil war in his absence. Andreu raised his shoulders and dropped the corners of his mouth as if to say, 'Nothing wrong with that. *Mais oui,* an easy mistake to make.' The trouble was, the Spanish authorities had had a different view of the matter. They judged that Andreu's father had been swanning about in the South of France when he should have been back home in Spain helping his *compatriotas* in their struggles. They promptly confiscated his savings, therefore, and threw him in jail. On his release, he was back where he'd started several years earlier – broke and with no prospect of work in his war-ravaged native land. So, back to Marseilles it was to do it all over again.

While Andreu paused to contemplate this sad turn of fortune, I squinted through the dazzling sunlight bouncing off the limpid water ahead of us. I could still see the scrub-mottled shape of Dragonera through the glare, but (and this troubled me) considerably less of it than a few minutes ago. What I had taken to be a mirage-like cushion of light at its base, had expanded horizontally upwards and was already covering half of the island.

Andreu caught my puzzled look. '*Brouillard*,' he calmly stated. 'Fog. How you say *en L'Écosse*, "Scotch meest", *c'est vrais?*' He laughed aloud.

I smiled weakly and nodded my head. Fog! What the hell next?

There was something strangely dream-like about the scene now – the sun glinting on the placid sea around us, the distant outlook blurred by the spreading mist, and still the tiny hermitage atop the summit of Dragonera floating on its own little cloud in an otherwise cloudless sky. The coastline, too, had become shrouded behind a drifting film of humid air, so that, looking around, we seemed to be totally alone, sailing on a surreal sea, silent except for the soporific rhythm of the engine and the quiet lapping of the wash fanning out from the prow of the boat.

My mind was transported back to those weird tales of Mediterranean mythology, which laboriously I'd had to translate from Virgil's *Aeneid* and the like in Latin classes at school. And, in this oddly illusory atmosphere, it wouldn't have surprised me to see Medusa or some hellish nine-headed sea serpent rising from the depths right there beside us.

The shrieks of Andreu's two children jarred me out of my fantasising. It wasn't the sudden emergence of a horrific Hydra that had excited them, though, but a dolphin – the beautiful creature joining our expedition in a joyous leap through the air, then leading us on our way by effortlessly riding the bow wave right beneath the children's feet. It was soon joined by two companions, one on either side of the boat, skimming through the water with consummate ease only an arm's length away from where we were standing. Like countless others, we had watched and delighted at the aquatic antics of dolphins in captive environments like Mallorca's own 'Marineland', but to see these enchanting animals close up in the wild like this was a wholly different experience.

'Magic!' was how Charlie described it. I couldn't have suggested a more apt description. And the realisation that the dolphins were swimming along with us by choice, and obviously enjoying it, made the spectacle even more special. Sleek, graceful creatures with a smile on their faces and a mischievous twinkle in their eyes, having fun while enthralling transient visitors to *their* very own domain. 'Magic!'

We continued to watch them while Andreu picked up the thread of his story…

His father's second Marseilles experience had proved to be very different from the first, in that this time he soon met and fell in love with a girl whom he eventually married. Domestic roots, naturally, had then to be established in France and, with a baby on the way, his father had been obliged to channel his ambition in a different direction from his original one of one day returning to his native Mallorca to grow oranges. With three mouths to feed, and still working as a fruit porter at the docks, the likelihood of being able to save enough capital to realise that dream was now nil. So, with a borrowed handcart and a tiny rented tin shed, he started his own fruit-importing company.

He had shrewdly spotted an opportunity in pineapples, which had been unavailable in much of post-war France, but which had started to arrive in limited quantities – often just a few boxes flung on board to fill up hold-space on merchant ships plying their trade between West Africa and Marseilles. Small, tentative beginnings, but the start of an enterprise which, in the space of a few years, was to see Andreu's father reaping handsome rewards in a rapidly expanding business. Before long, he did have enough money to return to Mallorca, not to buy an orange grove this time, but to invest in a strip of wooded hillside overlooking the sea on the edge of Port d'Andratx, then still a tiny fishing village. Locals had considered him a fool at the time. *Hombre*, what use was a piece of steep mountain and a chunk of rocky shore to anyone?

Andreu chuckled at the thought. Now that Port d'Andratx was rapidly becoming the Saint-Tropez of Mallorca, that same swathe of hillside, which his father had bought for a relatively insignificant amount of pesetas back then, was now worth *beaucoup d'argent*. '*Une fortune, mon Dieu!*' All the more so since his father had been quick to realise the potential of the site, had first had a hacienda-style holiday house built for himself right on the seafront, and had subsequently sunk capital into building four further villas at discreet intervals all the way up the pine-clad mountainside. And this, long before construction costs rose to current inflated levels. Now, comparatively tiny plots of land in that area were being snapped up for ridiculous amounts of money by royalty, millionaire film stars, pop icons and supermodels to have their luxury hideaways built on.

'So, the locals aren't calling your father a fool any more,' I concluded, marvelling at this tale of *mallorquín* ingenuity and perfect timing – jail term notwithstanding.

Andreu merely smiled modestly, and, although he was clearly proud of his father's achievements, I got the impression that he had been brought up *not* to take his family's hard-won wealth for granted. As if to underline this, he told us that he had been made to work his way up through the company, right from heaving crates about on the Marseilles docks to managing the firm's now-burgeoning French headquarters, to opening and supervising the development of their London branch, and now to doing the same here on Mallorca.

'You say that you've gone fishing in these waters before,' I half asked, looking anxiously at the solid wall of fog now masking the whole of Dragonera. The island had effectively disappeared, and wisps of the culprit mist were now swirling around us, dimming the sun and imparting a damp chill to the air.

'*Mais oui, certainement,*' Andreu affirmed. 'All of my life I have come to Mallorca for *les vacances*, and my father would always take me out here in just such a *llaud* as this.'

I noticed him glancing askance at me, a knowing smile on his lips.

'Do not worry, *mon ami,*' he said, 'I will not miss Dragonera.'

I felt like telling him that it wasn't inadvertently sailing past the island that bothered me, it was the possibility of driving straight into it. But I said nothing. Although I have to admit that, at that moment, I did put more faith in the dolphins piloting us clear of shipwreck than I did in Andreu steering blindly into a peasouper the way he was doing.

Within minutes we were enveloped in the thick fog. Visibility zero. Unconcerned, Andreu cut the motor and shouted to Josephine to drop anchor. The dolphins chattered their farewells and were gone. Silence. An eerie, claustrophobic silence, without even the drone of a friendly foghorn to remind us that there was other life out there somewhere.

'The lair of the dragon, my father calls this spot,' said Andreu, who was busying himself handing out fishing tackle to everyone.

'You mean you can tell where you are?' I queried, peering into the dense murk for the faintest sign of the huge island that he inferred we were lying alongside.

'*Mais naturellement*,' he said with a nonchalant shrug of the shoulders. 'The lair of the dragon. We are here, *sans doute. Voici!*' He handed me a baited fishing line. '*Et maintainent*, we must catch the fishes for the supper, *non? Allons-y!*'

Now, what I know about fishing could be inscribed on a pinhead. In a way, I envy the bloke with his flies on his hat who can sit the livelong day in what is obviously blissful relaxation, skilfully casting his line with dextrous flicks of the wrist, while puffing on a pipe and dreaming of 'the big one' that will be bending his rod double any moment now. But, although probably less fulfilled because of it, I've never been particularly attracted to that universally popular pastime myself. Something to do with lack of patience and no natural gift for dextrous wrist action, I suppose.

In fact, the one and only previous time I'd ever had a go at fishing had been many years earlier, when I was playing clarinet with the Clyde Valley Stompers jazz band during a summer season on the Island of Arran, off the West Coast of Scotland. Our renowned trumpet player, a chubby and incurable angling freak called Malky Higgins, managed to persuade me to put to sea with him one afternoon in a ridiculously tiny dinghy. It was powered (for want of a more appropriate word) by one of those put-put outboard motors that should carry a heart attack warning, requiring you, as they do, to yank endlessly on a piece of string in a usually fruitless attempt at jolting life into their wheezing innards. Malky had the required fisherman's doggedness, though, and despite all my misgivings as a devout non-swimmer, I was soon sitting two miles out in the Firth of Clyde, dangling my toyshop line and bent pin in the fathomless water. Malky, meantime, stood foursquare beside me in the bobbing tub, showing off his casting prowess with the latest of hi-tech game-fishing rods, mandatory pipe clenched firmly in his teeth.

'Ling,' he said resolutely.

'Come again?'

'Ling. Big long fish. Like a barracuda. A guy caught one out here yesterday. Saw it in the pub last night. Six foot if it was an inch. Fought like buggery, the guy said.'

OK, so Malky did have a tendency towards gross exaggeration, but hell, even if he hooked a fish only half that length, the chances of hauling it aboard without the bathtub boat capsizing seemed ominously slim to me. For the next three hours, I sat cursing my foolhardiness for allowing myself to be talked into this daft trip. But still Malky stood there and continued casting, pausing only occasionally to glug down a slug of McEwan's Export from his steadily diminishing stash of cans.

At about six o' clock I checked my watch. The ordeal was nearing an end at last. We'd have to start back for shore very soon, or risk being late for the gig. I told Malky so.

'One last go,' he said, drawing out armlengths of line from his reel in preparation for the cast of all casts. 'There's a ling about here somewhere. I can feel it in ma fuckin' water, man.'

I was both amazed by and despaired at the unflagging optimism of the man. Why on earth would he want to waste the best part of a sunny day floating on a watery wilderness when he could be having fun with his wife and kids back on the beach? A beach which we couldn't even see from way out there! I wound my junior fishing line round its little rectangular frame, then reached back and prepared to pull the outboard's start-up cord.

'YA-HEE-EE-EE!' came the frenzied yell. 'GOT YE, Y' BASTARD!'

The boat started to rock violently, and I turned to see Malky fighting with his fishing rod, struggling to keep its end up with one hand, while frantically reeling in the straining line with the other. The rod was already flexing fit to break. Malky's face was purple, sweat dribbling down his cheeks, veins on his neck standing out like the bloated lugworms in his bait bucket. His left foot was braced against the gunnel of the boat, which was now listing so far over that water was slopping in – and far too quickly for my liking.

'Watch it, Malky!' I shouted. 'You'll have us both over the bloody side, for Christ's sake!'

'Ling!' he panted, struggling for breath. 'Told ye! Must be a monster one an' all!' He continued his battle, deaf to my near-hysterical protestations. 'Just get ready t' grab the bastard as soon as it hits the surface, right!'

It was me hitting the surface that I was worried about. With *my* zero-buoyancy metabolism I'd shoot straight to the bottom like a rogue torpedo. Frantically, I started to bail the rising water out of the boat with cupped hands.

'Let it go, Malky! Cut it loose! It's not worth drowning for a bloody fish!'

'There's the bugger now, see? Fuckin' giant, right enough, eh!'

Malky's rod had now adopted the shape of an inverted letter 'u' – a wildly quivering letter 'u', the blunt end of which must have been doing his future paternal prospects no favours at all. His pipe fell from his mouth as he gulped in a shuddering lungful of air in one final, muscle-busting effort to defeat his fishy foe.

'Grab the – urghh – bastard, man! Quick!'

Terrified of what I would be faced with, I gingerly peeped over the side, one white-knuckled hand clinging for dear life to a rowlock on the high side of the lurching boat. I could see it now – just. A strange black shape about a metre down, its outline distorted by the rough water being whipped up by the bucking of the dinghy. As Malky heaved and grunted, his head thrown back to take the strain, the thing inched its way upwards, until its true form was finally revealed to my disbelieving eyes. I reached into the water and seized its long tail.

'Phew! Well done, Malky,' I gasped. 'They'll be impressed in the pub tonight, all right.'

'Yeah?'

'Yeah!'

I hauled his vanquished adversary from the sea. 'Look,' I chuckled, swamped by a great wave of relief. 'You've caught the bleedin' anchor!'

Andreu let out a reserved Gallic chortle after I'd told him this yarn while taking our fishing positions around the perimeter of the deck. And although his only comment was a rather superior, '*Quelle stupidité!*', I did notice that he made a point of claiming the stern of his boat for himself – the opposite end from the anchor rope.

A slight breeze had come up, wafting the fog into slowly moving drifts, and revealing fleeting glimpses of rocky shapes of indeterminate size and distance. But a change in the mood of the sea was happening, too. The *llaud*, until then floating immobile on a mirror-flat surface, started to roll on the rising swell. The white of waves breaking on a shore could just be made out through the dispersing mist, the sound of their splashing a welcome relief from the spooky silence in which we'd been marooned.

Little Michelle and Sasha chattered away to each other in French, each instructing the other on how best to go about the business of fishing, and both totally oblivious to this further change in the weather. They'd obviously seen it all before. Ellie, conversely, was already burping quietly into a clenched fist, little finger demurely raised, facial colour a delicate shade of chartreuse.

'Feeling OK?' I asked her.

No reply.

I saw that Charlie was also beginning to look a bit peaky. Not even the tantalising proximity to his face of Josephine's cleavage as she helped thread a maggot onto his hook drew his unblinking stare away from the heaving waters on which the boat was rocking and swaying ever more noticeably.

'*Alors*, Peter,' Andreu said, clearly unaware of the malaise threatening to overcome two of his guests, 'Your son Sandy here has told me that you have a fruit farm. *C'est vrais?*'

'Yes, that's right. A little *finca* between the mountains north of Andratx.'

'And will you sell me your fruits?'

Now we were talking! The very subject I'd been waiting for an opportunity to broach. Señor Jeronimo, who owned the only wholesale outlet for our produce that we'd so far managed to establish, had already warned me that he would have very little demand for our summer and autumn fruit – kakis, quinces, figs, apricots, loquats and so on – and come winter he wouldn't be able to guarantee taking *all* of our orange crop again. His business was small, catering mainly as it did for commercial customers in and around his local Peguera area, so there was always going to be a limit to what he could buy from us.

Andreu, on the other hand, was in the process of setting up a new branch of a huge business with established export outlets. He was going to need all the fruit he could get his hands on – and soon. And the fact that we would only be able to supply relatively small amounts of any one kind was going to be of no consequence... '*À condition que la qualité est excellente, naturellement.*'

'*Naturellement!*' I concurred, hardly able to conceal my Christmas-come-early delight. A real threat to our financial survival had been removed, and all an indirect result of Charlie having created an international brawl on the basketball pitch that morning.

'It's an ill wind,' I remarked to Andreu.

'*Non*, only another sneeze of the *climat Méditerranéen*,' he blandly replied, obviously mistaking my abbreviated version of the English proverb for a criticism of the deteriorating weather. '*Et regardez* – see how it improves the views!'

I looked towards where he'd gestured. 'Jeez!' I wheezed. 'It's frightening!'

While I gaped in awe, Andreu released another of his French-style nasal chuckles. '*Oui*, is very frightening, *non*? *Pourquoi* you think my father he is calling this the lair of the dragon?'

The freshening breeze had cleared away the fog that had been blanketing the area of water between us and Dragonera Island, leaving a clear view of sheer cliffs towering menacingly above us. From this acute angle I couldn't even see the top of them. The *llaud* was but a tiny bobbing cork in this scale of things, and the feeling of insignificance that had instantly hit me, escalated into one of heartstopping shock when I realised just how close we were to the boulder-strewn foot of those looming crags. No more than ten metres, by my reckoning. A fraction of a turn of the helm in the wrong direction when we'd been steaming through the mists and we'd have been flotsam and jetsam. Even now, the slightest change in wind direction would promptly see us doomed, the boat converted into matchsticks, anchor or no anchor. Well, that was my considered opinion as a non-cliff-climbing landlubber who got panic attacks in the bath and vertigo just watching *The Roadrunner* cartoons on telly. And I did know a bit about anchors, after all.

'*C'est magnifique, n'est pas?*' Andreu sighed.

'*Oui*,' I replied without conviction. But before I could voice my concerns about the safety aspect of our position, Sandy called out:

'Hey, I think I've caught something!'

He certainly had, judging by the animated twitching of his line as he pulled it in.

'*Cap roig*,' Andreu stated as soon as the victim exited the water. 'That's what they call them here. Scorpion fish in English, I think. Hmm, ugly, but *délicieux*.'

Ugly was right – a spiky red creature with a face so grotesque that it would have made Quasimodo pass for a heart-throb.

'It's a bit small,' I said, watching it flapping about on the end of Sandy's line and thinking to myself that it wouldn't have looked out of place in a goldfish bowl.

'Yeah, I'll throw him back in,' said Sandy.

'*Non, non, non!*' Andreu protested. 'You must keep it to make the bouillabaisse. Mm-m-m-wah! *Exquis!* But be careful how you hold him to remove the hook. '*Sacré bleu*, those long spines on his back are like swords.'

As if to object at the dastardly act of catching this miserable little specimen, the sea suddenly became more ruffled, angry rollers tossing the boat about quite violently now. While Andreu droned on about the other ingredients of his beloved Marseillaise fish soup, I watched Ellie and Charlie closely, their round-shouldered stance with heads drooping over the side of the boat a clear indication of how they were feeling. I pitied them, having been the victim of seasickness myself once or twice before. There can be few sensations more awful than being gripped by that affliction when trapped in a floating world which pitches and yaws incessantly beneath your feet, and even the faintest whiff of diesel turns your stomach even more.

Blissfully unmindful of their plight, Andreu rounded off his lengthy lecture on the perfect recipe for bouillabaisse by concluding that it was surely the most excellent seafood dish ever. 'Apart, that is,' he added after a moment's thought, 'from the luxury of raw oysters, *naturellement*.'

That was the last straw for Ellie. If she baulked at the sight of a tiny stewed snail that reminded her of something which had just dropped out of someone's nostril, the mere thought of raw oysters (giant gobs, she likened them to) slithering down her gullet was enough to make her gag. Except that, in her present state of advanced nausea, the gagging process was bypassed and a full-blown puke materialised. And that did it for Charlie. Side-by-side and with bums in the air, he and his mother then treated everyone to an accomplished display of formation vomiting, much to the amusement of Michelle and Sasha, who sniggered delightedly behind their hands.

But the *pièce de résistance* was still to come. On Charlie's final and most productive retch, a loud fart escaped his lofted backside, echoing off the nearby cliffs like a mini thunderclap and sending the two young children into fits of unrestrained laughter.

'The dragon roars,' I offered sheepishly to their embarrassed mother.

'The *mal de mer*,' Andreu smirked. 'I think perhaps it is time to head for home.'

It had been an interesting jaunt, I reflected on the return journey. Mutually beneficial business connections had been made and, I suspected, good friendships had been struck up, despite our having ruined our hosts' fishing trip. And while it had perhaps been wrong, despite Andreu's protestations to the contrary, to have taken that undersized scorpion fish from the sea, Ellie and Charlie had gone some way to making amends by treating its brothers and sisters to an unexpected feast. A sort of piscatorial karma, you might say.

I mentioned this thought to Ellie as we walked up the slipway at Sant Elm after waving goodbye to Andreu and his family. She declined to enter the debate.

'Something wrong with your legs, is there, Charlie?' Sandy enquired.

I turned to look at Charlie shuffling along on his own behind us. And, sure enough, he did have a rather awkward gait.

'Suffering a bit from the after-effects of the basketball brawl?' I asked, waiting for him to catch up.

He shook his head, the dejected look on his face strangely at odds with the twinkle in his eyes.

'Why are you walking that funny stiff way, then?' Sandy said.

There was a moment or two of silence, then Charlie muttered, 'Remember that backfire when I was spewing?'

We all nodded our heads, anticipating the inevitable.

'Major follow-through, I'm afraid,' confirmed Charlie, unable to suppress a silly titter.

Ellie clapped a hand to her mouth and made a beeline for the water's edge. The fishes, it seemed, were in for a second helping of *paella*.

Sandy held up the lifeless little scorpion fish by its tail. 'You've got a lot to answer for, mate,' he grunted, then threw it to the two stray cats that had been fighting over the spilled contents of a trash bag earlier in the day. 'Something tells me Mum won't be making us bouillabaisse for quite some time.'

- Nine -

A PIG IN A POKE – NO KIDDING!

Being the valley's most notable livestock farmer (his ramshackle little farmyard resembled a shipwrecked version of Noah's Ark), old Pep was interested in and a self-acclaimed expert on just about everything to do with animals. It didn't take him long, then, to come over the lane to Ca's Mayoral in order to cast a critical eye over Bonny, our recently acquired boxer pup. I was in the yard behind the house trying to teach her to sit and stay on command when Pep sauntered in. He leaned cross-legged against the gate pillar, saying nothing but watching everything, as was his wont.

After a few minutes, Bonny grew bored with what she obviously regarded as the pointless game of sitting and staying, and trotted over to say hello to Pep. Poker-faced, he looked down at her sniffing the Aladdin's cave of interesting animal odours that constituted the major component of his trouser legs, but kept his hands firmly in his pockets.

'They make good attack dogs, these mastiffs,' he eventually observed.

'Boxer, Pep. She's actually a boxer.'

'Same thing. *Coño*, I knew a man once who was attacked by one of these mastiffs. Bit his hand off in one mouthful. Strong jaws. *Muy potente*. Can't even prise them open with a crowbar once they get a grip of you.'

'Maybe that's a bulldog you're thinking about,' I said, scratching my nose to hide a smile.

'Same thing. *Es igual*.'

Bonny squatted down and had a pee at Pep's feet, the pongs wafting from his trouser legs clearly indicating to her that this was the right place to do it.

Pep watched her, expressionless. 'Better get her filleted before she's old enough to get herself pupped. Those randy mongrels along in the village there…' He paused for the skilful launch of a mucous missile villagewards from the corner of his mouth. 'Horny enough to shaft a knothole in a rotten tree stump, those *bastardos*. *Hombre*, first time they catch wind of her in heat they'll be swarming here like priests round a cartload of choirboys.'

He had a point there. And although he had conveniently neglected to mention it, there was also the possibility of his own goofy dog Perro coming a-courting when the time was right. Mind you, it was doubtful if Perro would have the smarts to know what the purpose of his visit was once he'd got here. Still, maybe we'd have to give serious thought to Pep's sterilisation suggestion all the same.

He re-crossed his legs, continuing to scrutinise Bonny as she reverted to sniffing his trousers. She was clearly enjoying this doggy quiz game of 'Guess-the-Guff'. All part of her education as a farm dog, I thought, and as Pep didn't seem to mind, I let her get on with it.

'Ears,' he said. 'Better get them done *pronto*. Leave it too late with these mastiff pups and it won't work.'

'Ears? Sorry, Pep, you've lost me.'

Pep slowly raised his eyes and glared at me from beneath the overhanging eaves of his black beret. '*Cuarenta putas!* What is the point of a dog having the face of a killer with silly, floppy ears like that on top? Neither one thing nor the other, *amigo!* Scare *bandidos?* Hah! She will be a laughing stock, and so will you!'

Now I got it. Pep was assuming that I'd follow the practice – popular with boxer owners in many countries, including Spain – of having the pup's ears cut into points to make it look more 'ferocious'. I'd seen several young boxers that had had the operation moping about for weeks with their 'trimmed' ears bandaged round corks until they stood erect (maybe!) on their own. I thought it was, if not cruel, then unnecessary, believing as I do that boxers' heads look perfect without any such cosmetic interference. And besides, I've never seen a boxer yet that had what Pep imagined was 'the face of a killer'. Quite the contrary, as behind those puggish features lies one of the gentlest, most fun-loving natures to be found in any breed of dog. That had certainly been my experience, and I explained all this to Pep as diplomatically as I could – adding (rashly, as I was about to discover) that cutting dogs' ears was forbidden in Britain in any case.

He looked as though he was about to have a seizure.

'*Gran Bretaña!*' he spluttered. 'Cutting the ears of dogs is forbidden in *Gran Bretaña!* Puh!' He made to take his hands from his pockets, thought better of it, and instead raised one dusty boot to point at Bonny's docked tail. 'And are you telling me that in *Gran Bretaña* it is forbidden to cut dogs' tails too?'

Uh-oh! I'd walked straight into this one, and the look of concession on my face was enough for Pep.

'So, in *Gran Bretaña* you frown upon making an attack dog look more macho by adjusting the shape of its ears,' he smirked, savouring the sweetness of the forthcoming kill, 'but you do not mind seeing it going about without a mudguard for its arse!'

He had me there, so I reckoned a slight change of tack was needed to steer me away from further trouble. We hadn't bought Bonny to be an attack dog as such, I said; to be a watchdog, certainly, but also as a family pet.

Pep shook his head in dismay. In typically reproachful fashion, he wagged a finger at me, pointing out that, in order to teach a dog to be aggressive towards unwelcome strangers, all thoughts of treating it as a pet must be banished from the trainer's mind. '*Hijo de puta*,' he scoffed, 'if I had a hundred pesetas for every dog I have successfully taught to defend his master's property – even to the death...'

Two thoughts came instantly to mind. Firstly, Pep, like many others who took them on 'face' value only, was obviously not at all comfortable with 'mastiffs'. Witness his reluctance to expose his hands in the presence of this baby of the breed. Secondly, it struck me that *he* was a fine one to boast about having aggression-training skills. After all, Perro, his own self-styled 'attack' dog, had almost licked me to death the first time I'd ventured into Pep's farmyard, and had then proceeded to urinate all over me in tail-wagging excitement. Could it be that Pep had trained him to drown trespassers?

I didn't want to get dragged into a verbal joust with him on that point, though, because I knew I'd come off second best, no matter what. Yet Pep still stared at me, waiting for my reaction to his last observation.

My bacon was saved by Perro himself lolloping into the yard, the usual gormless grin on his face, dribbling tongue dangling out of the side of his mouth. Perro was a *Ca de bestiar*, Mallorca's native all-purpose breed, resembling large, heavy-boned black Labradors, and used for everything from herding sheep to hunting wild goats. And, in keeping with the inherent qualities of the breed, which Pep was forever extolling, Perro was indeed a handsome lad. It's just that he had been at the end of the line when the savvy rations were being handed out. He stopped, took one look at Bonny sniffing his master's trousers, then trotted forward, lifted his leg and squirted a swift property marker on Pep's boot.

Bonny had never seen such a huge creature as this before, but instead of being fazed by his presence, she assumed – perhaps due to Perro's loopy mien – that there could be fun afoot. She lowered her head, front legs splayed, rear end in the air and wiggling wildly, then looked up into Perro's face and let out a mischievous '*YIP!*'

Startled, Perro jumped back, gave an unconvincing growl, and made a rapid exit back through the gateway, tail firmly between his legs.

'Sign of a good attack dog,' Pep advised with a confident nod of the head. 'Never plays games with pups. *Va bé.*'

'*Buenas!*' piped a little voice behind me.

'*Weh-ep!*' croaked Pep, looking past me and briefly doffing his beret.

I turned to see our other neighbour, old Maria Bauzá, looking over the wall that separated our two farms.

'I have something *muy importante* to tell you,' she said to me, then struck up a five-minute conversation in *mallorquín* with Pep, at the end of which silence reigned while they contemplated the gravity of whatever they had been talking about. The only words I'd understood were 'Don Pedro *ací*' and '*porcs*', which was a clue that pigs and I had been at least one topic of discussion.

I cleared my throat to remind Maria that I was still there.

'*Sí?*' she said enquiringly.

'Something important. You, ehm – you said you've got something important to tell me.'

'*Sí?* And what might that have been?' she demanded to know.

I pulled a 'search me' shrug.

'I see you have a dog. No good with sheep, that type.'

Before I could remind her that I didn't have any sheep, she launched into one of her lengthy discourses – this one on everything canine, from how to remove ticks from a dog's skin with a lit cigarette to the kindest way of drowning pups. Midway through, Pep yawned and bade us a muttered, '*Adéu.*' I envied him. I took a surreptitious glance at my watch. Dammit, I was already late for a meeting with Jordi, who had insisted that I go with him to buy tomato plants today. Still, not to worry, he'd be late, anyway. Everybody normally was (except Pepe Suau), and I was gradually getting used to it.

'And,' Maria ultimately declared, punctuating the end of her lecture with a resounding clatter of her trusty hoe on top of the wall, 'you would have been better off buying a German Shepherd!' With that, she turned to leave, all relevant points (and several others) having been firmly made.

'*Gracias*,' I called after her. '*Hasta luego*, Maria. See you later.'

Grateful that today's diatribe had been a relatively short one, I gathered up Bonny and headed for the house.

'Pigs!' It was Maria again, her squeaky shout ricocheting off the house wall. 'The farm supply store in Andratx has a litter of weaners in today. I chose the best one for you. Good price, too. I told the manager you would pick it up later. *Adéu*.'

Curses! I'd been putting off buying a pig since the first time Maria insisted I needed one months ago. Now she had craftily cornered me into it.

'How am I going to wriggle out of this without both offending her and letting myself in for a tongue-lashing?' I asked Ellie back in the kitchen.

'Why wriggle? There's an empty pen next to the tractor shed. Stick a pig in it. As Maria says, it'll fatten up nicely for nothing on fallen fruit and kitchen swill. Makes sense to me.'

Fair enough logic, I had to admit, although a touch incongruous coming from Ellie after her anti-carnivore stance at the Restaurante Ca'l Dimoni. But we'd once kept a few pigs back in Scotland and hadn't had our troubles to seek. Something told me it wasn't going to be any different this time.

Jordi was sitting outside the Bar Nuevo when I drove into the square in Andratx. Trust me to be late on the one occasion he'd been on time.

'Bloody 'ell! I being think you no baster coming,' he said by way of greeting.

I apologised and began to explain about having been waylaid by old Maria. But Jordi wasn't interested.

'I been being make one bloody fine bargain this morning,' he cut in, a self-satisfied smile creasing his face. '*Two* bloody fine bargains, man. Oh, yes. Up Jordi's *finca*. I take you seeing them.'

It was then that I noticed the half-empty glass of beer on the table in front of him. Still smiling at the thought of his bargains, he reached out and downed the contents in one gulp.

'Ones for the roads,' he said, then leaned round and shouted through the open bar door, 'Ay, Guillermo! *Dues cervesas, si us plau!*'

Jordi ordering two beers wouldn't have been at all unusual, of course – perfectly normal, in fact, if it hadn't been that he'd been warned off alcohol for life by his doctor just a few weeks earlier.

'Given up the orange juice, Jordi?' I pried.

He swatted the air. 'Pah! Bloody damn baster orange juices been being make Jordi's tripe nip.' He rubbed his midriff. 'Too many acid for me.' That look of glum self-pity returned to his face. 'Baster doctor he been telling me, OK then, Jordi, just drinking the waters now onwards.' He thought about that for a few moments, then said, 'Mayorky waters having too much limeys in it, oh yes. Blocking up every house pipes and making many boulders in Jordi's steaks.' He rubbed his kidneys to illustrate the point. 'Baster orange juices and Mayorky waters been being rot all Jordi's intesticles. Is bloody ridickliss...'

'So, it's back on the beer, eh?' I said, stifling a snigger.

Jordi chose to ignore that silly question, directing his attention instead to the two medium-sized glasses of draught lager that Guillermo was placing on the table.

'Bloody 'ell, Guillermo!' he erupted indignantly. 'I tol' you only to putting me a small ones now'days!'

Guillermo flashed me a knowing wink as he picked up Jordi's empty glass, which was exactly the same size as the two full ones.

'*Salud*, Jordi,' I said. 'Here's to your intesticles.'

Jordi raised his glass. 'Many cheer, man,' he beamed. 'Your very good health down the hatches.'

Jordi's *finca* or, more accurately, *huerto* – really just a vegetable patch with a tiny implement shed on it – boasted certain distinct advantages, despite its diminutive size. It was located an easy moped ride out of town, comprised a beautifully level wedge of deep, fertile soil, enjoyed the cool air funnelled through the Coll d'Andritxol pass, yet occupied the sunniest of spots sheltered by the mountains on either side. But the most fortunate feature of all was its proximity to the limitless supply of water from the commercially tapped spring right next door. Compared to the many thousands of gallons pumped into an endless stream of road tankers calling at the well every day, the amount of water needed for generous irrigation of Jordi's *huerto* was minuscule; but priceless, all the same. And the lush appearance of the vegetables that he was growing there provided ample proof.

'But I still be needing the shits,' he was at pains to point out while proudly showing me his rows of potatoes, beans and onions. 'And this is why Jordi been buying the big bargains this morning.'

I was fascinated.

He ushered me towards the *casita de aperos*, a windowless stone shack that backed onto the steep mountainside.

'I sometime be sleeping in here for the *siestas*,' he informed me while undoing the padlock, an expectant grin on his face. 'Many cool for the resting in pieces.'

He shoved open the creaky wooden door and beckoned me inside. Before my eyes had become accustomed to the darkness, my nostrils were invaded by the combined odours of dampness, petrol, stale cooking oil and animals. Something bleated in the gloom. Something else bleated in response.

Jordi nudged me. 'Damn baster bargains,' he chortled. 'Good ones.' He reached up and lit a paraffin lantern hanging from a woodwormy roof beam.

The inside of the *casita* was a shambles of handtools, sacks, tin cans, an ancient two-stroke cultivator, and a gas camping stove complete with well-used frying pan. Grinning broadly, Jordi gestured towards the back of the shed, where two black goat kids were chewing away contentedly at the stuffing of a mattress on the floor.

Unconcerned at the kids devouring what I presumed was his *siesta*-time resting place, Jordi gave a delighted chuckle.

'Tol' you, eh? Bloody good ones, and many cheapness. Now, with the shits of the goats, Jordi's *finca* gonna get the most better fertilisings for free.'

Right on cue, one of the kids laid a generous deposit of dung on his mattress.

'See,' Jordi laughed, 'him being started bloody working already.' He told me that, until he had made an enclosure for them, he would have to tie the kids to a post outside, then asked if I would help put tethering collars on them. 'Baster goats no liking the collars first time, oh yes.'

How right he was.

No sooner had he lifted the two ancient leather belts from a nail on the wall than the kids exchanged glances through mischievous eyes, bleated a unison declaration of intent and cleared the doorway in one elegant leap. By the time Jordi and I had stumbled out of the *casita* to grab them, the kids were already high-tailing it up the mountain, dancing over screes and scampering up rock faces with total disregard for the forces of gravity. We made a token effort to give chase, but soon had to admit defeat. We were knackered after clambering up only a few yards, leaning against tree trunks and gasping for breath, while the kids looked mockingly down at us from a ledge high above. They bleated one final goaty laugh and were gone – bounding away into the forest and a life of freedom.

'Baster!' Jordi wheezed, staring forlornly at the two empty collars in his hand. 'Now Jordi *still* be needing the shits.'

A fitting epitaph, perhaps, to his brief career as a goatherd.

But Jordi was nothing if not resilient, and by the time we had set out in the car to buy our tomato plants, he had shrugged off the loss of his goats, laughing, joking and swearing as if the incident had never happened. His spirits had been lifted, no doubt, by another beer at the Bar Nuevo en route, but his 'tripe' wasn't complaining, so what the hell! That was Jordi's attitude to life these days, and who could blame him? He was the most gregarious of characters, who liked nothing better than to while away a spare minute or thirty talking – preferably over a couple of drinks – to anyone who would listen to him. Jordi thrived on company, a commodity which had been in short supply at home since his English wife had gone back to Coventry to look after her ageing father a few years earlier. So, between tending his *finca* and doing spells of casual work practising his trade as a carpenter for visiting yachties down at the Port of Andratx, Jordi would be found indulging his twin hobbies of talking and sipping a social drink at any one of half a dozen favourite watering holes in the vicinity. Being barred from one essential ingredient of this laid-back lifestyle had clearly been a blow, therefore. But, to his credit, Jordi had given the medical sentence a trial run, didn't fancy it, had decided that *his* chosen way of living was right for him, and his 'intesticles' would just have to look after themselves. So be it. And who knows? If he stuck to having just a few beers and avoided Olympian brandy-guzzling sessions with the likes of Wayne Murphy, maybe his own prognosis would prove to be better than the doctor's after all. It was certainly proving to be more fun in the short term, anyway.

The village of Banyalbufar is reputed to be where the best tomatoes on the island are grown, so it followed that that was where the best plants could be bought, too. Besides, Jordi had an old chum there who, according to Jordi at any rate, was the undisputed *maestro de maestros* of the art of tomato culture. But there was one snag, Jordi pointedly advised; his pal didn't sell his precious plants to just anyone – only to a few skilful growers like himself who could bring out the best in them. Reputations, I would understand, had to be protected, quality of produce maintained.

'That counts me out, then. I haven't grown a single tomato in my entire life.'

Jordi gave me a just-leave-it-to-me wink of assurance, settled back in his seat and instructed me to take the Estellencs road north from Andratx.

Climbing steadily through pine woods, the road soon clears the Coll de Sa Gremola pass, then winds its way along the rugged flanks of the mountains, occasional breaks in the trees allowing glimpses of the Mediterranean glinting in the sunlight far below. This breathtaking corniche clings to the Tramuntanas' riven contours for mile after mile, disappearing into an occasional short tunnel, then re-emerging to reveal nothing but a low barrier between the road and a sheer thousand-foot plunge to the sea.

Jordi was in his element, singing the praises of the spectacular visual surprises that his native island now presented around every corner. 'Better than the bloody damn French Riviera any day, man! Jordi been being there! Jordi be knowing!'

I hadn't been there, so I didn't know. But I was inclined to believe him, as I found it difficult to imagine any comparable landscape more stunning than this.

Jordi told me that there were special *miradores*, or viewing points, built into the mountainside at strategic locations along this route, all the way to the Cape of Formentor at the northernmost tip of the island. After we'd passed through the village of Estellencs, he suggested that we stop at one such place, this one incorporating an old *talaia*, or watchtower, perched on the edge of a rocky outcrop high above the sea, before the road sweeps down towards Banyalbufar. It was already well past midday, and with so much still to do back at Ca's Mayoral, I would much rather have pressed on and left sightseeing stops till another time. But Jordi, sensing my unease, advised me in no uncertain terms to be bloody *tranquilo* like him and to stop the baster car where he tol' me to.

And I was soon glad that he had imposed this little example of the *mañana* syndrome. The outlook from the Mirador de Ses Ànimes proved to be truly out of this world. Even for someone who doesn't particularly like heights, it was impossible not to be mesmerised by the view from the top of the *talaia*. A panorama of rugged headlands faded into the distance along the entire coastline, from Dragonera Island in the south to the point of Cap Gros, which marks the entrance to Port de Sóller, away to the north. It was easy now to understand why these towers had been built on such promontories, serving many centuries ago as lookout posts from which approaching pirate ships could be spotted early, and the warning relayed along the coast by bonfires.

Looking over the parapet, the perpendicular drop of the cliff from the base of the tower made it impossible to gauge just how high we were above the sea. But it *was* dizzily high. High enough to be looking down on speck-sized seagulls lazily circling on upcurrents of warm air. High enough for an outstretched thumb to cover the outline of a large yacht sailing silently past almost directly below. Yet behind us, the majestic Tramuntana ridges rose higher still, serrating the sky and dwarfing everything beneath them. It was a truly entrancing experience, and I could happily have dallied there, lost in the spell of it all. And I probably would have, if it hadn't been for Jordi jolting me out of my trance by abandoning the *mañana* principle for once.

'Come on, Crice sake!' he urged. 'If we don' be hurrying now, Jordi's friend Tomeu the tomaty man be being already away from his *finca* for the bloody lunch hours!'

And so we continued our scenic journey to Banyalbufar. Nestling in a wide fold in the lower slopes of Mola de Planicie Mountain, the village is typical of those that dot this rugged coast of Mallorca – cosy settlements of warm-coloured stone houses huddled together in glens that lead steeply down to tiny hidden coves. The unique combination of tranquillity, the serenity of the mountains, the proximity of the sea, and the purity of light have long attracted writers and artists to live and work in these charmed little communities. Yet the vast majority of inhabitants still belong to local families who, for generations, have earned an enviable-if-modest living from working the land and harvesting the sea.

But what sets Banyalbufar apart from the other villages is the sheer scale of its cultivated terraces, the *bancales*, which climb in seemingly endless steps from the craggy shoreline all the way up to the foot of the mountains' steepest slopes. The beautifully crafted retaining walls of these fertile ribbons of land follow the eccentric contours of the valley precisely, thereby enfolding every inch of cultivable soil.

We pulled up at the entrance to the village, and Jordi pointed out a complex system of stone-lined channels directing spring water from the mountains to *cisternas*, or large holding tanks, again stone-built and cleverly situated to provide the means of irrigation for every terrace in turn. In Jordi's opinion, the *bancales* of Banyalbufar deserved to be rated as one of the engineering Wonders of the World. And the fact that this amazing example of man's ingenuity is believed to date back over a thousand years, to the Arab occupation of the island, would prompt few to argue with him.

The *finca* of his friend Tomeu occupied a couple of terraces above the village, a stiff climb from the road up a series of stone stairways. Tomeu, a rotund, cheery-faced little man of about sixty, had just finished harrowing a patch of land when we staggered, gasping, into the field. He and Jordi greeted each other with typical Mallorcan gusto – hearty hugs and backslaps accompanying outpourings of chuckled banter in which the word '*coño*' featured prominently, as usual. Interestingly, the literal translation of *coño* into English is the taboo 'C' word. Yet in Spanish it's an everyday term of chummy familiarity, friendly salutation, or at worst mild exclamation; an inoffensive expression used equally freely by both sexes. It's one of those anomalies of language which, although aware of it, I still hadn't plucked up sufficient courage to use when talking in Spanish to the local folk. Let's just call it Caledonian reserve!

Once the preliminaries in *mallorquín* between the two old friends were over, Jordi told Tomeu that the three of us would converse in Castilian Spanish from now on. *El escocés aquí* (the Scotsman here) could cope with that quite well, he stated, though I was still 'being bloody damn useless' at understanding their island tongue. Tomeu shrugged a typical *no problema* shrug. But for all that, Jordi couldn't resist translating into English every Spanish phrase that Tomeu then uttered, a linguistic talent which Tomeu's wide-eyed smiles of admiration had Jordi smirking smugly.

Having flashed me a sly wink, he proceeded to spin a yarn to Tomeu about *el escocés aquí* being one of the top tomato growers in *Gran Bretaña*, now with my own *finca* near Andratx, where I planned to continue practising my famous skills under the wonderful Mallorcan sun. While I silently cringed, Jordi went on and on with ever more exaggerated hype about my tomato-growing prowess. I was praying that Tomeu wouldn't ask me a question on the subject, but fortunately he seemed too much in awe of Jordi's lengthy recitation of my tomato-producing CV to interrupt.

'I am honoured to have you visit my humble *finca*,' Tomeu said with a gracious little bow once Jordi had finally run out of lies. He took me by the elbow and motioned towards a higher terrace. 'Come, I will show you this year's show of young plants. I would value your advice on some of the new varieties – disease resistance, optimum fertiliser regimes, cropping potential and so on.'

'Oops!' I thought. 'Caught!'

But Jordi was quick to come to my rescue – *and* his own.

'No!' he said firmly, laying a restraining hand on Tomeu's arm. 'No time. *El escocés aquí* is a busy man. *Hombre*, he has come all this way today to *buy* your tomato plants, not to inspect them.'

Tomeu's face lit up, his mouth widening into a delighted grin. '*Coño!*' he cried, then clapped my cheeks repeatedly with both hands. '*Ay-y-y, coño-o-o-oh!*'

I had broken the *coño* barrier – twice. Things were looking up.

He would consider it a privilege to sell me some plants, he gushed, then put on a serious face to confirm Jordi's earlier caution that he was very careful about who he sold them to these days. Respected growers only. *Carám!* only two years ago he had sold plants to a man he didn't know, only to find that the *bastardo* had then neglected to tend them properly. The crop, of course, had turned out to be a disaster – some of the plants even dying. 'It was very bad for my reputation, as you will appreciate, even although no blame could fairly be laid at my door.' The smile returned to his chubby face. 'But in your case, *amigo*, there will be no such worries. *Al contrario*, with your permission, I may even visit your *finca* to learn something of the most recent methods of tomato culture, which Jordi says you are a master of.'

'Thanks, Jordi,' I muttered, while faking a warm smile for Tomeu. 'You've dropped me right in it.'

But Jordi merely threw me one of his 'get *tranquilo*, for Crice sake' looks, then told Tomeu what our respective tomato plant requirements would be, reminding his friend that *el escocés aquí* was in a hurry. 'He has a pig waiting for him in Andratx.'

'*Por supuesto!*' Tomeu grinned, this time taking both Jordi and I by the elbow. 'Of course, but first you must come into my *casita de aperos* for a moment. *Sí*, I have something very *especial* to give you.'

His little implement shed was the customary clutter of tools, boxes and other agricultural paraphernalia, plus a small wooden cupboard mounted on the wall over a workbench. Tomeu unlocked the cupboard, lifted out three glasses and set them down on the bench. Then, winking conspiratorially, he reached inside the cupboard again and produced an old stoneware flagon with a little circular handle on the neck and a cork stopper in the top.

I noticed Jordi's face pale. 'Fuck me!' he groaned in English. 'Not the baster *orujo!*'

I twigged instantly what had spooked him. *Orujo* being the fabled moonshine liquor of Spain, Jordi's dicky liver had obviously gone into spasm at the very thought of it.

Oblivious to his friend's 'tripe' worries, Tomeu started to pour the slightly cloudy potion into the first glass, assuring me as he did so that, unlike the sissy commercial versions to be seen on the gantries of some trendy bars nowadays, this *orujo* was the genuine article. '*Hombre*, drinking this stuff separates the men from the boys!'

I attempted, as politely as possible, to decline a glass of the rare spirit myself – driving, Guardia Civil and all that. With an embarrassed smile, I said I hoped he'd understand.

He didn't. 'Guardia Civil!' he scoffed. 'Why worry about them? There has been no notice regarding the road to Andratx today.'

What he was referring to was the police's thoughtful practice of advertising the date and times of planned roadside checks for drink driving in the local press a day or two before the event. Too good to be true, in my cynical opinion, being more accustomed to the less user-friendly ways of the Scottish 'polis'. But saying so to Tomeu would most likely only have prompted a response of, 'You are not in *Escocia* now, *amigo*, so drink up!'

He went on to explain that, although newfangled laws imposed by spoilsport sons of whores in Madrid had made it all but impossible to find the real *orujo* these days, he was fortunate enough to be trusted by one *anciano* who continued to make it – an old chap who'd learned the secret when working in the province of Galicia many years ago. '*Sí*,' he concluded ruefully, 'only the still of old Vicenç now remains – up in the mountains there at…' His words dissolved into a cagey chuckle, and he handed us our generously charged glasses, reminding Jordi of the many happy times they had spent nipping away at this wonderful bootleg booze over the years.

I watched a look of confusion cross Tomeu's face as Jordi stared glumly at his glass. '*Qué pasa, amigo?*' he asked. 'What's up? The glass not big enough for you?' He gave his friend a comforting slap on the shoulder.

'A-y-y-y, *no problema*, Jordi! Plenty more in the *jarra*. *Salud y pesetas*, eh!' With that, he clinked both of our glasses and downed the contents of his own in one.

What would Jordi do now, I wondered? He evidently didn't like the idea of owning up to his old drinking chum that he had been warned off the hard stuff. At the same time, I could see that common sense was telling him not to drink it. Common sense lost out. '*Salud!*' he said, then poured the *orujo* down his throat, trying his best to suppress a grimace as it hit his stomach.

Both he and Tomeu then looked at my still-full glass. '*Salud!*' they said in chorus, staring directly into my eyes with expressions that dared me not to join in the fun.

'Ah, well,' I reasoned. 'When in Rome. *Salud!*'

My attempt at suppressing a grimace was a lot less successful than Jordi's. The involuntary shudder saw to that. Rough brandy was my initial assessment of the *orujo*, but barely a second later my taste buds were telling me: 'Paint stripper with a hint of battery acid.'

'Damn baster good stuff, eh?' said Jordi.

'Uh-huh,' I wheezed, blinking the tears from my eyes.

'*Una copita mas*,' grinned Tomeu. 'One more glass.'

Jordi sang Mallorcan folk songs all the way back to Andratx, while I concentrated on choosing which of the three white lines down the centre of the road to keep to the right of. Tomeu's one more glass had been repeated another four times (that I can remember). Surprisingly, Jordi's 'tripe' seemed to have withstood the punishment well. He even invited me to join him for 'ones more for the baster roads' when I dropped him off with his tomato plants outside the Bar Nuevo. But I had a date, thank God – the first and last time my bacon would be saved by a pig.

I couldn't claim to be an expert on pigs, but what little experience I'd had of keeping them had taught me that every one has a different character, and in any group of them there is most definitely a pecking order – if the word 'peck' isn't a misnomer when applied to our snouted friends.

'He is a very fine *porc, sí?*' smiled Josep, the manager at the farm supply depot.

He was, and he was obviously a boss pig, too, barging his way through the others in the pen to stand up, front trotters draped over the hurdle, in order to have a good look at me. This little pig exuded self-confidence and, judging by the hoity-toity expression on his face, suffered from a massive superiority complex as well. I had crossed personalities with pigs like him before… and I'd come a poor second every time. But he *was* the pick of the litter, without doubt, so if I was going to be lumbered with a pig at all, it was just as well to go for the best one – inevitable battles of will notwithstanding.

We climbed into the pen.

'Sit him on his *culo*,' said Josep, 'and I will tie his feet.'

Round one went immediately to the pig. As I tried to grab him, I missed, slipped on the sawdust-covered floor and landed on my behind in a dollop of pig muck.

'Do not worry, *señor*,' said Josep. 'No harm done. I will hold him. You tie his feet.'

Now, the amount of noise that a pig can make when he's not happy about something is quite amazing. And this pig was most certainly not at all pleased about suffering the indignity of being sat on his arse in front of his inferiors and, worse still, being hogtied by an amateur. The squeals could have been heard in Palma.

'Lift him up, *señor*,' said Josep, once phase one of the contest was over, 'and we will put him into this sack to keep him controlled for the journey home in your car.'

A deceptively strong and exceedingly wriggly creature is a weaner pig, and the five glasses of *orujo* were soon gushing from my pores. But eventually, thanks to the assistance of two elderly *campesinos* who had watched our futile performance until they could laugh no more, we managed to bundle the bagged piglet into the back of my car. The short journey back to Ca's Mayoral was ominously uneventful, with neither a grunt of protest nor the merest sound of a struggle from within the sack. Maybe something to do with the soothing aroma of the tomato plants, I thought, ever hopeful.

'Give me a lift out with him,' I called to Sandy back in the yard. 'We'll get him out of the sack and shoo him down to the sty at the *casita de aperos*.'

'So you have a pig at last,' said old Maria, appearing from nowhere to take up her customary position looking over the wall. 'I picked you an excellent one, no?'

'Yes, well, I've had a bit of bother with him, to be honest, but he seems to have settled down OK now.'

Wrong! The moment I untied the neck of the sack, the pig shot out like a screeching streak, feet miraculously unhobbled, and made a dash for the open gate.

For some reason known only to themselves, horses don't seem to like pigs. I knew this from bitter experience when a pair of our pigs back in Scotland had escaped and put the frighteners so far up a Shetland pony that the chase was several miles old before we caught up with them in the car. I'd learned that pigs and ponies can run very fast when it suits them. However, I didn't know whether mules suffered from the same 'porcuphobia' as their horsey half-brothers. I was soon to find out, though.

It was old Pep's habit to do his shopping in Andratx in the evening, when the shops re-opened after the afternoon *siesta*. Sometimes he would go on his moped, but if it was a particularly pleasant evening and he wanted to impress the *paseo*-givers in the square, he would yoke up his mule instead, standing proudly in his cart all the way and shouting his usual '*Weh-ep!*' greeting to passers-by. I'd seen him do this a few times, and I must admit that he did cut quite a dash, particularly when he had succeeded in goading the mule into going at a trot.

How unfortunate, then, that on this occasion he just happened to be exiting his farmyard when the escapee porker was exiting ours. The mule took one look at the pig, reared up, almost decanting Pep backwards out of the cart, then took off at the gallop along the lane with the pig in hot pursuit. Sandy and I gave chase, too, but we were no match for the speed of the stampeders. At the junction with the main road, the terrified mule turned right for the village, bolting down the street at full tilt, with Pep stumbling about in the cart behind and straining on the reins like a rustic Charlton Heston. The pig, meanwhile, had turned left, cleared a low wall, and disappeared up the wooded mountainside.

We never saw it again, although we did hear rumours of an unlikely gang of two black goat kids and their pink accomplice raiding some of the more remote mountain *fincas* for goodies of a dark night. I thought it prudent not to check out the verity of the story. And even old Maria never mentioned her belief in the necessity of my having a pig again, perhaps having been warned not to by Pep in the wake of his ignominious chariot charge into town.

- Ten -

CURRENT AFFAIRS AND ODOROUS AIRS

The spot that had been earmarked for planting our tomatoes had three things going for it: it would be protected from the fiercest rays of the summer sun by the outer branches of a row of fig trees, it wasn't too far from the source of irrigation, and (most gratifying of all, I felt) it was right behind the *casita* of Tomàs and Francisca Ferrer.

For different reasons, none of us had been at home for much of the previous day, and it was only on opening the bedroom shutters the following morning that Ellie had noticed two ugly blots on the beautiful view from the upstairs windows. Our laneside wall, some six feet wide at its base and all of twelve feet high, had been there since

Roman times, it was said. It had served originally as an aqueduct, carrying mountain water to the old mill which the Ferrers were in the process of 'converting' into their *casita fin de semana*, their weekend country cottage. Why anyone would even dream of mounting an unsightly water tank and a TV satellite dish on top of such a priceless historic relic was beyond me. Yet that's exactly what had been done in our absence the day before, *and* on a part of the wall which was inside our property, adjacent to the Ferrers' house but conveniently out of sight from it.

We'd had a feeling for a while that our weekend neighbours, while having gladly accepted our money for their former home, still regarded it as their own. This suspicion stemmed from one occasion when Sandy had been in bed suffering from flu, and Ellie and I had taken Charlie to one of his Saturday morning sports fixtures at the school. No sooner had we left, Sandy informed us, than he'd heard the Ferrers inside the house, wandering about and casually discussing all the changes we'd made. What made matters worse was that we had locked the house doors behind us when leaving, pointing to the fact that the Ferrers had sneakily kept a set of keys for themselves when selling us the property.

To say that I was incensed would be a gross understatement, but as nothing had been touched, Ellie persuaded me to let the incident pass without even letting on to the nosy so-and-sos that we knew what they'd been up to. Better not to risk getting involved in bad blood within the close community in which we now lived. That was her way of looking at it. Just change the locks and keep an eye on the Ferrers from now on.

When we'd struck the original bargain to buy the farm, we had bought the maximum amount of '*rustica*' land that foreigners were permitted to own on the island at the time, with the Ferrers' promise that more land, plus the old mill, would be sold to us as soon as the expected relaxation of the laws allowed. We had therefore been disappointed to discover, on taking possession of the farm a few months later, that the Ferrers' own 'conversion' of the mill was already well under way. Worse still, none of the original building now remained, the ancient stonework having been demolished to make way for a fairly characterless breeze block construction. Even the most sympathetic restoration of old country properties is covered by strict regulations in Mallorca, and their destruction absolutely prohibited, except under very special circumstances. So, we wondered, how had Tomàs managed to obtain planning permission for such a vandalising project as his?

He had a reputation locally of being somewhat 'careful' with his money, so it had surprised me when, immediately after we'd moved into Ca's Mayoral, Tomàs offered to pay a proportion of our electricity bills. He would cover the cost, in effect, of all the electricity usage recorded by the agricultural meter in our tractor shed, leaving us responsible only for the domestic charges logged in a separate meter in the house. According to him, until such time as the electricity company had given him a domestic supply of his own, the only way he could provide mains power for his cottage would be by plugging a cable into a socket connected to our agricultural meter. This had seemed a reasonable enough arrangement to me at the time, although hardly likely to constitute much of an immediate financial saving for us, as significant use of 'agricultural' electricity wouldn't begin until we started using the well pump at the onset of the irrigation season. But with that time of year almost upon us, canny Tomàs was going to be hit quite painfully in the pocket if he didn't get the ongoing situation quickly resolved.

When I mentioned this to him, he just shrugged and said, '*No importa* – it doesn't matter.' And today, when I'd tackled him about the tank and TV dish which he'd had installed on top of the old wall, he'd given a similarly nonchalant response: '*No importa*. I will pay the workmen to put them somewhere else.'

Something didn't add up. Then I spoke to Jaume, old Maria's avuncular and portly son-in-law, during one of our impromptu chats over the march wall.

'Aha, Don Pedro,' he said when I'd steered the conversation in the required direction, 'there are *aspectos* of this matter which you are best to turn a blind eye to.'

As a retired waiter, Jaume was probably only exercising a bit of the art of dining room diplomacy which he'd picked up in a lifetime working in one of Palma's poshest hotels. But, despite his alleged lack of interest in the 'parochial' ways of his native valley, there wasn't much he didn't know about them, as I'd perceived from the exemplary way he worked old Maria's *finca* for her. So, I was sure he could throw some light on the subject of Tomàs's new easy-going attitude towards spending money. And interestingly, although Jaume's peaceable nature had always prevented him from talking ill of anyone to me so far, on this occasion, it took only a touch of gentle encouragement to make the temptation too great for him to resist.

He glanced furtively about, leaned in closer and whispered, 'He is actually breaking the law, Don Pedro.'

Now we were getting somewhere! I pressed him for more.

GESA, the electricity company, operated two tariffs on farms, he explained – the normal urban rate for the house, and a special cheaper rate for agricultural use. Hence the need for two meters, and hence the prohibition of using the agricultural supply for domestic purposes.

I was starting to get the picture. 'So, why have GESA taken so long to connect the Ferrers' *casita* to a domestic supply? I mean, the longer they delay, the more money they're losing. And it's not as if their cable doesn't pass right over the Ferrer's gate.' I was tempted to say that this sounded like the *mañana* syndrome gone mad, but thought better of it, Jaume being a procrastinator *par excellence* himself.

He seemed genuinely reluctant to divulge any more, but after thinking about it for a moment or two, he raised his shoulders and said, '*Bueno*, I do not want to stab anyone in the back, my friend, but if *I* do not tell you, someone else will soon enough.'

'Go on,' I urged, hardly able to wait for the next instalment.

Jaume leaned further over the wall to adopt an even more confidential position. 'You see, you must have full planning permission to build a new house before GESA will provide an electricity supply for it.'

The final piece of the jigsaw. Suddenly everything was crystal clear. Rather than go to the extra trouble and expense of converting the original stone-built mill to a dwelling, Tomàs had evidently decided to ride roughshod over regulations in the hope that his lofty position in local government would ultimately help him have the rules bent in his favour. This had been his attitude when having the so-called septic tank installed at Ca's Mayoral years ago, as we had quickly discovered to our cost. He'd got away with it then, would be his view, so why not on a larger scale now?

'But surely he runs the risk of being made to knock that new house down,' I said. 'Town hall planning departments usually have eyes everywhere.'

Jaume said nothing, but the slow raising of his eyebrows spoke volumes.

'And what if I suddenly decide not to give him access to our agricultural electricity supply any more – or if I see fit to drop a word to GESA that he's been defrauding them all this time?'

Jaume looked at me over the rims of his glasses and stated sagely, 'Aha, Don Pedro, but you forget something.' He tapped the side of his nose. 'Señor Ferrer is a shrewd judge of character, and he knows that you are too good a neighbour to do such things.'

'Hmm, he thinks I'm too soft a neighbour, more likely. Which reminds me, Jaume – I've got tomatoes to plant.' I gave him a warm smile and a pat on the back. '*Hasta luego*, and thanks for the information. We'll see what happens, eh? *Vamos a ver.*'

'*Sí, claro*,' he called after me in hushed tones, 'but when dealing with Tomàs, just remember the old proverb about the little woodworm: At first he makes only one tiny hole. But given time…'

I waved my hand in acknowledgement of his carefully couched words of advice. But he needn't have worried. I'd already got the message loud and clear.

Jordi and Tomeu had shown me (between shots of *orujo*) the correct way to plant tomatoes Mallorcan-style, so Sandy and I followed their instructions to the letter. With our little tractor we threw up ridges in the well-tilled soil, then carefully trowelled in one plant on either side of the drill, repeating the process at carefully measured intervals along each row. It was important to insert the plants just below the apex of the ridges, so that when the intervening troughs were flood irrigated, the roots would be encouraged to reach down for sustenance while leaving the stems of the plants dry and free from the possibility of rotting off.

Despite the dappled shade of the fig trees, the morning heat was intense, our chosen part of the field being tucked away in a corner sheltered on one side by the high old wall and by the back of the Ferrer's new *casita* on the other. So, although not particularly arduous, it *was* extremely hot work, and before we had firmed in even half of the two hundred or so plants, Sandy and I had retreated back to the house to swap our jeans for shorts – the first time we'd felt the need to until then.

Our deathly pale Scottish legs did seem strangely out of place in this exotic setting of citrus orchards, though, and I think we both secretly hoped that nobody would see us. For all that, we hadn't resumed our tomato planting work for long before the shirts had to come off as well, exposing our milk-bottle upper bodies to potential ridicule, too. By that time, however, we couldn't have cared less, thoughts of sipping cool drinks by a swimming pool like other less 'adventurous' Brits on the island now totally to the fore. But there was still plenty more work to do.

After the planting was finished, we had to fetch bundles of canes cut from a grove of bamboo growing wild by the dry *torrente* a little further up the valley. The canes were tied criss-cross at intervals down the entire length of each drill, then connected by a series of horizontals until a sort of elongated teepee framework was established. This would provide the essential support needed by the tomato plants as they grew to maturity and bore fruit.

'Right,' I said once the job was complete, 'let's give them a good drink. I'll go and switch on the pump.'

'Are you really going to do this?' Sandy laughed.

'Of course! It's common practice in hot countries like this to use septic tank liquid for irrigating things. Full of nutrients, too. Worth its weight in... well, you know what I mean.'

'Yeah, but the pong. I mean, right here beside the Ferrers' house.'

'That's the object of the exercise. It may seem anti-social, but Tomàs should've thought about that before he lied to me about the house's so-called sewage filtration system. It's nothing but a hole in the ground that'd cost us fortunes to have emptied every time by the sludge wagon. That, plus all the other liberties he's taken since he sold us this place.'

Sandy gave a nervous snigger. 'Well, *I'll* go and switch on the pump, then. I wouldn't want to be here when Señor Ferrer comes out of his house.'

'Fair enough,' I shrugged. 'I'll stand by the end of the hose here and make sure it doesn't jump out of the furrow when the stuff comes through.'

I'd always thought that pig slurry had the worst smell that you could encounter in the countryside, but a couple of minutes later I found out otherwise. Take it from me, we humans come top of the effluent stench league… by a long way. Holding my nose, I waited for Tomàs to appear. I had been looking forward to the moment for months. He'd be furious, most likely, but I was prepared for that. Being incomers and anxious to get along well with *all* of our new neighbours, we'd kept quiet about a lot of things which we could have griped to the Ferrers about. Everything from the weedy state of the land when we arrived, to the collection of clapped out furnishings and domestic appliances which they'd fobbed off on us. Even being saddled with feeding their menagerie of dogs and half-wild cats every weekday. And not forgetting their sly snoop inside the house, or the water tank and satellite dish dumped on top of our wall. Oh, and there had been that business about the poisonous caterpillars, too. Yes, Tomàs had asked for this, and he'd finally get a piece of my mind the moment he complained.

'Ah,' he smiled when he eventually showed up at the other side of the fence, '*parfum de Paris!*' Then he gave a chuckle and wandered nonchalantly off to do some hoeing.

Dammit! Was there no way to ruffle this man's feathers? He was a cool customer, without doubt, and very likely mindful of the fact that any beef from him about the stink might result in his septic tank scam (and others) finally being reported to the authorities. That was my considered opinion, anyway.

But I was wrong. The very next morning brought further evidence that Tomàs didn't give two hoots about the authorities – or that we were now the owners of Ca's Mayoral, for that matter.

We were sitting on the balcony having breakfast, when Ellie noticed something draped between the fruit trees down at the bottom of the second field from the house.

'It looks like a rope,' she said.

'Strange,' I replied. 'Come on, finish your coffee and we'll go and have a closer look.'

What Ellie thought had been a rope was, in fact, a cable. An electricity cable. One end of it, the end with the plug, was inside our *casita de aperos*, the little equipment shed that housed our tractor and, more significantly, our agricultural electricity supply. We followed the cable from there, hooked as it was over the branches of our fruit trees, all the way to the wall between old Maria's farm and our own. And it didn't stop there. As far as we could make out, the cable continued on through the branches of Maria's lemon trees as far as her little farmstead.

'God, don't tell me *she's* planning to syphon off our power now as well,' I groaned. 'What the hell's going on here?'

'Only one way to find out,' said Ellie. 'Let's go and ask her.'

Maria was plucking a hen. '*Hola, Señora de Escocia,*' she grinned at Ellie, looking up from her bench outside her *casita*. 'This hen is for you.' She cast me a disparaging glance. 'Until *Señor de Escocia* here eventually buys you some of your own, I will give you the occasional old bird for boiling up. *Va bé?*'

I was waiting for an equally barbed comment about my pig-handling efforts, but none was forthcoming.

'Sorry to bother you, Maria,' I said, 'but I wondered what that cable running over here from our place was for.'

Ignoring me, she said to Ellie, 'A nice plump bird this one. And the flavour – *estupendo!* Feeding on the grubs in the fallen fruit, you see.' With a mischievous wink, she then added, 'And you know what they say – an old hen makes the best broth.' There was obviously an element of double entendre in that last quip, because Maria threw her head back and let rip with one of her tinkling giggles that soon had us laughing along as usual.

'Ehm, about that cable, Maria,' I ventured once the chortles had subsided.

'Ah, *sí*,' she said to Ellie, 'the best broth. '*Sí*, and that reminds me – did I ever tell you how to make chicken giblets soup?'

We sat down and resigned ourselves to a long wait. Twenty minutes later, we had been tutored in the culinary possibilities of just about every part of a hen's anatomy, but were no further forward regarding the mystery cable. Indeed, it was only when Jaume arrived on the scene that I managed to get a response to my question, while Maria continued to bend Ellie's ear with further poultry matters.

The cable, Jaume told me, had been put there by Tomàs Ferrer.

'I don't get it, Jaume. Why would Tomàs want to run a wire from our *casita de aperos* over here to yours?'

'Aha, Don Pedro,' Jaume replied, giving me that wise old owl look over the top of his glasses again, 'it is not our *casita* that the cable comes to, but to there.' He gestured towards their well.

I was more confused than ever now, but Jaume went on to reveal that the Ferrers had a right to draw water from Maria's well one day a week. This had been the case for generations, Maria's farm once having belonged to an ancestor of Francisca Ferrer, who had sold most of it to a predecessor of Maria's. The part which Francisca's forebear had retained just happened to be the field which she and Tomàs still owned.

I was still puzzled. 'So how come our farm, Ca's Mayoral, lies right between these two blocks of land? It seems a funny layout.'

Jaume had a quiet chuckle at that. 'Such awkward divisions of land are quite common in Mallorca, *amigo*. Marriages, deaths, dowries and wills, debts being recovered, wagers being honoured – that type of thing. *Hombre*, it is quite normal today for a farmer to own a couple of fields at one end of the valley, another one in the middle and yet another at the far end. And, naturally, the sharing of water rights has become equally complicated, as you are discovering for yourself.'

'But why does Tomàs Ferrer still want to draw water from your well? He already has sole access to ours at weekends, and that should be more than enough to irrigate the little field he's left with now.'

Jaume's ample midriff wobbled as he had another little chortle to himself. 'Ho! Enough is not a word associated with water here, Pedro. Just wait another month or so. You'll see.'

I was beginning to see red. 'OK, but Ferrer's going to have to take his bloody cable off our trees. It's downright dangerous for a start, *plus* he's got another think coming if he reckons he can keep plugging into our power supply whenever he wants without even asking.'

'Ay-y-y-y, *tranquilo, tranquilo, tranquilo*, my friend,' Jaume crooned, patting the back of my hand. 'Tomàs Ferrer is not worth having a heart attack over. His cable runs through our trees as well, but I just ignore it.' He gave my shoulder a hearty slap. '*Oiga!* Let me bring you a glass of my *vino*. That will cheer you up, eh!'

He really was the kindest of souls, but I'd had an inelegant sufficiency of Jaume's home-made wine once before, so, wanting to keep a clear head this time, I restricted myself to one glass before thanking him for everything and standing up to leave. I waited a few moments while Maria finished off her hen lecture to Ellie, who was now looking distinctly glassy-eyed.

Noticing me at last, Maria glanced up and said, 'The cable is for Ferrer to pump water from my well.' She then turned back to Ellie, smiled and asked, 'Did I ever tell you how this arrangement came about back in the old days?'

We politely took our leave, complete with plucked hen, before the onset of the history lesson.

I spent the next hour carefully pouring over the Ca's Mayoral title deeds, Spanish dictionary much in use.

'It's here,' I eventually said to Ellie. 'Look at the plan of the farm – these dotted red lines. They mark the Ferrers' right of way round the perimeter of that field to get to our well at weekends.'

'Hmm, but that one there, which happens to run alongside where he's strung his cable, also takes him right up to Maria's wall.'

'Yeah, well, I'd noticed all that before, but what I'd missed when the lawyer was reading out the main details in English was this clause here. What it says is that he's also allowed maintenance access to his water pipe which runs under that same path.'

'Is that a problem?'

'No, none whatsoever. It obviously runs from Maria's well, but I hadn't even twigged there was a pipe there until a minute ago. No, there's only one problem, and that's the cable he's strung through our trees without as much as a by your leave. Picking fruit, a careless moment, and one of us could very easily cut through that with our secateurs. Tomàs Ferrer's gone too far this time, and I'm off to see the power company right now!'

The counter clerk at the GESA office sighed despairingly when I told him the purpose of my visit. He gave the distinct impression that tales like this were ten a penny at the approach of every irrigation season. 'There is nothing we can do about a cable running through your trees, *señor* – entirely a private matter between you and your neighbour.'

'Maybe, but there are other things going on which are entirely a matter between *you* and my neighbour. I don't want to put you to any trouble, but I'd be really grateful if you could arrange for one of your engineers to call next weekend – Saturday morning, when Señor Ferrer is sure to be at his *finca* next door.'

The clerk pulled one of those 'oh, well, if you really insist' shrugs; the type of shrug that tells you he's bored stiff, hates his job with a vengeance, and wishes he'd never sprogged the wife and had all those money-draining brats of kids. '*Si, señor,*' he intoned, 'one of our men will telephone you to make an appointment.' He gave me a weary smile, then ambled off to file my details, scratching his behind as he went, and thinking, no doubt, that I was damned lucky that a silly cable was all I had to worry about.

I have to admit to having approached the meeting with Tomàs and the GESA man with some trepidation. Firstly, Tomàs wasn't even going to know that a meeting was about to take place until I arrived at his door with the engineer. It seemed a sneaky way of going about things, but I knew that, given advance warning, Tomàs would probably use his connections in high places to somehow gain the initiative. Secondly, the proceedings would be conducted in Spanish, if not *mallorquín*, so I'd have to be on my mettle not to get totally bamboozled. I looked up a few key words in advance and did my best to memorise them – words like planning permission, trespass and sue. But deep down I hoped I wouldn't have to use them.

I'd had experience of a similar confrontation back in Scotland – a run-in with a self-important bully of a neighbour who'd seen fit to demolish several hundred metres of stone wall between our two farms when I'd been away for a few days. The wall was situated on the highest and most exposed part of the farm, and had provided the only means of shelter for our grazing cattle in bad weather.

Taking legal action almost certainly wouldn't have resulted in the wall being rebuilt. I was realistic enough to concede that. So, all I could do was give the boor absolute hell verbally, and an enemy was made out of someone who, until then, I had at least managed to suffer. The last thing I wanted was for the same to happen in this much more intimate situation. But, at the same time, Tomàs Ferrer had to be made aware that we were wise to his little ploys and wouldn't put up with them any more.

If he was surprised by my arrival at his house with the GESA engineer, he certainly didn't show it. In fact, it appeared that they knew each other well, greeting one another affably and exchanging casual pleasantries. I already felt like the odd man out.

Then Francisca appeared at the door and, on seeing me, threw her hands in the air and welcomed me to her home with her usual outpourings of compliments and enquiries after the wellbeing of Ellie and the boys. She had heard that we had a puppy, she informed me with one of her coquettish looks, and I must be sure to bring it over to meet her two darlings, Robin and Marion, without delay. It was good for little dogs to have nice doggy neighbours too, *si*?

While Tomàs and the engineer continued to chat away, Francisca popped back inside the house and re-emerged with a basket of new potatoes. 'The first of the season,' she smiled. 'Tomàs dug them up only this morning, and I was just about to take them over to your wife. Please, take them with our compliments.'

Suddenly, I was on the back foot, totally disarmed and in the worst of positions to make complaints that might start a dispute.

Tomàs was quick to take advantage of the moment. 'And what can I do for you this morning?' he asked me, a smile of carefully tempered superiority on his lips. 'No more problems, I hope. You will notice that the water tank and television dish have been moved, as you requested.' He gave the engineer a telling look, as if warning him that I was an inveterate nitpicker.

I could see that this wasn't going to be easy, but there was no backing off now. 'If we walk down to my tractor shed, I'll be able to explain fully,' I said, noting that the supercilious smile on Tomàs's face never wavered.

Francisca decided to come along, too, ostensibly to continue her genial conversation with me, but more likely to provide back-up for Tomàs in the showdown which they must have realised was about to take place.

'I was wondering why this electric cable came to be looped through the trees,' I said for openers when we reached the *casita de aperos*.

Without batting an eyelid, Tomàs told me precisely why.

'We have been leading that cable through our trees for years,' Francisca piped up, her attitude every bit as matter of fact as her husband's, but playing right into my hands, nonetheless.

'Ah, but the difference now,' I quickly pointed out, 'is that they're not *your* trees any more. Nor is the power supply which you presumed you could plug into again.'

Tomàs gave a dismissive snort. 'But we already have an agreement about that. Surely you are not going back on it.'

'We have an agreement for you to use my agricultural power supply for your new house, but that's all.'

Feeling certain that I had just given the power company his head on a plate, I waited for Tomàs to panic. He didn't. Nor did the engineer show any sign of concern at my revelation that Tomàs was swindling his employers. He simply turned to Tomàs and started to converse calmly with him in *mallorquín*.

'Can we keep it in Spanish, please?' I cut in, trying to control the anger building up inside me. 'And why hasn't GESA given Señor Ferrer here an electricity supply for his new house?' I asked the engineer, who merely raised a shoulder and said it wasn't his department.

'We are paying your agricultural bill for you,' Francisca said, becoming suddenly aggressive. 'Why are you complaining?'

Ignoring that, I asked the engineer bluntly, 'When will Señor Ferrer be given his own power supply to his house?'

He didn't get a chance to reply. A crack showing in his veneer of indifference for the first time, Tomàs snapped at me, 'That is none of your business, *señor!*'

'Maybe not, but this farm is now – a fact which you seem to forget at times.'

Francisca tutted as if appalled that I should suggest such a thing. But I had the bit between my teeth now and wasn't about to stop before I'd said my piece.

'I have no objections to you running your cable through this farm to old Maria's well,' I went on, 'but unless you take it down from those trees and have it safely buried underground, I'll have to think again about letting you use our agricultural electricity supply for your house.'

Having regained his composure (on the surface, at least), Tomàs slowly nodded his head and said, 'As you wish, *señor*. As you wish.'

Then he, Francisca and, interestingly, the engineer turned and strolled calmly back to their *casita*.

'I'm afraid I've come away being made to feel like the villain of the piece,' I confessed to Ellie when I got back to the house. 'And I've dropped the Ferrers in it with the power company. Their man now knows exactly what's going on.'

'Well, the Ferrers are the ones in the wrong, so why should you feel bad about it?'

'I know, but I still hope my spouting off won't lead to them being prosecuted or something. I could very easily end up being looked upon around here as the typical superior Brit. You know the type, in a foreign country for five minutes and already throwing his weight about. That certainly wasn't my intention. I only wanted to –'

'You only wanted to stop the Ferrers taking so much for granted and acting as if they still owned this place. That's all you've done, and even if it does get them into trouble, nobody in these parts will feel in the least bit sorry for them. They'll regard you as a hero, in fact.'

What Ellie said was probably absolutely correct, I knew, but I still hoped I hadn't made enemies of Tomàs and Francisca. That would only result in creating a terrible atmosphere when they were living so close by at weekends. Also, whatever their faults, they had been extremely kind to us on occasions, too – like when Francisca had come over to console Ellie after the trauma of the housebreaking, or when Tomàs had given me his old Spanish text books to help me learn the ways of Mediterranean fruit farming. They were essentially good people – if inclined to take a mile, given an inch, as old Jaume had tactfully warned me – and I did worry that my having taken such a deliberately confrontational course would have soured our relationship permanently.

My concerns were unfounded. The following Saturday morning, Tomàs was his usual imperiously genial self, arriving at our front door to ask permission (permission!) for a workman to bury his tree-mounted electric cable there and then. Shortly after, Francisca came over with a gift of her infamous almond ice cream – a ploy to introduce herself to Bonny, who immediately took to her with unrestrained delight. Her airy ways with humans aside, Francisca genuinely loved animals, and animals, it seemed, loved her back. She certainly formed an instant bond with Bonny, which, though touching to see then, was to lead to many an exasperation as time went by.

Nothing was said by either of the Ferrers about my having exposed their improper use of 'agricultural' electricity to the GESA man, however, so I still suspected that this unexpectedly refreshing rapport with us would vanish the moment the consequence of that deed reared its legal head.

Wrong again.

'I have to inform you, *señor*, that the electricity supply cable to your property is sub-standard.' It was the same engineer who had been present at my 'meeting' with the Ferrers just ten days earlier. 'We will renew it immediately, at the same time as installing a supply to Señor Ferrer's new house.'

I was flabbergasted. How could Tomàs have applied for and obtained retrospective planning permission for his mill 'conversion' as quickly as this? I knew such applications were notoriously slow to be processed in my own country, and this was supposed to be *Mañana*land, after all. Strange. Still, it wasn't for me to question the machinations involved. Tomàs had managed it somehow, and we were going to be rid of the irksome power-sharing arrangement at last, in addition to enjoying the benefit of new supply cabling ourselves. Marvellous. Although, to be frank, I couldn't help thinking it odd that our allegedly obsolete mains cable had never been mentioned by the electrician who had done extensive upgrading inside the house a few months earlier. But anyway – if the power company wanted to renew it, I wasn't about to look their gift horse in the mouth.

And as it turned out, it wasn't a particularly big undertaking in any case. The work took barely half a day, and only involved running a new overhead cable from a pole in the lane to the gable of the house, then along under the eaves to an existing hole in the wall behind the fuse box. It wouldn't have cost the power company much, and I concluded that they had merely decided to take the opportunity of doing a routine cable replacement for us while they were undertaking the Ferrers' installation next door. *Va bé*, as they say in *mallorquín*. Fine.

And then the envelope arrived.

'The equivalent of two thousand bloody quid!' I wailed at Ellie when I'd taken a look at the bill. 'For that little job, which we didn't even ask to be done!'

'But I thought they were doing it for nothing,' said Ellie, peering incredulously at the invoice.

'Mm-m-m,' I grunted, 'me too. But worse than that, I wouldn't be surprised if crafty Tomàs pulled strings so that we're being charged for his work as well. Uh-uh! No way, José!'

And so I paid my second visit to the jaded clerk at the electricity company's office.

After a cursory glance at the bill, he shook his head and mumbled, 'No *errores* have been committed here, *señor*. Standard charge for the job, nothing more.'

'But I didn't ask to have the cable replaced!'

'Such matters are for our engineers to decide.' He handed back the bill and looked at me through tired eyes. 'There are strict safety standards to uphold with regard to cables, and as that was precisely the reason for your last visit, I cannot understand your problem. *Adiós.*'

Game, set and match.

I still felt I should bring all this to Tomàs Ferrer's attention, however, so I made a point of walking over the fields to his *casita* the next time he was there. I showed him the bill.

'Hmm, such work is not cheap, my friend,' he said, and I thought I caught a hint of sympathy in his voice.

'You're not wrong there. And, uhm, don't think me rude, but can I ask how much you paid for everything involved in laying on your entirely new supply?'

'Much more,' he said gravely. '*Ah, sí – mucho, mucho más.*'

His poker-faced mien told me that it would be pointless to attempt eliciting any further information on the subject. And despite my misgivings regarding what we'd been charged, I could hardly voice them to Tomàs without implying collusion between him and the electricity company. That, I immediately decided, was one can of worms that I most definitely did not want to open.

After all, the whole exercise had achieved what we wanted – respect for our ownership of Ca's Mayoral from the Ferrers, and, it seemed, the beginnings of a new feeling of mutual deference. Cheap at the price of a length of grossly overvalued cable, when all was said and done. Or had I just been taken for a complete *loco extranjero*? I'd probably never know, and by then I didn't really want to, anyway.

- Eleven -

SUMMERTIME, AND THE LIVING IS... *HOT!*

It isn't easy for northern Europeans like us, living for the first time in a Mediterranean climate, to tell when summer really starts, especially on an island like Mallorca, where even our first winter had seemed more benign and reliable than the summers we were used to in Scotland. But if Sandy and I thought that planting tomatoes in the lee of the old wall at the end of April had been hot work, we were in for a few surprises.

Like millions of others, we had spent holidays on the island in high summer and knew how oppressive the temperatures can be. But there is all the difference in the world between loafing about on a beach with the refuge of an air-conditioned bar nearby, and doing physical work in an open-air oven. Soon enough, we found out why our valley, shut off as it was from cooling northerlies by Ses

Penyes Mountain, was referred to locally as *Sa Calenta* –
The Hot One.

By early June, even some bemused Scottish vegetables
that we were attempting to grow were beginning to show
signs of heat exhaustion. Among the old books given to
me by Tomàs Ferrer, I had found a Mallorcan farming
almanac, which gave month-by-month details of what
to do on the land – including a disclosure of the ancient
waxing/waning moon rules of timing held so dear by old
Maria. I was pleased to see that the almanac also gave
recommendations for the best times to 'bake your bricks
made from mud', 'assemble your billy goats with their
nannies', and even the ever-handy 'when to sow your
opium poppies'. But not a mention of Swedes – the turnip
variety, that is. And so we had our first crop failure.

Jock Burns had long been organising a regular Mallorcan
'Burn's Night' honouring his namesake Rabbie, Scotland's
national bard. These lighthearted Caledonian fiestas had
become a firm social favourite every January, when Jock
would lay on the traditional dinner of haggis, neeps and
tatties, plus a dance band, piper and entertainers, all
imported (except the potatoes) from Scotland for the
occasion. Hundreds of expat and native revellers would
pack a heather-decked function hall for the grand tartan
knees-up every year, and a great whisky-soaked time
would invariably be had by all.

The only problem was caused by the Swedes – the neep
variety, that is. This essential accompaniment to haggis just
wasn't available in Mallorca, and it wouldn't have been
viable to airfreight from Scotland enough fresh turnips for
the numbers of diners being catered for. Jock, therefore,

had had to resort to having the dried type brought over. But, being an incurable neep purist, he had never been entirely happy about this situation. 'Nah, cannae whack the real thing, son,' was his annual lament.

So, I offered to grow him enough for his requirements, my philosophy being that, if you can't raise a few neeps for a Burn's Night friend in need, things have come to a sorry pass indeed. Trouble was, the turnips had other ideas. As I'd done many times before in Scotland, I sowed the seeds in May and, with ample watering, the seedlings duly popped their tender green heads through the soil – and quicker than I'd ever known before, too. But, after sampling the Mallorcan June sunshine, the baby plants heaved a homesick sigh for cooler climes, spread their little green leaves on the earth... and died.

'*Coño*,' croaked old Pep when asked for his opinion on the disaster, 'you should have sown the seeds in the autumn.'

And, of course, he was dead right. Why hadn't I thought of it? The seeds would have mistaken the ensuing Mallorcan winter for a Scottish summer and would, therefore, have grown happily on. Obvious. Another lesson learned.

The failure of our maize crop wasn't quite so simple to diagnose, however. Although we'd had no experience of growing the warm-climate corn before, we'd sowed the seeds according to the correct principles, at the right moonphase (having consulted the almanac), and had provided them with the recommended amount of fertiliser and water required to make them flourish and, we confidently expected, to grow as high as the proverbial elephant's eye. They didn't even get beyond the height of a worm's eye. Nothing. Not one solitary shoot appeared through the soil.

Even Pep was puzzled this time. 'Where did you buy the seed?' he asked, looking out over the barren corn patch.

'I didn't. I was given a bag of it as a present from a visiting friend from Australia.'

That told Pep everything. 'Forty whores!' he scoffed. 'There is the answer. How could you have been so stupid?'

'Stupid? How do you mean?'

'Australian seed, *guapo*,' he spluttered through chortles of derision. 'Simple. The *bastardos* are growing downwards!'

Well, at least our tomatoes were thriving, as were our peppers, onions, garlic and other plants well suited to the Mediterranean climate. And as the temperatures started to soar, the pace of life in the valley slowed down correspondingly. Being *tranquilo* wasn't an effort any more, it was a must, and even the most work-ethic-indoctrined *extranjero* could become sorely tempted to join the *mañana* brigade. But, as the almanac stated for June: 'In the first days of the month, the remaining reserves of water in the soil are normally exhausted, and it is necessary to irrigate.'

Just as Pepe Suau had predicted, the fruit trees had responded wonderfully to his severe pruning and were now looking in prime condition, but, without further human intervention, would soon succumb to the summer drought. We had already opened up irrigation channels round every tree on the farm, a long and energy-sapping operation, even using the tractor and plough method that Sandy had experimented with earlier. How the local folk found the stamina to do this backbreaking job by hand in such a heat was a constant source of wonder. But they did, and seemed to think no more of it than we had when feeding outwintered cattle in the midst of a Scottish snowstorm. Just a question of what you're used to, I suppose.

Whether it was the languor-inducing effect of the heat or the result of our power cable showdown I don't know, but Tomàs Ferrer had become noticeably more neighbourly of late, happily giving help and advice whenever asked. Sometimes even without being asked. Relationships had become so cordial, in fact, that we had stopped using the septic tank soup to irrigate the tomatoes when he and Francisca were in residence at their weekend *casita* – a gesture of goodwill which I'm sure they appreciated greatly. And, who knows, maybe it was the very thought of waking up to the aroma of our '*parfum de Paris*' again every Saturday morning that was keeping him sweet. Whatever the reason, it was a welcome relief for us to be rid of the tensions that had previously existed between the Ferrers and ourselves.

'You must never allow it to fall below eight *palmos* from this knot,' said Tomàs. He was instructing me on how to gauge the amount of water in our well by measuring the level on a length of rope dangling down the shaft from a cleat on the parapet. He spread his hand and indicated the span between little finger and thumb to make sure I knew exactly what he meant by one *palmo*. 'If you extract any more water than that at one time, you have extracted too much, and it will take too long for the level to recover. Never forget that. *Muy importante.*'

Somehow, I wasn't particularly surprised when Tomàs himself pumped out almost ten *palmos* worth on the first Sunday he used the well. And, just as he'd warned, there wasn't enough water for me to irrigate our trees the next day. Maybe my assumption that he'd turned over a new leaf had been a touch premature after all. But rather than risk getting drawn rashly into one of those all-too-common water wars that old Maria had told me about, I opted to let the incident pass without comment – this once! And, to be fair, Tomàs never overstepped the watermark again that summer. Perhaps he had merely made a mistake on that occasion. Or maybe, giving him further benefit of the doubt, he had overdrawn the well on purpose, just to drive home the rule of the eight *palmos* to me. I was happy to leave it there, although I noted that, from then on, Tomàs always drew the absolute permitted maximum of water from the well every weekend – much more than he really needed, I was sure. But that was clearly just the nature of the man; if he couldn't have a mile, he was sure as hell going to take the full inch.

And I could have no complaints about that. Pepe Suau had advised me that, in order to satisfy their needs, every tree on the farm would require having its irrigation trench filled to capacity at least once every ten days. There proved to be more than enough water in the well to comply with that rule of thumb, so neighbourly harmony with the Ferrers was thankfully maintained.

Only once was this welcome status quo slightly threatened...

'*Madre mía*, you have stolen my shoes!' Francisca warbled, standing at our front door with a basket of broad beans in one hand, the other pointing at a pair of grubby espadrilles lying on the doormat. She looked at me with an expression on her face that went most of the way to accusing me of being a grade-one pervert. 'I come to give your wife these beans,' she continued, bottom lip quivering, 'only to find that you have stolen my new shoes.' She bent down to pick them up, gripping them tentatively between forefinger and thumb as if they'd just returned from an AWOL walkabout in Chernobyl. 'I have been searching for them everywhere – and now look at them. Filthy!'

I was taken aback to the point of being struck temporarily speechless.

Then Francisca noticed something tucked under a chair further along the *porche*. 'And look!' she squawked. 'My red rubber boot! It has been missing since yesterday! *Jesús, María y José!*' She crossed herself and muttered an invocation that sounded more defamatory than pious.

I didn't know the Spanish word for 'kinky', but I made it absolutely clear all the same that I wasn't into nicking women's footwear.

'Your sons, then,' Francisca ventured, on the verge of tears. 'Boys of that age – you know...?'

I was on the point of telling her that, even if either or both of the boys happened to be developing a shoe fetish, it was extremely unlikely that they'd be attracted to such outstandingly unattractive items as the ones she claimed to be hers. But I decided it was best not to add insult to injury. An assurance that all three of us were innocent was all I could give her – take it or leave it.

She wasn't having that, though. 'But it could not have been your wife,' she protested, before revealing the basis for such a sweeping conclusion: 'My shoes would be much too small for her.'

Again, all I could do was plead innocence, stress my ignorance of the whole affair and silently ponder that it was just as well for Francisca that Ellie hadn't been around to hear her catty insinuation about the size of her feet.

Just then, Bonny came bounding over the wall from old Maria's place. She was getting on for five months old now, and had already developed into a fine, muscular young boxer, brimming with all the fun and energy so typical of the breed and revelling in the freedom that life on the *finca* afforded her.

'Bo-nee-ee-ee!' squealed Francisca, her sour expression instantly mutating into a grin. '*Oh, mi pequeña querida!*' she crooned, spreading her arms to welcome her mutual admirer. But her greeting of 'My little darling' was swiftly followed by a startled gasp of '*Dios mío!*' when she saw what Bonny was carrying in her mouth. One of old Maria's well worn flip-flops.

Suddenly, the shoe-stealing mystery was solved, and Francisca received the revelation with cascades of laughter, though not offering one word of apology to me for having implied that my two offspring and I were but one stop short of being clothes-line bandits.

Maria, however, didn't share Francisca's delight. While Francisca cooed objections to my giving Bonny a firm scolding, she arrived breathless round the corner of the house, one wrinkled foot naked and dust-covered. She was not a happy neighbour.

'Nipped it right off my foot,' she panted. 'I was sitting there wringing a duck's neck, when your dog gallops up and makes off with my shoe! *Hombre*, it should be taught to respect its elders!'

With that, she and Francisca exchanged hostile glances, collected their respective bits of footwear and promptly set off home in opposite directions. Their animosity towards one another had saved me from a proper tongue-lashing on this occasion, and although I inwardly shared Bonny's amusement at the results of her newfound prank, I realised that something would have to be done to curb it. Ironically, we had bought Bonny to deter would-be thieves, only to discover now that she had sticky fingers (or teeth) herself.

'Tie an old boot to her collar,' Ellie suggested. 'That might put her off.'

We'd tried a similar remedy with a previous boxer of ours in Scotland. Her weakness wasn't footwear, but hens – live ones. Well, they were when she stole them. Invariably, the poor creatures had died of fright by the time Copper proudly delivered them from a neighbouring farm to our back door.

'Tie one to her collar,' somebody suggested. 'That always puts them off.'

Trailing a dead hen on a piece of string for days on end hadn't put Copper off, and trailing an old boot didn't do anything to discourage Bonny, either. She thought it was all part of the game and, until she tired of it in her own time, we had to get used to a regular routine of returning pilfered shoes to our two lady neighbours. It didn't help that Francisca punished her thieving 'little darling' with a giggle, a titbit and a tickle behind the ears, of course, and Maria's futile attempts to behead our '*loco animal*' with her hoe merely added to Bonny's enjoyment.

Only when she started to take an interest in our irrigation work did she eventually decide to mend her ways and put her shoe-plundering days behind her. Savaging water as it gushed from the end of a hosepipe was much more fun.

Bonny's unintentionally disruptive attentions aside, watering the trees turned out to be not entirely the drudgery I'd been told it would. A tad tedious at first, but actually quite enjoyable once I learned to combine the job with a bit of serious inactivity. The system was simple. A length of wide-gauge hose was connected to a series of take-off taps on a galvanised pipe that ran the entire length of the farm from the well to the lane. Throwing the switch of the well pump then started the process off. I'd fill the channels surrounding the trees nearest the metal supply pipe first, then couple several extensions to the hose until I finally reached those by the fence which separated us from the Ferrer's place.

This task was performed in the evenings, when some of the heat had gone out of the sun and the risk of evaporation had consequently receded. The routine was to start at the far end of the farm, irrigate a pre-determined number of the trees, then progress in stages towards the lane every evening until all the trees had had their required amount of water – exactly ten days later, as prescribed by Pepe Suau. Then it was time to repeat the process all over again.

Apart from lugging a cumbersome hose about, the hardest (and most boring) part of the job was standing watching the water pouring into the channels. But I was soon struck by a flash of true *tranquilo*ness. Why not *sit* and watch the water instead? That would give me ten minutes rest out of every twelve or so. Time to sit and think, or, more often as it turned out, time to just sit. At last I was learning to yield to the ways of the Mallorcan country folk, not to fight them, and I was warming to the experience.

Indeed, I told myself, there were many more unpleasant things for a fella to be doing than sitting on a plastic crate in an orange grove on a balmy Mediterranean evening, listening to the gurgle of running water, breathing in the heady scent of the citrus trees and gazing dreamily at the majesty of the surrounding mountains. The idyll was completed when Charlie was coaxed into the habit of bringing me out a large bottle of ice-cold beer on coming home from school every evening. He'd then take Bonny away to play with a burst football which had become her favourite post-footwear toy, and I'd be left in solitary bliss to contemplate nothing more exacting than the strange golden colour of my once-snowy Scottish knees. Then, as dusk beckoned, I'd be surrounded by a million dancing lights – a flying ballet of insects, hovering and flitting between the trees, their tiny wings radiating the glow of the setting sun.

If this was drudgery, then *viva* drudgery!

As the weeks passed, our mornings became increasingly taken up with picking the summer fruits, beginning with cherries, which, no matter how early we started, the birds always seemed to beat us to. The advice old Pep had given us about not encouraging our feathered friends into the orchards was finally sinking it. Little burrowing wasps threatened to plague a variety of small dessert pears, earwigs were the enemy of our apricots, slugs attacked the plums, and fruit flies took a great fancy to our loquats, but by following the simple spraying regimes laid down by Pepe Suau, we managed to keep most of the parasites at bay.

With both our new French friend Andreu and Señor Jeronimo now providing ready markets for the produce, our early worries of commercial ruin were easing by the week. The output of Ca's Mayoral was never going to make us rich – that we had accepted from day one – but at least we were now making ends meet... almost. And a lot sooner than had seemed likely just a couple of months before. Though Sandy, as Ellie and I had suspected all along, did have reservations about his continued participation in our Mallorcan adventure.

'I know things are going OK,' he said one day while we were loading boxes of fruit into the back of the Panda, 'but, you know, the future...'

I could tell by his ill at ease approach that he had been thinking deeply about what he wanted to say, but still found it difficult to come right out with it.

'It's all right,' Ellie smiled sympathetically, 'if you're having second thoughts about all of this, that's not a crime. It's your life, and you've got to do what's best for you.'

'I mean, it's not that I don't like it here,' he said, obviously relieved that the ice had been broken. 'It's really great. But, well, I'm not sure if growing fruit is what I want to do for a living.' He shuffled his feet, feeling awkward again. 'I... well, it's just... nothing against the dinky tractor and fields full of trees and everything – I've sort of got used to that. But...'

'But this way of farming maybe isn't really your cup of tea?' I prompted. 'Can't fault you for that. I had my own doubts for long enough, believe me.'

Sandy lowered his head dejectedly and mumbled, 'I'm just not sure any more. I know there's still an awful lot of work to do to get this place sorted out, and I don't want to let you down or anything...'

I gave his shoulder a reassuring pat. 'Tell you what – why don't you take a trip back to Scotland for a couple of weeks – say early September? Pick up a bit of *real* tractor work during the harvest. Have a chat with the folks at the agricultural college. See how everything back there grabs you again, then make up your mind. What do you say?'

Sandy's face lit up like a kid's on Christmas morning. 'You wouldn't mind?'

'Of course we wouldn't,' said Ellie, putting on an encouraging smile. 'As I said, it's your life, and we'd be the last to stand in your way.'

'Well, that's great,' Sandy grinned. 'Right, that's what I'll do, then – go back home for a spell and see what's what.'

Ellie and I said nothing, but I knew we were thinking the same thing. You didn't have to be Freud to read something into Sandy's use of the word 'home'. But only time would tell. Perhaps a reminder of what it could be like to battle against spiteful weather while cutting the last of the Scottish grain crop – a not uncommon occurrence – would convince Sandy that continuing his involvement in our little farming venture in the sun wasn't so difficult to settle down to after all.

I said as much to Ellie after he had set off in the Panda to make the day's deliveries. We had shared the same vision of the four of us carrying on as the close family unit that we'd always been. But chicks find their wings and fly the nest when their time comes. If that time had come for Sandy, then of course, no matter how saddening the wrench, we would accept his decision, wish him well and give him all the support we could.

But for the moment, we were still all together in Mallorca, it was summer, and we were determined to enjoy it.

Fickle weather conditions certainly weren't something that Pep had to worry about for *his* grain harvest. In fact, so favourable is the Mallorcan climate that he started cutting his oats two months before the combine harvesters would have tackled the same crop in even the earliest areas of Scotland. But it wasn't a combine harvester that was clattering away on Pep's *finca* that sunny late June morning. It wasn't even a binder, an implement that the first combines had superseded on most British farms by the early fifties. No, the machine that Pep was using to cut his oats was a reaper, the primitive precursor of the binder. The reaper had been revolutionary when introduced, rendering the scythe obsolete, but I'd only ever seen one before in an agricultural museum. To actually see one working was akin to having been transported back to another age, as was looking at the harvest scene depicted by Pep and his four helpers.

Pep was holding the bridle of his mule, goading the testy beast with shouted curses into pulling the ancient, noisy reaper, and attempting to lead it in orderly lines between the field's scattering of almond trees. No mean task. On the machine sat a man with a three-pronged wooden pitchfork. His job was to rake the cut oats back from the reaper's reciprocating knife, gather them neatly onto a platform behind the cutter bar, then, when a suitable amount had accumulated, to fork them backwards onto the stubble. These loose bunches were then picked up and tied with straw into sheaves by the remaining two men. This would all have amounted to hard, energy-sapping work even in a temperate climate, but in the full summer sun of Mallorca, it struck me as being on the verge of purgatory. Yet Pep was still wearing his trusty leather bomber jacket and black beret!

Another thing that surprised me was that the men who were tying the sheaves didn't then set them up into stooks, as I remembered doing back in Scotland when I was a boy. This was an essential part of the whole operation, crucially keeping the grain heads off the ground. I shouted to Pep, asking him if he wanted the boys and I to lend a hand with that, but his reply was preceded by a dismissive swat of the hand.

'*Gracias, amigo*, but they are fine where they are.' He pointed to the sun. '*El bon sol* will see to that. *Va bé.*'

I knew that Pep wasn't lazy – far from it. But I still found it strange that he would risk leaving his precious sheaves lying in such a way that the grains would be susceptible to drawing dampness from the soil, and without the safeguard of rain run-off which stooking would afford. The fact of the matter was, of course, that the soil was as dry as tinder, and the risk of rain at this time of year was so remote as to be not worth bothering about.

Even the almanac backed up Pep's lack of concern. For the coming period it stated: 'On average, only one day of rain is registered during the month. You can say, therefore, that the precipitation of July is nil.'

Both Pep's laid-back attitude and the almanac's bold forecast proved to be totally justified. For the next three weeks the sheaves lay where they had been dropped, and no harm befell them – save, perhaps, for the attentions of a few fieldmice, and not even stooking would not have protected the tasty oats from those determined little nibblers.

I was driving back down the lane after a shopping trip with Ellie one day, when we were confronted by another scene from yesteryear on Pep's *finca*. In front of his ramshackle farmstead was parked an old mobile threshing mill, of the type that used to travel from farm to farm in Britain in pre-combine harvester days. Another sight that I hadn't seen since my childhood. Those I remembered had been hauled and powered by great, smoke-billowing steam engines, but Pep's mill – identical to but somewhat smaller than those I recalled – was being driven by a belt connected to an ancient Fordson tractor. A tractor? On Pep's place? So much again for his assertion that he would never have one of the oily, air-polluting contraptions on his land.

Dismissing Pep's fibs about his farm's 'green' credentials as just harmless examples of what, I now suspected, was his contrived quirkiness, I stopped the car and gazed fascinated at this living picture-postcard from the past. The out-of-shade temperature in the valley on that July day would have been well in excess of forty Celsius, with perhaps ninety per cent humidity. Yet Pep, who must have seen seventy summers if he'd seen a day, was standing atop the mill forking sheaves into its hungry mouth as energetically as someone half his age. His only concessions to the stifling working conditions were shirt sleeves (the first time I'd seen him without his image-promoting bomber jacket) and a handkerchief, knotted at its four corners, replacing the beret on his head.

Two other men were bringing the sheaves in from the field with Pep's mule and cart, while a fourth man stood at the back of the mill, bagging off the threshed oats. Old Pep, then, with his pitchfork and the heart of a lion, was keeping three men and a mule going. And they say the Spanish are an idle race? Without doubt they've turned the *mañana* syndrome and their ability to be *tranquilo* into art forms, but when needs must, their country folk, at least, can work anyone into a cocked sombrero. And Pep bore witness to this on that roasting summer's day, when I admit to breaking into a sweat just thinking about picking a couple of baskets of apricots.

I told Pep this when he had called a short halt to threshing operations in order to give his helpers, and the mule, a breather – and himself enough time to roll and smoke one of his pyrotechnic *cigarrillos*.

'*Hombre*, you have to be born to it,' was his immediate reaction, before adding an admission of: 'But, *tío*, put me in your country and I would be frozen knackerless before I had pitched a single sheaf!'

Point made.

The pending successful completion of his oats-harvesting season seemed to have put Pep into an unusually genial mood, so I thought I'd take the opportunity to tease him about breaking his much-vaunted no-tractors-on-my-farm maxim. His excuse for allowing the old paraffin-drinking Fordson onto his place was short and sweet…

'*Coño*,' he snorted, 'if I had kept threshing corn with a flail like we used to in my father's day, I would have been dead twenty years ago.'

Point taken.

'OK, but what about asking Sandy to rotovate your land with our little Barbieri tractor that time?'

'A matter of practicality,' said Pep, clearly preparing for an even more blunt reply. 'I needed to have a fine tilth cultivated in an awkward corner of a field. An awkward corner, but a secure corner… for my rare tobacco plants, you understand.'

I nodded my head and awaited the inevitable killer punch.

Pep winked a mischievous wink at Ellie, then said to me, 'Harrows behind a mule make a cumbersome combination in a tight corner, *sí*?'

'*Sí*.'

'*Bueno!* Try stuffing the drive shaft of a rotovator up a mule's arse and see what you get!'

Point understood.

The end of Charlie's summer term – or semester as they called it, within the strongly transatlantic ethos of the school – was marked with the annual sports day. An athletics ground with adjoining swimming pool on the outskirts of Palma had been hired for the occasion, the school's own sports facilities being limited to a little indoor gym and a basketball pitch in the playground. Although the participants' family members were small in number (there were only about two hundred pupils in the entire school), they made up for it in enthusiasm and noise. And the kids, each competing for his own 'house', revelled in the big-time atmosphere of doing their stuff in a *real* stadium and Olympic-size pool.

The oppressive late-afternoon temperature within the confines of the sports ground meant that track events were limited to sprints and relays for the older pupils, and short egg-and-spoon and three-legged races for the younger ones. Spain being Spain, there was a bar within the ground, so that sunstroke-susceptible parents (exclusively fathers, I noticed) could enjoy viewing their children's sporting efforts over the rim of a glass of chilled beer in air-conditioned safety. The idea appealed to me strongly, but Ellie was quick to remind me that, before any such indulgence, I had to talk to the headmaster about Charlie's earlier misdemeanour on the basketball pitch.

Contrary to what Sandy had been told at the time, no one from the school had been in touch with us about it, so I presumed that the whole matter had been regarded as a storm in a teacup. Still, better to make it known that we disapproved of Charlie's behaviour, anyway.

'Boys will be boys,' smiled the headmaster, a much more convivial and less officious chap than the despotic old 'beaks' I remembered from my own schooldays. He was busy helping his staff to organise events at trackside, but was happy to take time out to give us an update on Charlie's progress after two full terms at his school.

On the subject of the basketball punch-up, he explained that, although he couldn't condone violent behaviour of any kind in a school such as his, with a fairly high turnover of pupils from many cultural backgrounds, such scuffles as the one Charlie had been involved in were not that uncommon.

'We make a point of encouraging harmony between all the students, no matter what their nationality, but, as in any school, there's always going to be one youngster who throws his weight around and makes life miserable for anyone who backs down to him. Strictly between ourselves, the lad your Charlie had the, er, disagreement with is just such a boy. But, although the PT teacher knew that Charlie was probably only standing up for himself on that occasion, he had to enforce the school's code of discipline.'

'As long as Charlie took it to heart,' I said.

'You need have no worries about Charlie's general behaviour, I assure you. He's a lively lad with an outgoing nature, prone to let his attention wander at times in class, but very popular with pupils and staff alike.' Lowering his voice, the headmaster smiled and added confidentially, 'And his basketball adversary keeps well out of his way these days.'

'How about his school work?' Ellie asked. 'Is he sticking in – making good progress?'

'We'll be giving them their report cards to take home later today, so you'll get all the details from that. But, generally speaking, I'd say that Charlie is very good at subjects which interest him, and not so good at those that don't. It's not an uncommon trait in kids of his age, but in a small school like ours the teachers have time to work on it, and we're doing just that with Charlie.'

'We'll certainly back that up at home,' I assured him, more than a little relieved that the bottom academic line on Charlie was no worse than the old 'can do better' chestnut. At least the school fees weren't being *totally* wasted.

'Oh, only one other thing,' the headmaster said while readying himself to return to race-organising duties. 'On a matter of attitude, if you could also advise Charlie that we suspect that he thinks that some of us teachers are complete idiots. And we may well be. But,' he paused to give a little laugh, 'we don't want to be reminded of it, no matter how subtly, by a twelve-year-old, do we?'

I resolved to mention this to Charlie, but within myself I was pleased that he was already developing an ability to judge character. And who better on whom to practice his nascent skills than schoolteachers? A rich vein of diverse originals, if ever there was one!

Whilst totally different from school-playing-field sports days in Britain, where the sweet smell of cut grass on a pleasantly warm afternoon creates an abiding memory, this stadium-housed version did manage to generate the same end-of-term feeling of elation. Although occupying only one small section of the terracing, the little crowd of cheering parents created a charged atmosphere that spilled over onto the track. As ever, a few athletically talented kids scooped most of the honours, but everybody had a real go – even the inveterate tail-enders, who invariably looked as though they trained on cream cakes, burgers and chips.

But they were all enjoying themselves, and by the time the proceedings had moved over to the pool, the sense of competition between the houses had reached fever pitch. I can't claim to be the most avid watcher of 'professional' swimming on TV, but I admit to having been so caught up in the excitement of this little contest that I completely forgot to visit the bar like other heat-afflicted dads. Praise indeed for the quality of the racing, where even the infants entered wholeheartedly into the spirit of the occasion – albeit that a few novices with water wings got no further than floundering about at the edge of the pool. They were taking part, though, and that was what mattered most.

There may not have been the smell of newly-mown grass to savour, but it was more than compensated for by the infectious enthusiasm of those happy youngsters, tanned skins reflecting the healthy outdoor life which is so much part of growing up in a climate like Mallorca's. Charlie was a lucky lad, and he had obviously taken to this way of life like a duck to water. It was a touch ironic, though, that going to a new school, a necessity which he had previously dreaded, had been the prime factor in helping him settle so well into this new environment.

If only Sandy had had the good fortune of being thrown into such a social melting pot.

But thoughts of long-term family unity would wait for another day. For the moment, the relief imparted by the headmaster's assessment of Charlie's scholastic 'progress', combined with the euphoria of the school sports day, had prompted Ellie to suggest rounding it off by taking the boys out for a celebratory dinner. And, rabbit being her current culinary favourite, she further suggested that the Restaurante Mirador de Na Burguesa would be the place to go.

Curiously, it was young Ali, the Egyptian boy who had backed Charlie up after the basketball tussle, who recommended this particular eating place to us. It was a favourite of his parents, not just because of the excellent Mallorcan game dishes which were its speciality, but for the stunning views from its windows, too. The only snag, he pointed out, was that the restaurant was on the summit of Na Burguesa Mountain, and the road up there was so hair-raising that his mother always got out of the car and walked!

We were soon sympathising with her. Leaving the village of Gènova to the west of Palma, the narrow track zigzags up the face of the mountain and, with no barricades, negotiating the seemingly endless series of switchback corners becomes increasingly perilous the higher you drive. I noticed that Ellie had her eyes tightly shut, and the groans from the back suggested that the boys weren't particularly enjoying the experience either. As for me, white-knuckling it behind the wheel, I was only thankful that the climb was so steep that I didn't have to change from first gear. Concentrating on manoeuvring those crazy hairpins was more than enough for me to be going on with.

And then the inevitable. We met a delivery van head on at the sharpest bend yet. There simply wasn't enough room for two vehicles to pass, so one of us was going to have to reverse out of the way. All credit to the van driver who tried to do just that, but the gravel-strewn surface of the tarmac was so slippery that his rear wheels started to spin, without moving the van one inch up the steep incline.

'I'll have to back up,' I said, purposely not looking at the sheer drop into oblivion at my left elbow.

'I'm getting out!' Ellie quavered.

'So am I,' said the boys in unison, scrambling out of the passenger's door hot on their mother's heels.

'Thanks a million,' I muttered, trying very hard to control the urge to jump ship myself. 'Don't even *think* about putting the bloody thing in reverse,' I told myself. 'If your foot slips off the clutch you'll be...' I swallowed hard and eased my foot ever so gently off the brake pedal, tweaking the handbrake too – just in case.

'STOP!' three frantic voices yelled. I looked in the rearview mirror to see Sandy and Charlie waving desperately, Ellie standing with her hands over her eyes.

'You're only about an inch from the edge,' Sandy shouted. 'Pull forward a bit and try again. I'll guide you back, so don't worry.'

Don't worry? God, I was already wishing I was wearing incontinent pants, never mind just worrying!

I don't know how long it took to complete the tricky manoeuvre – probably only a minute or so, but to me it seemed an eternity. I was still shaking, sweat dripping from the end of my nose, when I finally pulled into the car park at the top.

'Glad you could make it!' I shouted to Ellie and the boys when they came puffing over the rise. I pointed a quivering finger at the statue of Jesus that stands looking out to sea from the very summit of the mountain. 'And remind me to say a few prayers to him if we make it back down again.'

But my nerves soon settled once I was seated with a glass of robust country wine inside the rustic comfort of the restaurant. It only took a couple of sips of the fortifying red liquid to persuade me that the view from the room's wall of picture windows made the whole scary trip worthwhile. We had a Jesus's eye view of the entire bay of Palma. The whole city was laid out far below us, all the way round to the cathedral, looking like a matchbox model in the distance, and beyond to Es Pla, the vast central plain. We were so high that we could even look down on toy-like passenger jets taking off and landing at Palma airport away beyond the farthest outskirts of the city. Young Ali's tip had turned out a winner.

But what of the food?

'Well, I know what I'm having,' said Ellie, not even bothering to look at the menu. 'If Ali says the rabbit here's fantastic, that'll do for me.'

Her restaurant-speak Spanish was steadily improving. So, full of confidence and gastronomic anticipation, she decided to order for herself.

'*Hola!* Eh, good evening, *señor,*' she cheerfully Spanglished to the waiter. 'I've heard that they're really *fabuloso*, so I'd like one of your lovely *cojones*. Uhm, a *grande* one, *por favor.*'

Sandy and Charlie started to snigger, so I threw them a swift 'control yourselves' look. This was shaping up to be one of Ellie's classics. Too good to put down at birth.

'*Perdón?*' enquired the waiter, glancing at the boys and me in turn for the slightest sign that this was a send-up.

We gave him none.

'Your marvellous *cojones*,' Ellie repeated with a charming smile. 'I'd like *uno* of them, *gracias*.'

The waiter arched his eyebrows and raised an apologetic shoulder. '*No es posible, señora*,' he stated po-faced.

Ellie's face fell. 'Oh, dear. Are they off?'

'No, no, *señora*, they are on. And, hey, I gonna keep them that way!' He thrust a menu into Ellie's hand. 'I come back in a coupla *minutos*, eh?'

I could sense that, like me, the boys were trying desperately hard to keep a straight face.

Frowning, Ellie scanned the menu. 'I don't understand what he's on about. The rabbit's down here in black and white.' She pointed to the entry on the bill of fare. 'Look – *cojones!*'

That did it. Sandy and Charlie were purple in the face, tears welling in their eyes, snorts of hilarity escaping from their nostrils.

'Well, Ellie,' I said, sniggering myself now, 'the letters are right.'

'But?'

'It's just that you're saying them in the wrong order.'

'Which means?'

'Which means that *conejos* is the word for rabbits, while *cojones* is the word for…' I paused to pull myself together. '*Cojones*, dear, is the word for… testicles.'

'I've heard plenty people talking bollocks,' Charlie wheezed after Ellie had made a sharp exit to powder her nose, 'but Mum's version is in a class of it's own!'

When the waiter returned, I ordered up her rabbit.

The waiter coughed circumspectly, smiled nervously, then politely enquired, '*Castrado, señor?*'

'*Sí,*' I replied, acknowledging his shaft of gentle wit with a nod of the head, '*no cojones, por favor.*'

Epilogue

HASTA MAÑANA

The Mallorcan calendar is liberally peppered with fiestas; holy days when all businesses except the bars close down to honour one saint or another with parades and, usually, boisterous celebrations. Perhaps the most important summer fiesta in the Andratx area is the one dedicated to *La Virgen del Carmen*, the patron saint of fisherfolk. It takes place in mid-July down in Port d'Andratx, where the boats of the local fishing fleet are bedecked with bunting, streamers and balloons, and the village's quaysides and narrow streets are crammed with people who come from all over the island to witness the colourful event.

The daytime highlight is the sole annual appearance of the saint herself – or, to be absolutely accurate, a lavishly robed, lifesize effigy of her, which is carried aloft on a palanquin from the little church behind the village all the way down to the waterfront. Hidden somewhere among the cheering masses, a brass band leads the procession to the particular fishing boat chosen to carry *La Virgen* out to sea, where she will bless the water and, in so doing, ensure a safe and profitable year ahead for the local fishermen.

In keeping with the family-oriented tradition of most Spanish fiestas, children are encouraged to board the boats and are treated to sweets and the entertainment of musicians as the little fleet makes its way out of the harbour and beyond the headland to the open sea. Charlie, having teamed up with Toni, his Mallorcan chum from our own village, had managed to get onto the leading boat, not, I suspected, because it carried the wooden *Virgen*, but rather because she was accompanied by the fiesta's adolescent beauty queen and her entourage of equally nubile handmaidens. Sandy elected to remain aloof from such juvenile pursuits. Instead, he wandered off to the fairground which had been set up for the occasion on the edge of the village, there to impress, no doubt, some of the more mature local *chicas* with his Dodgem-driving skills.

For Ellie and I, it was now a matter of whiling away a leisurely hour or two, first sitting outside the tiny Bar Tur overlooking the harbour, where Pau, the genial host, would present Ellie with his habitual gift of an *ensaimada*, while addressing her tongue-in-cheek as *La Reina de Las Malvinas* – the Falklands Queen. Although this grand title had originally been bestowed by the Spanish on Maggie Thatcher and occasionally, you'd suspect, on some rust bucket of a tramp steamer, Ellie took the dubious honour in good part. Everyone has his or her price, and in Ellie's case it just happened to be a one hundred peseta pastry.

While the crowds, which had drifted away on the departure of the fishing fleet, began to re-assemble on the quayside to welcome the boats back to port, we took an evening stroll to a quiet little hideaway on the other side of the bay. The Bar Lovento was originally little more than a fisherman's shack, a tiny stone building which still forms the basis of the hostelry, now enlarged by a covered terrace reaching to the very edge of the sea. And there we sat, sharing a plate of *boquerones*, fried fresh anchovies, while throwing scraps of bread to little shoals of grey mullet scrummaging for titbits right beside our table. What better setting from which to watch the glow of sunset on the bay, as the returning fishing boats appeared round the point, the reflection of their celebration lights dancing like fireflies on the rippling waters?

With nightfall, a fireworks display signalled that fiesta celebrations proper were about to begin in Port d'Andratx. Time to leave little fishes and tranquillity behind and rejoin the rejoicing throngs over there on the quayside. The night was yet young, and the emerging stars would soon be lighting up a sparkling street party that would last till the wee small hours.

August brought with it the devitalising heat that Francisca Ferrer had described as '*terr-ee-blay, horr-ee-blay*' when she first showed Ellie and I around the farm exactly a year earlier. And if she, a native of the valley, found the August temperatures difficult to bear, what chance did we recent immigrants from the chilly north have? The conditions which drive even the most seasoned Mallorcans into praying for relief are those that prevail when a southerly wind known as the *Mitjorn* is blowing, carrying on its hot breath the sand of the Sahara. Everything – cars, boats, even the leaves of trees – becomes covered in a film of the red desert dust as the sweltering air of Africa wafts over the island. What makes things even worse is the moisture that the *Mitjorn* accumulates on its journey across the sea, raising the ever-present humidity of Mallorca to almost unbearable levels.

'We'll have to build a swimming pool,' I puffed, slouching into the kitchen after watering the trees on just such an oppressive evening. I was wearing only shorts, but still sweating profusely while doing nothing more energetic than lifting a bottle of cool water from the fridge.

'But you can't even swim,' Ellie said, peeping out from behind her feverishly fluttering fan.

'No, but I can melt. Look at me. I must be on the verge of dissolving right now!'

'Can we afford it – a pool, I mean?'

'We won't know until we find out how much it'll cost. But anyway, we could look at it as an investment – adding value to the place, that sort of thing.' I opened the fridge door again and stuck my head inside. 'I'm telling you, I'm going to start getting quotes first thing tomorrow morning. This is bloody torture.'

Fortunately, as with the chilling *Tramuntana* gales of winter, the *Mitjorn* usually only blows for a day or two at most, and we were soon back in the 'normal' cauldron of August heat which brings sun-seeking holidaymakers flocking in their millions to Mallorcan seaside resorts every year. With most of the summer fruit already picked, we had at least a month's respite from that aspect of work until the autumn-ripening fruits, like quinces and pomegranates, would be ready. At last we had some time on our hands, particularly at weekends when there was no irrigating to do. So, whenever other work about the place permitted, we would escape the often suffocating heat of the valley to drive away, car windows opened wide, for the comparatively fresh air of the coast.

But we didn't head for the teeming tourist traps, where the gentle onshore breezes are flavoured with the aromas of a hundred brands of suntan lotion, and the sand of the beaches is hidden under a blanket of baking humanity. Nothing better, if that's what you come to the island for. But we had already discovered a little of the real Mallorca; the pre-tourist-boom Mallorca, where the natural beauty of the island remains relatively unspoiled, and where you can still enjoy a dish of freshly-caught sardines in the repose of a simple waterside *tasca*, in which the waitress may well be the wife of the fisherman who caught your lunch. A few such priceless places do still exist, tucked away in little coves like Port de Canonge, for instance, far from the madding summer crowds on the rugged northern coast.

Or we would drive into the mountains, where the air is clean and refreshingly cool, even at this sultry time of year. One of our favourite destinations was the Bar S'Hostalet, an isolated little tavern in the Coll de Sóller, the high pass between the mighty Sierra del Teix and Sierra d'Alfabia ridges. This remote inn was, in times past, a resting place for muleteers transporting goods between Palma and the town of Sóller on the other side of the Tramuntana Mountains. And, despite a new road tunnel swallowing up most of its former passing trade many kilometres below the pass, the Bar S'Hostalet is still open for business.

On the most recent occasion that we stopped there, however, the only other customer to wander into the yard in front of the *hostal* was a baby goat, roaming free, happy with life and keen to be sociable. It homed in on Ellie, who just happened to be eating a small *madelena* sponge cake. Instantly won over by the cute little animal's acrobatic antics, she offered it a morsel, which it quickly gobbled, then snatched the remainder of the cake from her other hand. Worth it, she reckoned, for the company of a friendly creature whose presence only served to enhance the rustic charm of the surroundings.

We were sitting at a table in the shade of a spreading evergreen oak, sipping iced drinks and looking out over the deep valley where the road winds its twisting way up towards the pass. Above that, the craggy bluffs of Alfabia Mountain dominated the scene and cast welcome shadows over the scrub-mottled slopes below. Nothing stirred, and even sparrows sheltering among the oak leaves above our heads gave scarcely a chirp. It would have been easy to linger there all day, but *siesta* time was beckoning, and it was a long drive back home to Andratx.

The affectionate little goat accompanied Ellie down the steps to the car park while I went to pay the bill. On either side of the tavern's front door were two little cane cages containing one red-legged partridge each.

'Pets,' said the barmaid.

'And the young goat?'

'*Sí*, a pet also,' she smiled.

While she rummaged in the till for my change, I took a quick look at the dinner menu hanging on the wall, and – surprise, surprise – the two current specials were noted as 'Partridge With Wild Mushrooms' and – horror of horrors – 'Roast Kid Mallorcan Style'.

I didn't tell Ellie, for fear of being arrested for aiding and abetting a kidnapping.

'The September sign of Libra depicts a set of scales,' stated the almanac, 'signifying the equal length of days and nights. The entrance of the sun in this sign marks the end of summer and the start of autumn.'

Well, the sun and Libra could have fooled me. The heat was still intense, Spanish flies still bounced like mini bungee jumpers in the middle of the kitchen, ants still patrolled the terrace in endless armies, little geckos still clung to the sun-baked house walls, and two cockroaches still took part in nightly races over the *almacén* floor. Mosquitoes, too, continued to remind us that we were a long, long way from our idea of autumn when, the almanac claimed, 'It starts to nip and the cold chafes.' We were actually looking forward to it!

But we had made it through our first summer in the valley, and were a little wiser and a whole lot browner. Our pace of life had slowed right down, too, thanks to the hot weather, and we had become accustomed to planning plenty, doing little and taking much needed daily *siestas* without the slightest twinge of work-ethic conscience.

Winter and the labours of orange-harvesting would come round soon enough.

We hadn't seen much of our neighbours for a while, the ferocity of the daytime heat driving them indoors in search of shade and a coolish corner to sit in. Even the midday streets of Andratx had been deserted for weeks. Only at sundown would the pavements become crowded with townsfolk, not risking anything as energetic as a *paseo*, but sitting on chairs watching TV through the downstairs windows of their houses.

Jordi, too, had been keeping an uncustomary low profile, although I'd spied him on the odd occasion when driving through the square – ensconced just inside the doorway of the Bar Nuevo, glass of beer in hand, and looking none the worse for it. He'd be back to his old companionable ways just as soon as temperatures fell sufficiently to make moped trips round his other haunts possible, of that there was no doubt.

Despite the recent lack of conversation opportunities in the valley, word had filtered through the grapevine that Pepe Suau's worries appeared to be over. A rumour was about that an American couple had bought the estate of Es Pou and, being only interested in the big house, had asked Pepe to continue farming the place as before. The couple had twin daughters who were in Charlie's class at school, it transpired. Sugar and Spice they were called, and you couldn't help but feel that people who had chosen such cheery names for their kids would make good landlords for Pepe. We certainly hoped so, but we'd get all the news first-hand from Pepe when he came back to prune the trees again in the spring.

'Sandy flies back to Scotland tomorrow,' Ellie reminded me when I was just about to nod off one night, my face luxuriating in the cooling air from an electric fan on the bedside table. 'I wonder if he'll come back.'

'Hmm, it'll all work out for the best, never fear.'

'Charlie starts the new school term tomorrow, too. It's going to be quiet around here.'

'Hmm.'

Ellie fell silent for a while, and I knew she was already missing Sandy. Did she have some sort of mother's intuition that he wouldn't return to Ca's Mayoral? Perhaps, but for now all I wanted to do was sleep. It had been a long and tiring day.

'Goodnight, Ellie.'

'You'll have to do something about those cockroaches.'

'I did,' I mumbled. 'I scattered walnut leaves, like old Maria told me to.'

'Well, it hasn't worked. The cockroaches are still there – and the flies, too.'

'Hmm, I've put slices of salty lemon here and there in the kitchen. Maria says that'll fix the flies.'

'But it hasn't. And listen to that!'

'What?'

'There's a mosquito in here. So much for old Maria's trick of sticking a flowerpot of basil on the windowsill.'

'Maybe we should try burning a lump of donkey dung instead, then.'

'Don't be silly. You really will have to do something about it, though.'

'Mmm, I'll go to the hardware store and get some insect spray tomorrow.'

'You said that yesterday… and the day before!'

'Goodnight, Ellie.'

'And what about getting quotes for building a swimming pool?'

'Yes, I'll do that tomorrow as well.'

'You've been saying that for the past month.'

'Tomorrow, Ellie,' I mumbled, pulling the sheet over my head to thwart the attentions of the mosquito. 'It'll all get done tomorrow.'

'I think I preferred it before you perfected all this tranquiloness,' Ellie grumped, snuggling down to sleep at last. 'Goodnight!'

'Goodnight, Ellie,' I yawned. 'Hasta mañana. See you in the morning…'

SNOWBALL ORANGES

ORANGES

One Mallorcan Winter

PETER KERR

SNOWBALL ORANGES
One Mallorcan Winter

Peter Kerr

ISBN: 978-1-78685-042-3   Paperback   £9.99

When the Kerr family leave Scotland to grow oranges on the island of Mallorca they are surprised to be greeted by the same freezing weather they thought they had left behind. They then realise that their new orange farm is a bit of a lemon... *Snowball Oranges* is hilarious, revealing and full of life and colour, set against the breathtaking beauty of the Mediterranean.

'This should do for Spain what A Year in Provence *did for France.'*
THE SUNDAY POST magazine

'Kerr writes with a combination of nice observation and gentle humour.'
THE SUNDAY TIMES

SPAIN
TO
NORWAY
ON A BIKE CALLED
REGGIE

ANDREW P. SYKES

SPAIN TO NORWAY
ON A BIKE CALLED REGGIE

Andrew P. Sykes

ISBN: 978-1-84953-990-6   Paperback   £9.99

Meet Andrew: French teacher,
writer and long-distance cyclist.

Now, meet Reggie, his bike.

With two European cycling adventures already under his belt, Andrew was ready for a new challenge. Exchanging his job as a teacher in Oxfordshire for an expedition on Reggie the bike, he set off on his most daring trip yet: a journey from Tarifa in Spain to Nordkapp in Norway – from Europe's geographical south to its northernmost point. Join the duo as they take on an epic ride across nearly 8,000 km of Europe, through mountains, valleys, forests and the open road, proving that no matter where you're headed, life on two wheels is full of surprises.

Have you enjoyed this book?
If so, why not write a review on your favourite website?

If you're interested in finding out more about our books,
find us on Facebook at **Summersdale Publishers** and
follow us on Twitter at **@Summersdale**.

Thanks very much for buying this Summersdale book.

www.summersdale.com